Marriages
of
Patrick County
Virginia
- 1791-1850 -

Compiled By:
Lela C. Adams

Southern Historical Press, Inc.
Greenville, South Carolina

SOUTHERN HISTORICAL PRESS, INC.
PO BOX 1267
Greenville, SC   29601

ISBN #0-89308-357-7

Printed in the United States of America

3 Aug 1819   John Abington and Elizabeth Thomas. Sur. William
             F. Abington. Min. John C. Traylor. M.R. 6 Oct. 1820.

21 Mar 1827 Joseph F. Abington and Ruth Penn. Sur. Peter L.
             Penn.

27 Dec 1813 John Abshier and Margaret Blancet. Sur. Jarrard
             Branson. Min. Thomas Whitlock.

12 Feb 1800 Bartholomew Adams and Pegge Going. Consent of
             James Going. Sur. Caleb Going.

 8 Jul 1796 Daniel Adams and Sarah Ingram. Sur. Joshua Adams.
             Min. Robert Jones.

28 Jan 1807 Henry Adams and Rebekah Dinkins. Sur. Jarrard
             Branson. Min. Thomas Whitlock.

13 Oct 1808 Isaac Adams and Ony Ingram. Sur. Daniel Ross.
             Min. Lewis Foster. M.R. 10 Nov. 1808.

14 Jan 1832 Isaac Adams and Exoney Foster.

23 Sep 1847 Isaac C. Adams, Jr. and Exoney Conner. Consent of
             father James Conner. Min. G. W. Conner. M.R. 22
             Sep 1847.

25 Feb 1830 James Adams and Leony Reynolds. Sur. Barnabas
             Baliles. Min. Joshua Adams.

31 Aug 1809 Joseph Adams and Nancy Barton. Min. Bret Stovall.
             M.R. 11 Sep 1809.

28 Nov 1807 Joshua Adams and Elizabeth Fuson. Min. Lewis Foster.

16 Dec 1809 Joshua Adams and Elizabeth Corn, daughter of Samuel
             Corn, who gives consent. Wit. John Adams. Sur.
             John Spencer.

11 Dec 1823 Notley Adams and Seley Akers. Sur. Nathaniel Akers.
             Min. Jesse Jones. M.R. 19 Jan 1824.

15 Feb 1828 Paul C. Adams and Esther Pilson. Sur. Richard
             Pilson. Min. Joshua Adams. M.R. 7 Feb 1828.

31 Aug 1795 Peter Adams and Ann Tittle. Sur. Anthony Tittle.
             Min. Jesse Jones.

12 Aug 1841 Samuel G. Adams and Lucy Ann Barnard. Sur. Isham
             Barnard. Min. Joshua Adams. M.R. 7 Sep 1841.

 2 Sep 1801 William Adams and Biddy Nowlin. Sur. Francis
             Nowlin.

31 Jan 1843   Austin Agee and Eliza J. Hensley. Consent of father,
Nathan Hensley. Sur. William Ayres. Min. G. W.
Conner. M.R. 2 Feb. 1843.

8 Feb 1847   James Agee and Judy Thomas. Sur. Joseph Thomas.

3 Jul 1798   John Agee and Senney Hilton. Consent of Nathaniel
Newman Hilton. Sur. same. Min. Jesse Jones.

20 Jan 1844   John Agee, age 22 and Lucinda Wood. Consent of
fathers: Joshua Agee and Henery Wood. Sur. Samuel
Agee. Wit. Alexander Wood. Min. Jesse Jones.
M.R. 12 Jan 1844.

29 Mar 1821   Joshua Agee and Sarah Brammer, daughter of John
Brammer, who consents. Wit. Jonathan Hubbard.
Min. Stephen Hubbard. Wit. James Brammer.

28 Dec 1843   Lewis Agee and Ann Wade. Sur. John Massey.
Min. Jesse Jones.

28 Jul 1829   Nathaniel Agee and Mary Ma---ens. Min. John Conner.

15 Aug 1833   William Agee, consent of John Agee,Sr. and Lucinda
Spencer. Sur. William Spencer. Min. Joshua Adams.
M.R. 22 Aug 1833.

20 Sep 1822   Adam Ahart and Elisabeth Tune. Sec. Thomas Whitlock.
Min. Thomas Whitlock.

9 Apr 1822   Burres Ahart and Abigail Gregsbay. Sec. Martin Cloud.
Min. Thomas Whitlock.

23 Dec 1826   Henry Aistrop and Matilda Glasgow, consent of Robert
Glasgow, Sr.. Sur. Jesse Aistrop. Wit. Robert
Glasgow, Jr.

10 Jan 1816   Blackburn Akers and Betsey Lesueur, daughter of
Martel Lesueur. Sur. John Akers.

13 Mar 1848   Creed Akers and Martha Belcher, daughter of Benjamin
Belcher, who consents. Sur. Fleming Akers. Min.
G. W. Conner. M.R. 16 Mar 1848.

17 Nov 1836   Featherton Akers and Elizabeth Edds. Consent of
Jesse Edds. Sur. A. Gunnell. Wit. James H. George
and Leftwich Edds.

14 Sep 1820   Hudson (Hutsin) Akers and ----- Sur. James Via.

11 Aug 1825   James Akers and Thena Slaughter. Sur. Dandridge
Slaughter.

10 Aug 1836　James Akers and Agnes Houchins, consent of mother
Margaret Houchins. Sur. Fleming Clark.
Min. John Conner.

17 Feb 1835　John Akers and Elizabeth Adams, consent of father,
Isaac Adams. Sur. John D. Cheatham.
Wit. Tarlton Carter. Min. John Turner.

3 Dec 1844　Nathaniel Akers and Sarah Jane Crews. Sur.
David Cruise.

9 Dec 1814　Robert Akers and Rebecca Hollandsworth. Consent
of her mother, <u>Sarah Craddock</u>. Sur. James Craddock.

18 Nov 1845　Samuel Akers and Elizabeth Akers. Elizabeth Akers
signs her own consent. Sur. Nathaniel Akers.
Wit. Burrel Akers. Min. Jesse Jones. M.R. 27 Nov
1845.

7 Sep 1801　Stephen Akers and Nancy Via. Consent of William
Via. Sur. James Via. Min. Samuel King.
M.R. 10 Sep 1801.

9 Oct 1838　Andrew Jackson Allen and Susanah Anglin. Consent
of her father, Phillip Anglin. Wit. Robert Tuder.
Sur. Anderson Allen. Min. Joshua Adams.

10 Mar 1815　Care Allen and Tempy Daniel. Sur. Thomas Whitlock.
Min. Thomas Whitlock.

26 Dec 1805　John Allen and Nancy Daniel. Sur. Meredith Smith.
Min. Thomas Whitlock.

26 Aug 1844　Madison Allen (Charles Madison Allen on M.R.) and
Mary (Polly) Corn. Sur. Andrew Allen.
Wit. Charles M. Allen. Min. Joshua Adams.

5 Jan 1843　Robert Allen and Elvira Deen. Sur. Joel Mankin.

6 Sep 1853　John W. Alley, born Rockingham, N.C. and Mary W.
Saunders born Patrick Co.,Va., Consent of her
father, Jesse Saunders. Wit. W.T. Akers.
Min. Samuel J. Lacky.

9 Sep 1834　Frederic Alterman and Rosesey Watson. Sur.
William Harrle.

8 Nov 1848　Elisha Anglin and Mary Hubbard. Consent of her
father, Johnathan Hubbard. Sur. Alfred Elgin.

21 Jan 1811　John Anglin and Polly Hannah. Sur. William
Hannah. Min. Brett Stovall. M.R. 25 Jan 1811.

23 Feb 1846   John L. Anglin and Mary Critz, daughter of
              William Critz. Min. Joshua Adams.

30 Jul 1807   Phillip Anglin and Polly Reynolds. Sur.
              Moses Reynolds.

16 Sep 1799   John Arnold and Milly Hollandsworth, consent
              of her father, John Hill. Sur. James Hollands-
              worth.

16 Mar 1832   John Arnold, Jr and Nancy Griffin, daughter of
              Richard Griffin, who gives consent. Sur. Henry
              Trent. Min. Joshua Adams. M.R. 22 Mar 1832.

21 Nov 1829   William Arnold and Ann Cherry, daughter of John
              Cherry, who gives consent. Sur. William Hill.
              Min. Joshua Adams. M.R. 23 Nov 1829.

13 Mar 1850   Daniel Arrington and Sarah Hall. Sur. John D.
              Cheatham. Min. Joshua Adams. M.R. 21 Mar 1850.

 8 Mar 1829   Edmond Arrington, son of John Arrington, who gives
              consent, and Ony (Laony) Boyd, daughter of Elizabeth
              Boyd, who gives consent. Sur. John Arrington.
              Wit. Brice Edwards, John Arrington, Jr. John Hall,
              Lewis Arrington. Min. Stephen Hubbard.
              M.R. 8 Mar 1829.

24 Nov 1831   John Arrington, Jr. and Anna Helms. Sur. Jacob
              Helms. Min. John Conner.

 3 Sep 1834   Leroy Arrington and Rachel Blancett. Sur.
              William Blancett.

19 Dec 1848   Lafayette Ashby and America Edwards, consent of
              her father William Edwards. Sur. James M. Hughes.
              Min. Joshua Adams. M.R. 20 Dec 1848.

 8 Apr 1839   James E. Ashly and Polly Carter, oldest daughter of
              James Carter, who gives his consent. Sur. John D.
              Cheatham. Min.Joshua Adams. M.R. 9 Apl 1839.

23 May 1848   Granville H. Ashworth and Nancy King, daughter of
              Elizabeth King, who gives consent. Sur. Madison
              D. Carter. Wit. George L. King. Min. Samuel
              Hill. M.R. 26 June 1848.

21 Jan 1801   Daniel Askew and Mary Thomson. Sur. Samuel Staples.

19 Sep 1827   George Askew and Nancy Finney. Sur. Phillip Askew.
              Min. Nathaniel Thomson. M.R. 20 Sep 1827.

27 Jan 1811   Obediah Askew and Leony Harris. Sur. Barnard Harris. Min. Brett Stovall. M.R. 3 Jan 1811.

4 Sep 1830   Obadiah Askew and Franky Ayres, a widow, gives own consent. Sur. J.W. Hylton. Min. John Washburn. M.R. 5 Sep 1830.

15 Jun 1832   Phillip Askew and Lucinda Gilbert. Sur. Richard Nowlin.

2 Mar 1826   Braxton Athisson and Mary Flippen. Sur. Samuel Flippen. Min. Joshua Adams.

8 Aug 1806   Stephen Atkinson and Sally Frans. Sur. Gabriel Penn. Min. Maning Hill.

12 Mar 1827   Thomas Austin and Nancy Martin. Sur. John Tuggle.

26 May 1821   William Austin and Mary Spaulding. Sur. Andrew Boyd, Jr.

5 Oct 1820   Hugh Ayrs and Frances Murphy. Consent of fathers, Murphy Ayrs and James Murphy. Min. Peter Frans. Sur. Moses Harris.

7 May 1843   James Ayers of Rockingham Co. N.C., and Martha R. Tatum, daughter of John Tatum. Sur. A.A. Moir.

14 Feb 1822   Lemuel Ayres and Nancey Dennis. Min. Thomas Whitlock.

11 Dec 1817   Leonard Ayrs and Elizabeth Harris. Sur. Moses Harris.

11 Sep 1849   Parris Ayres and Embersetta Smith. Sur. Samuel G. Staples.

14 Feb 1822   Samuel Ayres and Nancy Dennis. Sur. Thomas Whitlock.. Min. Thomas Whitlock.

8 Oct 1818   Thomas Ayers, Jr. and Rebecca Harris. Sur. Joseph Cummings. Min. Peter Frans.

27 Aug 1826   Thomas Ayres and Mahala Turner. Sur. Augustin Jones. Min. Maning Hill.

4 May 1821   William Ayres and Frances Davis. Sur. William Crum. Min. Stephen Hubbard. M.R. 6 May 1820.

16 Nov 1849   William H. Ayers and Emily E. Sheppard. Sur. James Sheppard. Min. Joshua Adams. M.R. 18 Nov 1849.

10 Aug 1814 William P. Ayers and Catherine Yats. Sur.
Stephen McMilian. Min. Thomas Whitlock.

23 Oct 1806 Robert Baged and Elizabeth Rakes. Min.
Ruben Short.

31 Jan 1805 Thomas Bailey and Sally Adams. Sur. George
Clark. M.R. 29 Jan 1805.

10 Nov 1835 Andrew J. Baker and Jane Foster, daughter of
Lewis Foster, who consents. Sur. William R.
Sims. Min. Joshua Adams. M.R. 12 Nov 1835.

13 Dec 1827 Burton Baker and Polly C. Shelton. Sur. Absalem
Shelton. Min. Bird Lowe.

26 Nov 1808 James Baker, Jr. and Catherine Koger. Sur.
Jacob Koger. Min. Lewis Foster. M.R. 15 Dec 1808.

 2 Apl 1830 Norman Baker and Nancy Nance. Jane Sims states
that Nancy Nance is 21 years of age. Sur. John
Sims. Min. John C. Traylor.

20 Mar 1811 Barnabas Balisle and Milley Reynolds.
Sur. Jesse Reynolds.

11 Aug 1853 Lee Balisle, son of Barnabas Balisle and Mildred
Balisle and Nancy J. Morrison, daughter of Thomas
and Jane Morrison. Min. Joshua Adams.

12 May 1811 James Ballard and Rebecca Fitzpatrick. Sur.
James Dickerson.

 8 Sep 1829 John Banks and Mary Adams. Sur. Giles Martin.
Min. John Conner.

19 Feb 1838 Joseph Banks of Grayson Co. Va., son of William
Banks and Mary W. Scott. Sur. Thomas Scott.
Wit. P. Boman and Frederick Quisinberry.
Min. William Lawson. M.R. 28 Feb 1838.

12 Nov 1807 Thomas Banks and Elizabeth (betsy) Critz. Sur.
William Frans. Min. Lewis Foster.

 4 Feb 1808 William Banks, Jr. and Elizabeth (Betsy) Penn.
Sur. William Frans. Min. Peter Frans.

15 Jun 1815 William Banks and Polly Martin. Sur. Giles
Martin.

12 Oct 1814   William Banks,Jr. and Frances Penn. Sur. Martin
              Miller.

24 Jul 1804   Edward Barmer and Charlotte Harris. Min.
              Stephen Hubbard. M.R. 25 July 1804.

14 Jan 1830   Archilous Barnard and Ifa Lawson. Sur. Rowland
              Hurt. Min. Nathaniel Thompson.

17 Sep 1852   Isham Barnard and Elitha Mankins, daughter of
              William Mankins. Isham Barnard the son of Tinea
              Barnard. Min. William Lawson.

31 Aug 1852   Emanuel Barnes, son of Sinai Barnes and Oney Massey
              daughter of Ancil Massey. Min. Jeremiah Burnett.

23 Feb 1808   Daniel Baringer and Martha Covington. Sur. Charles
              Vancel. Min. Thomas Whitlock.

21 Jan 1808   John Barrett and Elizabeth Riddle (Ridely). Sur.
              David Fain.

15 Nov 1833   William Barrett and Nancy Barrett. Sur. John Barrett.
              Min. Brett Stovall.

24 Jul 1841   James Bartee and Elizabeth Clark, daughter of John
              Clarke. Sur. H. Critz and N.P. Adams.
              Min. Joshua Adams. M.R. 27 July 1841.

25 Jul 1811   Thomas Bartlett and Frances Clark. Sur. William
              Fuson.

20 Apl 1818   Alexander H. Bassett and Polly Koger. Sur. Jacob
              Koger.

14 Feb 1850   Woodson Bassett and Julia A.F. Prunty, daughter of
              John Prunty. Sur. John L. Dillard. Wit. Ann E.
              Pinkard. Min. William Schoolfield.

 1 Nov 1796   John Bates and Frances Burnett, daughter of Phillip
              and Mary Stephens, who give consent. Sur. James
              Dehart. Wit. William Fuson and Richard McClary.

 9 Aug 1816   James Bays and Nancy Cannon. Sur. Isham East.
              Min. Thomas Whitlock. M.R. 1 July 1816.

 4 Aug 1838   Obediah Bayse and Elizabeth Jane Cloud, daughter
              of Martin Cloud who gives consent for his under-
              age daughter. Sur. John Boyd.

20 Oct 1821   Enoch Beasley and Martha Overby (Overty) Sur.
              Isham Slate. Min. William Davis. M.R.22 Oct.1821.

3 Nov 1821   Henry Beasley and Ossie Collings. Sur. Micajah
             Collings.

6 Nov 1794   James Beasley and Sarah Harris. Consent of Mathen
             Harris. Sur. James Taylor. Wit. John Harris.

10 Nov 1798 James Beasley and Sally Rea. Sur. John Rea,Sr.

18 Oct 1819 Ruben Beasley of Stokes Co., N.C. and Mary W.
             Puckett. Sur. Micajah Collings. Min. Bret
             Stovall. M.R. 9 Oct 1819.

22 May 1799 John Bedwell and Sarah Agee, daughter of John Agee.
             Sur. James Henderson.

16 Sep 1800 Bartlett Belcher and Ailsey Lawson. Sur. Richard
             Davidson.

22 Jun 1823 Benjamin Belcher and Sally Jones. Sur. Thomas
             Belcher. Min. Peter Frans.

22 Jan 1833 Francis Belcher and Nancy Dunn. Sur. Joshua Finney.

3 Mar 1853   Harden Belcher and Elisabeth Hylton. Min. G.W.Conner.

18 Sep 1813 John Belcher and Permely Bigers. Sur. James Vandever.

27 Jan 1845 John Belcher, son of Benjamin Belcher and Nancy
             Brammer, daughter of John Brammer. Sur. James Dillion.
             Wit. William Dillion. Min. G.W. Conner. M.R. 13 Feb
             1845.

3 Mar 1831   Noah Belcher and Jane Maynor. Sur. Richard Maynor.
             Min. John Turner.

5 May 1824   Thomas Belcher and Catherine Stanley, daughter of
             Thomas Stanley of Franklin Co. Va., who is 20 years
             of age. Sur. Richard Mayner.

19 Jan 1812 Aaron Bellar and Susana Handridg. Sur. Alexander
             Penn.

21 Jul 1805 Elias Bellar and Elisabeth Strang. Sur. Eli Bellar.
             Min. Thomas Whitlock. M.R. 4 July 1805.

23 Apl 1828 Uel (Nel) Bellar and Frances Thompson. Sur. Kneel
             Thompson and Isaac Adams. Min. John Conner
             M.R. 1 May 1828.

26 Jan 1853 Alexander Bennett and Elizabeth Ann Brammer, daughter
             of John Brammer.

5 Jun 1841 James Bennett and Mary Hines, daughter of Henry Hines. Min. John W. Lewis. M.R. 8 Jun 1841.

15 Sep 1813 Howel B. Beville and Sally Fuson (Fulse). Sur. Thomas Whitlock. Min. Thomas Whitlock.

14 Aug 1798 Douglas Biggs and Nancy Saunders. Sur. John Nunns. Min. John Nunns. M.R. 12 Aug 1798.

3 Mar 1825 Edward Bingham and Nancy (Rosey) Keller. Sur. Thomas Whitlock. Min. Thomas Whitlock.

6 Dec 1829 Benjamin Bird and Lucy Grady. Min. Jesse Jones.

10 Apl 1849 William Blackard and Susanah Malinda Dehart, daughter of Gabriel Dehart, Sr., Sur. Alexander A. Shelton. Wit. Richard A. Wood. Min. G.W. Conner. M.R. 12 Apl 1849.

23 Jun 1853 Willoughby Blackard and America Dehart, daughter of Stephen Dehart. Wit. William Blackard. Min. G. W. Conner.

11 Dec 1815 John Blackburn and Sally Cox. Sur. Joseph Vaughan. Wit. William Walden.

17 Dec 1845 Enoch Blancett and Mary Jane Arrington. Sur. John Arrington. Min. G.W. Conner. M.R. 23 Dec 1845.

24 Jan 1849 William Blancett and Stacy Fitzgerald. Sur. James T. Fitzgerald. Min. Joshua Adams. M.R. 30 Jan 1848.

30 Oct 1799 Archibald Blanchett and Polly Hammons. Sur. William Yeatts and Thomas Branson.

7 Apl 1824 Joel Blanchett and Sarah Phillips. Min. Thomas Whitlock.

19 Sep 1849 Thomas R. Blankenship and Ann T. Potter, daughter of William Potter. Sur. J.R. Brown. Min. G.W. Conner.

14 Feb 1822 Thompson Blanks of Rockingham Co., N.C. and Mary Harris. Sur. Elijah Harris. Min. Brett Stovall.

7 Apl 1824 Joseph Blanset and Sarah Phillips. Sur. Joshua Haynes.

11 Feb 1852 Samuel Blanset and Elizann Dehart. Min. Samuel J. Lackey.

22 Dec 1818 James Boaz, Jr. and Elizabeth Rogers. Sur. Clement Rogers. Min. Maning Hill.

Bolen, Boling, Bowlen, Bowling, Bolling

18 Jan 1849   Andrew B. Bowling and Lucinda Bolling.
Min. John Conner .

21 Mar 1835   Andrew W. Bowlen and Martha Handy, dau of
William Handy. Sur. Obadiah Boling.
Wit: Marvel Bowlen.

11 Jan 1849   Andrew W. Bowlen and Lucinda B. Foley, consent of
Lity Foley. Sur. John C. Bowlen. Wit. Marvel Bowlen.

14 Dec 1813   Gabriel Boling and Elizabeth Tuggle.
Min. Jesse Jones.

17 Nov 1846   Gabriel Boling and Aminta Adams.
Sur. Notley P. Adams.

 6 May 1839   Henry J.(T.) Boling and Elizabeth Eleanor Burnett,
daughter of Jeremiah Burnett. Sur. Gabriel Boling.
Min. Jesse Jones. M.R. 8 May 1839.

30 Jan 1801   James Bolling and Elisabeth Morrison. Sur. William
Morrison. Min. Nathan Hall. M.R. 1 Feb 1800.

19 Nov 1825   James Bowling and Jemima Ratliff, consent of
Isaac Pennington, her step-father. Sur. Isaac
Pennington.

29 Jul 1848   James Boling and S.(Arency) Parr. Sur. Samuel Terry.
Min. G. W. Conner. M.R. 3 Aug 1848.

 8 Feb 1837   James Bowlen and Ruth Foley, daughter of Lity Foley.
Sur. Marvel Bowlen.

31 Mar 1835   James Luke Bowling, consent of James Boling, and
Sally Nowlin, consent of Samuel Nowlin. Sur. Alfred
Shelton. Wit: Mary Boling, Lucy Boling, Eliphas Shelton.

17 Oct 1848   James M. Bowling and Mary Pendleton, daughter of
Prier Pendleton. Wit. Wilson Pendleton.
Min. Joshua Adams.

17 Sep 1815   John Bowling and Lucy Clay. Sur. Jourdon Clay.
Min. Stephen Hubbard.

20 Mar 1830   John Boling and Sarah Handy, daughter of William Handy.
Sur. Marvel Bowlin. Wit: Peter Handy. Min. Jesse Jones.
M.R. 23 Mar 1830.

25 Aug 1836   John W. Bolling and Elizabeth Hubbard, daughter of
Benjamin Hubbard. Sur. Gabriel Bolling.
Min. John Conner.

7 Feb 1841   Marvel Boling and Lity Foley. Sur. R. Thomas

27 Dec 1843   Nathan G. Boling and Jane Burnett. Sur. Moses
Burnett. M.R. 31 Dec 1843.

6 Apl 1817   Thomas Boling and Polly Smith, consent of Sarah
Smith. Sur. John Boling. Min. Jesse Jones.
Wit. Dandridge Slaughter.

27 Sep 1832   Westley Bowlen, consent of father Joseph Bollen,
for his son Wesley Bollen and Elizabeth Cooper,
daughter of Mary Walden. Sur. William Edwards.
Wit. William Akers.

10 Feb 1846   William Bowling and Joanna Collings, daughter of
Edward Collings. Min. Julius Terrel.
M.R. 14 Feb. 1846.

15 Aug 1833   William G. Bolling and Nancy Moles. Sur. William
Keith. Min. Joshua Adams.

16 Dec 1852   William W. Bowling, the son of Poley G. Bowlen,
and Nancy Clifton, daughter of Emanuel Clifton.
Min. Austin J. Cassell.

1 Jan 1796   Charles Bolt and Molley Barnard, consent of Lucy
Barnard. Sur. John Nunns. Min. Nathan Hall.

7 Jan 1813   Charles Bolt, Jr., and Levina Harbour. Sur.
Thomas Harbour. Min. Jesse Jones.

28 Jan 1807   John Bolt and Rebecca Dillard. Sur. Charles Bolt.
Min. Thomas Whitlock. M.R. 20 Jan 1807.
++
26 Mar 1844   Stephen H. Bolt and Serna Hall. Sur. A. Bowman.
Min. J. Boyd.

Boman, Bowman

28 Jan 1851   Austin Bowman and Mary Arrington. Min. William
Lawson.

15 Jun 1835   Ely Bowman and Nancy Harris. Sur. John H. Bowman.
Min. Thomas Whitlock.

14 Jul 1848   Fewell Bowman and Sintha Hamm. Sur. Norman Bowman.

23 Oct 1805   Gilbird Bowman and Lucy Brimm. Sur. David Roark.
Min. Thomas Whitlock.

7 Apl 1827   George Bowman and Betsy Lewis. Sur. James Pack.
Min. Nathaniel Thompson. M.R. 18 Apl 1827.

++ 29 Jul 1803-John Bolt and Celey Amos. Sur. Samuel Staples.
Min. Nathan Hall. M.R. 21 Aug 1803.

25 Feb 1810   Hamon Bowman and Kesiah Brim. Sur. Aaron Bowman.
Min. Thomas Whitlock.

22 Nov 1847   Jefferson Bowman, son of George Bowman and Martha
Harris, daughter of William Harris. Sur. William
Lawson, John Monday and H.B. Terry. Min. John
Conner. M.R. 25 Nov 1847.

17 Apl 1816   John Bowman and Seley Chaney. Sur. Thomas Whitlock.
M.R. 9 Sep 1815.

10 Oct 1808   John Bowman and Mary Bellar. Min. Thomas Whitlock.

 1 Dec 1852   Madison Bowman and Martha Pack.

29 Jan 1849   Nicholas Bowman, son of Samuel Bowman and Eliza
Harris, daughter of William Harris. Sur. William
Harris. Wit. Madison Bowman and Madison Edwards.
Min. G. W. Conner. M.R. 1 Jan 1849.

13 Apl 1813   Norman Bowman and Jane Simson. Sur. Aaron Bowman.
Min. Thomas Whitlock. M.R. 13 Apl 1813.

30 Aug 1816   Norman Bowman and Rachel Bons. Sur. Martin Duncan.

 3 Mar 1831   Peter Bowman and Nancy Strange. Sur. Gilbert Bowman.
Wit. Daniel Blackburn. Min. Brett Stovall.

21 Jan 1836   Rowland Bowman and Rebecca McMilian. Sur. Parker
Hall. Min. Nathaniel Thompson.

18 Aug 1812   Samuel Bowman and Betsey Harrel. Sur. Jesse Harrel.
Min. Thomas Whitlock. M.R. 13 Aug 1812.

10 Jan 1821   Tyre Bowman and Margaret Vaughters. Sur. H.H. Moore.
M. Thomas Whitlock.

11 Oct 1837   William Bowman and Sally Thompson. Sur. John Bowman
and Austin Thompson. Consent of Jesse Thompson.
Min. William Lawson.

31 Jan 1838   Anderson Bond of Grayson Co.,Va., and Mima Bowman.
Sur. Norman Bowman and Pleasant Bowman. Min.
William Lawson. M.R. 5 Feb 1838.

15 Feb 1815   Isaac Bonds and Nancy Goard. Sur. Thomas Whitlock.
Min. Thomas Whitlock. M.R. 9 Feb 1815.

 6 Feb 1820   Edward M. Booker and Elizabeth Anglin. Sur. John
Thompson. Wit. Abraham Penn. Min. Peter Frans.

17 Aug 1815 Abijah Booth and Lucy Hubbard. Sur. Jesse Hubbard.
Min. Stephen Hubbard. M.R. 26 Aug 1815.

13 May 1819 Austin Booth and Lucy Harris. Consent of Reuben
Harris. Sur. Reuben Harris and William Ayres.
Min. Jesse Jones. M.R. 29 Apl 1819.

28 May 1805 Daniel Booth and Sarah McAlexander. Min. Jesse Jones.

24 Apl 1806 Daniel Booth and Mary McAlexander. Sur. William
McAlexander.

26 Dec 1836 Daniel Booth of Floyd Co.,Va., and Susanna Hubbard.
Sur. Samuel McAlexander. Wit. James McAlexander.
Min. Jesse Jones. M.R. 27 Dec 1836.

 4 Jul 1853 Harvey L. or S. Booth age 21, and Nancy Winfree age
20, daughter of Stephen Winfree. Min. George W.
Rilley.

 3 May 1807 Isaac Booth and Nancy McAlexander. Min. Jesse Jones.

30 Apl 1807 Isaac Booth, consent of father Isaac Booth,and Agnes
McAlexander. Wit. Tamer McAlexander. Sur. William
McAlexander.

 1 Jan 1813 Isaac Booth and Mary Brammer, consent of Guen...Brammer.
Sur. Samuel Brammer.

 6 Sep 1837 Isaac Booth of Montgomery Co.,Va., and Nancy Hix,
daughter of Margaret Hix. Sur. William Ayres.
Wit. H.R. Hall, Martha Hall, Samuel McAlexander.
Min. Jesse Jones.

12 Feb 1852 Caleb Boyd and Rachel Brammer. Min. Wm. Lawson.

12 Jun 1832 David Boyd and Elizabeth Dillon. Sur. William Ayres.
Min. Stephen Hubbard.

 1 Apl 1843 Hearon Boyd and Sarah Cockram, daughter of S. Cockram.
Sur. Henry Boyd. Min. William Lawson.
M.R. 10 Apl 1843.

10 Sep 1836 Henry Boyd, son of Jesse Boyd, and Nancy Cockram.
Sur. Spencer Cockram.

21 Sep 1853 James Boyd, son of John Boyd, and Maza Hiatt, daughter
of Josiah Hiatt. Min. Martin Cloud.

13 Sep 1828 Johnathan Boyd and Polly Burnett. Sur. Prier Pendleton.
Min. John Conner. M.R. 18 Sept 1828.

 5 Feb 1819 Joseph Boyd and Sarah Mankens. Sur. Elkanah Ayers.
Min. Thomas Whitlock.

4 Mar 1830   Joseph Boyd and Sally Herd. Min. Stephen Hubbard.

4 Aug 1838   Obediah N. Boyd and Elizabeth Jones, daughter of
             Martin Cloud. Sur. John Boyd.

23 Oct 1806 Robert Boyd and Elizabeth Rakes, daughter of Charles
             Rakes. Sur. Isham Cockram and John Spaulding.

19 Oct 1853 Sparrell Boyd, age 28, born 28 Feb 1825, the son of
             Andrew Boyd, and Malvina Graham a widow aged 28, born
             31 May 1825. Married at the home of John J. Light.
             Wit. Samuel Light. Min. Austin J. Cassell.

14 Nov 1844 William Boyd and Jane Hill age 20, the daughter of
             John Hill. Sur. Henry Boyd. Wit. S. Cockram.
             Min. William Lawson. M.R. 13 Nov 1844.

16 Sep 1824 Caleb Bradley and Rebecca Morris, daughter of Samuel
             C. Morris,Sr. Sur. Benjamin Morris.

8 Dec 1828   Orlando Bradley and Susanah Carter. Sur. Thomas
             Whitlock. Min. Thomas Whitlock.

4 Feb 1814   James Brammer and Anna Hubbard, daughter of Jesse
             Hubbard. Sur. John Hubbard. Min. Stephen Hubbard.

11 Dec 1834 Johnathan Brammer and Moriah Laymons(Lemmons).
             Sur. George Laymans. Min. Jesse Jones.
             M.R. 1 Jan 1835.

30 Apl 1795 John Brammer and Sarah Lee. Sur. John Lee.
             Min. John Pedigo.

11 Jan 1823 John Brammer and Anna Hall. Consent of Thomas R.
             Hall. Sur. Randolph Hall. Min. Stephen Hubbard.
             M.R. 7 Jan 1823.

31 Jan 1816 John Brammer and Nancy Davis. Sur. Gabriel Bolling.

15 Sep 1843 John Brammer,Sr. and Dorcas Winphrey(Winfrey).
             Sur. James Brammer. Min. Michael Howry.
             M.R. 17 Sep 1845.

19 May 1801 Malaey Brammer (Malachi Brannon) and Lucy Amos.
             Sur. Samuel Amos. Min. Nathan Hall.

12 Apl 1809 Robert Brammer and Hannah McAlexander, daughter of
             William McAlexander. Robert (Robin) Brammer, the
             son of Mary Brammer. Sur. Samuel Clark.
             Min. Jesse Jones.

6 Jan 1806   Shadrick Brammer and Frances Tuggle. Sur. Henry
             Tuggle.

7 Nov 1808   William Brammer and ---- Tuggle. Sur. John Tuggle.

11 Mar 1852   William D. Brammer and Lucinda Dehart.
              Min. G. W. Conner.

3 Jun 1824   Oliver M. Branch and Lydia Moles, daughter of
             Joseph Moles. Sur. John C. Clark, Jr. Jesse
             Corns will pay for the license by July Court.
             Min. Joshua Adams.

15 Nov 1836   Olive Branch and Rachel P. Goard. Sur. John
              Goard. Min. Joshua Adams.

12 Mar 1807   Jarrard Branson and Frances East. Sur. Jesse
              Mankins. Min. Thomas Whitlock.

15 Dec 1803   John Branson and Sarah Dillard. Sur. Meredith
              Smith. Min. Thomas Whitlock.

17 May 1827   John Branson and Sally Surrat. Sur. Jesse Mankin.

   May 1807   Vallentine Branson and Susanah East. Sur. Thomas
              Farmer. Min. Thomas Whitlock.

15 Apl 1798   Joseph Breden and Polley Bartlet. Min. John Pedigo.

              Briant, Bryant

26 Jul 1821   Abner J. Bryant and Sally Bridges. Sur. John Moles.
              Min. Stephen Hubbard. Wit. John Harrison.

5 Jun 1848   Alexander Bryant and Rebecca Moorefield. Sur.
             Wright Moorefield. Min. Joshua Adams.
             M.R. 8 Aug 1848.

29 Jun 1813   Elias Bryant and Delany Price. Sur. Jerman Baker.

4 Oct 1847   Henry L. Bryant and Mary White. Sur. Thomas White.
             Min. Joshua Adams. M.R. 5 Oct 1847.

13 Oct 1838   John Bryant and Frances Jones. Sur. John Cruise.

11 Nov 1819   Lewis D. Bryant and Polly Akers. Sur. Hudson Akers.

12 Jan 1828   William Bryant and Peggy Lewis. Sur. Soloman Wash-
              ington and Elias Bryant.

17 Nov 1811   Edward J. Brickle and Elizabeth Maginess. Sur.
              John Switzlan. Min. Brett Stovall.
              M.R. 20 Nov 1811.

23 Mar 1809   Benjamin Brim and Gillah Bowman. Min. Thomas Whitlock.

14 Jul 1842   James Brim and Martha Hall. Sur. James Dillard. Min. Martin Cloud.

23 Mar 1809   Joseph Brim and Gelah Bowman. Sur. Hamon Bowman.

14 Sep 1853   Price (Rice) O. Brim and Martha Clark, daughter of Edie Clark. Min. D. G. Taylor.

10 Jan 1811   Richard Brim and Jencey Bowman. Sur. Aaron Bowman. Min. Thomas Whitlock. M.R. 15 Feb 1811.

20 Dec 1809   William Brim and Susanah Jenkins. Min. Thomas Whitlock.

25 Jul 1843   Asa G. Britton and Eliza L. Staples. Sur. John D. Cheatham. Min. William Anderson. M.R. 26 Jul 1843.

10 Feb 1850   John Brooks and Mary Mitchell, daughter of James H. Mitchell. Sur. John Mitchell. Min. William Schoolfield.

10 Aug 1842   Thomas B. Brooks and Sarah A. Hairston, consent of Hardin Hairston of Mayo Fort. Sur. Samuel Staples. Min. Joshua Adams.

25 Apl 1794   Augustine Brown, Jr. and Jemimah Hall. Sur. John Hall.

10 Nov 1803   John Brown and Sarah Smith. Sur. Harmon Harel.

1 Jul 1844   Johnathan B. Brown and Nancy Joyce. Sur. Martin Cloud. Min. John Boyd.

11 Feb 1840   Samuel Brown of Rockingham Co., N.C. and Susanah N. Smith. Sur. Munford Smith. Min. Joshua Adams.

30 Oct 1825   James Bulling and Jemima Ratliff. Min. Bird Lowe.

15 Dec 1808   Robert Burch and Judith Harris. Min. William H. Robertson.

2 Dec 1852   Robert Burge and Elizabeth Moorefield, daughter of Wright Moorefield.

13 Dec 1796   William Burge and Polly Cox. Sur. Isaac Dodson.

28 Jan 1836   Woody Burge and Martha New, daughter of George New. Sur. John F. New. Min. Julius Terrel.

22 Dec 1822   Archibald Burnett and Liddy Ayres. Sur. Thomas Whitlock. Min. Thomas Whitlock.

26 Feb 1846   Benjamin T. Burnett and Mary Elvira Harbour, daughter of Richard Harbour. Sur. Pulaski Pedigo.

12 Aug 1836   Beverage Austin Burnett and Judith Slaughter, daughter of Dandridge Slaughter. Sur. Valentine Burnett. Min. John Conner.

19 Nov 1809   Cornelius Burnett and Milly Stone. Sur. Richard Stone.
Min. Lewis Foster. M.R. 22 Nov 1809.

29 Dec 1810   Crawford Burnett and Veny Sharp. Sur. William N.Sharp
and Leonard Sharp. Min. Brett Stovall.
M.R. 2 Jan 1811.

11 Mar 1842   Henry Burnett and Polly Hall. Sur. Harden H. Moore.

13 Aug 1818   Isham Burnett and Anna Hall. Sur. James Tuggle.

 5 May 1853   Jacob J. Burnett and Mary Nolen. Min. G.W. Conner.

 6 Jan 1807   Jeremiah Burnett and Patsy Hughs, daughter of
Beveridge Hughes. Sur. Beverage Hughes. Wit.
Benjamin Hubbard. Min. William H. Robertson.

23 Jul 1810   Jeremiah Burnett, Jr. and Elizabeth Cox, daughter
of James Cox. Sur. Erskine Cox. Wit. Jabez Cox.
Min. Lewis Foster. M.R. 7 July 1809.

15 Sep 1853   Jeremiah Burk Burnett age 20, born 5 Jan 1833, son
of Moses Burnett, and Sally D. Vipperman age 16,
daughter of Daniel Vipperman. Min. Austin J. Cassell.

 4 Jun 1835   Jeremiah Burnett, Sr. and Jane Turner. Sur. Richard
Turner. Min. John Turner.

 7 Oct 1806   John Burnett and Nancy Penington. Sur. Thomas
Spaulding. Min. Stephen Hubbard.

28 Sep 1839   Lewis Burnett and Susannah Cannaday.
Sur. William Cannaday.

20 Oct 1807   Neeley Burnett and Peggy Turner. Sur. Adam Turner.
Min. Lewis Foster.

26 Mar 1844   Obediah M. Burnett, Jr. and Ann Sutphin. Sur.
William Lawson. Wit. Madison Lawson.

11 Mar 1817   Obediah Burnett and Polly Terry. Sur. Richard
Hopkins. Min. John Conner.

16 Aug 1827   Obediah Burnett, Jr. and Milly (Mildred) Hurt,
daughter of Mary Hurt. Sur. Dandridge Slaughter.
Min. John Conner.

10 May 1802   Reuben Burnett and Nancy Tuggle, daughter of
John Tuggle. Sur. Robert Sharp.

11 Aug 1813   Samuel Burnett and Leah Cox. Sur. James Cox.

29 Dec 1812   Valentine Burnett and Agnes Hughes, daughter of Nancy Hughes. Min. Jesse Jones. M.R. 7 Jan 1813.

2 Jul 1821   William Burnett and Garten Thompson. Sur. Henry Thompson.

11 Feb 1793   Zacheriah Burnett and Darkas Small. Sur. John Burnett. M.R. 14 Feb 1793,

8 Apl 1809   John Burress and Deley Thomas. Sur. John Thomas.

7 Jun 1797   Peter Burress and Mary (Martha) Going, consent of David Going. Sur. Edmond Bolling. Min. John Nunns. M.R. 1 June 1797.

22 Mar 1810   Phillip Buzzard and Stacy Fitzgerald. Sur. John Hughes. Min. Brett Stovall. M.R. 28 Mar 1810.

8 Jan 1823   John Cahill and Jane Philpott, consent of father Edward Philpott. Sur. David Philpott. Min. Othniel Minter. M.R. 14 Jan 1823.

12 Nov 1842   Caleb C. Campbell and Martha Jane Jarratt, daughter of Wiatt Jarrett. Sur. Addy Jarratt. Wit. Joshua H. Clark. Min. Arnold Walker.

13 Jul 1837   James W. Campbell, son of John Campbell, and Jemima A. Kasey, daughter of John N. Kasey. Min. Joshua Adams.

27 May 1841   John Campbell and Frances Brammer. Sur. William Cassell. Min. John Conner. M.R. 29 May 1841.

4 Jun 1803   John Campbell and Elizabeth Beller. Sur. Eli Beller.

23 Jan 1845   Thomas K. Campbell and Mary C. Clark, daughter of Henry Clark. Sur. William B. Smith. Min. A. Walker.

27 Nov 1841   William Campbell, son of James & Lucinda Campbell, and Nancy Collings, daughter of Edward & Hannah Collings. Min. Joshua Adams. M.R. 7 Dec 1841.

13 Jul 1798   Ceaser Camron,   negro, and Hander Fender.

7 Jan 1839   Fleming Canaday and Susanah Thomas, daughter of Pleasant Thomas, Sr.. Sur. Pleasant C. Thomas, Jr. Wit. James Thomas. Min. Jesse Jones. M.R. 15 Jan 1839.

26 Dec 1843   Isaac Cannaday, son of Elizabeth Cannaday, and Mary Rakes, daughter of Samuel Rakes. Sur. John T. Griffith. Wit. Peter Canaday.

12 Nov 1840   John Cannaday and Lilly W. Bartlett. Sur. J.Bartlett.

24 Sep 1849   Pleasant Canaday and Deborah Hall. Sur. David McAlexander.

7 Jan 1841   John Canley and Martha Ross. Min. John Conner.

9 May 1807   Samuel Carrol and Elizabeth McAlexander. Sur. William McAlexander. Min. Jesse Jones. M.R. 14 May 1807.

17 Nov 1803   Talton (Zalton) Carrol and Mary Dockery. Sur. Elihu Ayers. Min. Thomas Whitlock. M.R. 7 Nov 1803.

22 Apl 1821   Abraham Carter and Salley Bondurant. Sur. George Sprouse. Min. Maning Hill.

29 Dec 1810   Alexander S. Carter and Liddy (Elizabeth) Deal. Sur. Jacob Grigg.

30 Aug 1838   Austin Carter and Leveny Edens. Min. John Conner.

27 Apl 1817   Banes Carter and Julia B. Philpott, consent of B. W. Philpott. Sur. A. Stovall. Min. Peter Frans.

25 Feb 1813   Benjamin Carter and Nancy Reynolds. Sur. Moses Reynolds. Min. Lewis Foster. M.R. 29 Feb 1814.

8 Jul 1847   Christopher C. Carter and Martha Crowder. Sur. J.T. Turner. Min. W.W. Nesbitt. M.R. 13 Jul 1847.

29 Oct 1818   Elijah Carter and Amelia Sprouse. Sur. George Sprouse. Min. John Conner. M.R. 28 July 1818.

5 Jan 1821   George Carter and Sally Fulkerson. Sur. Fredrick Fulkerson. Min. Peter Frans. M.R. 4 Jan 1821.

24 Nov 1852   George R. Carter and Sarah Jane Carter. Wit. Samuel Carter. Min. Joshua Adams. M.R. 2 Dec 1852.

11 May 1805   Jedediah Carter and Susanah Reynolds. Sur. Moses Reynolds.

28 Aug 1806   Jesse Carter and Sarah Haynes. Sur. Thomas Farmer. Min. Thomas Whitlock.

26 Aug 1830   Jesse Carter and Ruth Adams. Min. Joshua Adams.

7 Feb 1851   Jerman W. Carter and Sophia Hagood. Min. William M. Schoolfield. M.R. 11 Feb 1851.

12 Feb 1852   John Carter and Nancy Joyce. Min. Joshua Adams.

22 Mar 1832   John B. Carter, son of John Carter, of Floyd Co.,Va.
              and Rozinah Adams. Min. Joshua Adams. Sur. Rowland
              Adams. Consent is given by Joshua Adams, guardian
              for Rozina Adams. Wit. Lewis Spencer. M.R. 21 Feb
              1832.

 1 Oct 1824   John P. Carter and Polley Lackey, daughter of George
              Lackey. Sur. James Bartlett.

27 Nov 1849   John P. Carter and Adaline Ayers, consent of father,
              Francis Ayers. Sur. J.W. Gates. Min. J.H. Jefferson.

 9 May 1848   Lewis Carter and Permelia, daughter of Thomas W. Turner.
              Sur. Joseph L. Turner.

 6 Jan 1829   Lewis Carter and Ann C. Bartlett. Sur. John Massey.
              Min. Jesse Jones.

28 Feb 1842   Robert Carter and Roady(Rhody) Keaton. Sur. Samuel
              Carter. Wit. Solomon Keaton, Hirum Keaton and James
              E. Ashley. Min. Joshua Adams. M.R. 27 Feb 1842.

 9 Jan 1854   Samuel Carter, son of Nancy Carter, and Sally Stegall,
              consent is given by John G. Lee, guardian. Sur.
              William Stegall.

13 Apl 1821   Samuel Carter and Nancey Daniel. Sur. Robert Daniel.
              Min. John C. Traylor.

21 Oct 1810   Thomas Carter and Nancy Cother, daughter of Isaac
              Cother. Sur. Benjamin Howell.

14 Nov 1804   William Carter and Lucy Edwards, daughter of Thomas
              Edwards. Sur. John Carter. Min. Jesse Jones.

10 Feb 1822   William Carter and Nancy Booker. Sur. Edward Booker.
              Min. Peter Frans. M.R. 10 Feb 1822.

18 Sep 1819   William Carter, Jr. and Elizabeth Moore. Sur. Thomas
              Whitlock. Min. Thomas Whitlock. M.R. 15 Sep 1819.

 1 Mar 1819   Peter Cassaday and Prudence Harris. Sur. Elijah Harris.
              Min. Brett Stovall. M.R. 5 Mar 1819.

 8 Dec 1843   William A.J. Cassaday and Jane Dalton. Sur. Coleman
              Dalton. Min. Joshua Adams. M.R. 11 Dec 1843.

29 Aug 1838   Austen Cassell and Leviny Edwards, daughter of Brice
              Edwards. Sur. William Cassell.

20 Dec 1819   John Cassell and Polly Gilbert. Sur. Samuel Gilbert.

NOTE: Original Book had a hand-numbered page 20A. This threw pagination off at
      printer, so we have now numbered page 20A as Page 134. Hence names start-
      ing with Cassell and ending with Cheatham are now on Page 134.

8 Oct 1850   Benjamin Cherry and Mary Carter. Min. Jeremiah Burnett.

17 Feb 1804   Isaac Cherry and Lottey Harris. Sur. James Taylor.

2 Mar 1805   John Cherry and Nancy Hill, daughter of John Hill.
Sur. John Gossett.

10 Feb 1842   Rev. Nicholas Chevalier of Montgomery Co.Va., and
Bethenia F. Stuart. Sur. Arch. Stuart.
Min. Dugald McIntyre.

30 Apl 1852   William Childers and Maryann Elizabeth Stanley,
daughter of Richard B. Stanley.

18 Oct 1794   Henry Chiles and Polly Reynolds, consent of mother
Susanna Clark. Sur. Jesse Reynolds. Wit. John
Medley. Min. George Dodson. M.R. 19 Oct 1794.

25 Feb 1813   Joel Chitwood and Susannah Corn. Sur. Thomas Reeves.
Min. Thomas Whitlock.

12 Feb 1798   John Chitwood and Sally Farrell, daughter of John
Farrell. Sur. William Farrell. Min. Isaac Adams.

28 Apl 1814   William Chitwood and Nancy Corn. Sur. John A. Corn
and Wilson Penn.

18 Oct 1826   Tully Choice and Susannah Hagood. Sur. Gregory Hagood.

6 Nov 1848   George W. Clanton and Mary Ann Hylton, daughter of
J. Hylotn. Sur. George W. Hylton. Min. Joshua Adams.
M.R. 8 Nov 1848.

4 Feb 1840   Alexander B. Clark and Sarah Goins (Gaines), daughter
of George W. Gaines. Sur. Thornton Gaines.
Min. Joshua Adams.

22 May 1845   Andrew J. Clark and Martha Stone. Sur. John Stone.
Min. Joshua Adams.

13 Feb 1843   Andrew Jackson Clark, the widow of John Clark consents,
and Malinda Spencer. Sur. William Spencer. Min.
Joshua Adams. M.R. 16 Feb 1843.

21 Jan 1840   Cardwell W. Clark and Ruth A. Smith, daughter of
Munford Smith. Sur. Hamilton Joyce.

18 Jan 1839   Edward Clark and Sally G. Salmons. Sur. George W. Lewis.

2 Nov 1826   Fleming Clark, consent of mother Lucy Clark, and
Margaret (Peggy) Houchen. Sur. Isaac Adams. Wit. T.R.
Hall.

8 Feb 1843   George N. Clark and Mary Dehart. Sur. Thomas Dehart.
Min. William Schoolfield. M.R. 11 Feb 1843.

7 Aug 1852 George W. Clark and Elizabeth P. Ross, daughter of Daniel Ross. Min. Bird Turner.

17 Mar 1825 Henry Clark and Ruth Mize, daughter of John Mize. Sur. Harden R. Hall. Min. Stephen Hubbard.

1838 Henry Clark and Miss Jarrott. Min. John C. Traylor.

8 Apl 1825 Jacob Clark and Jane Stovall. Sur. Madison R. Hughes.

15 Dec 1846 James Clark and Mary Bowling. Sur. Thomas H. Markham. Min. Joshua Adams. M.R. 14 Dec 1846.

30 Jan 1849 Jerman Clark and Frances J. Law, daughter of William Law,Sr. Sur. John H. Washburn. Min. J$_o$shua Adams.

25 Mar 1801 Jesse Clark and Lucy Peddigoe, daughter of Edward Pedigo. Sur. John Hall.

15 Aug 1835 Jesse Clark and Lydia C. Bartlett. Sur. James Bartlett. Min. John Conner.

21 Dec 1809 Joel Clark and Elizabeth Cardwell. Sur. Thomas Cardwell. Min. Brett Stovall.M.R. 2 Jan 1810.

25 Apl 1811 John Clarke and Elizabeth Wright, daughter of Salley Wright. Sur. Sally Wright and Cornelius Thomas. Wit. Frankey Clarke and Jesse Clarke.

10 Dec 1839 John Clark, son of Michael Clark and Diona Mize, daughter of John Mize. Wit. John T. Dodson. Min. Joshua Adams. M.R. 12 Dec 1839.

23 Sep 1841 John B. Clark and Elmira Hudnall, daughter of Richard Hudnall. Sur. Charles Hudnall. Min. John Washburn. M.R. 28 Sep 1841.

24 Apl 1816 John Clark, Jr and Eliza B. Sandefer, daughter of M. Sandefer. Sur. John Clark. Min. Brett Stovall. M.R. 12 May 1816.

5 Apl 1852 John R. Clark and Sarah Jane Dodson, daughter of Elisha Dodson. Min. Joshua Adams. M.R. 8 Apl 1852.

30 Jan 1838 Joseph H. Clark, James Clark gives consent, and Louisa Jarratt. Sur. Robert Jarrott. Wit. John Fretwell.

2 Apl 1814 Landford Clark and Sally Clark. Min. Brett Stovall.

28 Jul 1830 Moses S. Clark and Nancy Edwards. Sur. William Clark. Min. Bird Lowe. M.R. 29 July 1830.

29 Jun 1848   Robert M. Clark and Exoney E. Hall. Sur. Samuel G. Staples. Min. Joshua Adams.

19 Nov 1829   Samuel Clark and Elizabeth Tatum. Consent of J. Tatum. Sur. Thomas J. Tatum. Min. Bird Lowe.

31 Mar 1814   Sanford Clark and Sally Clark. Sur. John Clark. Min. Brett Stovall. (See Lanford Clark).

9 Feb 1851   Stephen Clark and Elizabeth Clark. Min. D.G. Taylor.

28 Jul 1814   William Clark and Patsy Carter. Sur. A. Staples. Min. Peter Frans.

26 Nov 1808   Caleb Clay and Sarah Morrison. Sur. Thomas Morrison. Min. John Conner.

20 Jun 1806   Soloman Clay and Polly Hancock. Sur. John A. Hancock. Min. William H. Robertson. M.R. 3 July 1806.

7 Nov 1804   Charles Clements and Nancy Hanby. Sur. Samuel Hanby,Jr. M.R. 17 Nov 1804.

22 Dec 1828   Martin Clifton, son of John Clifton, and Susan Barrett. Sur. William Cassell. Wit. Clayborn Barrett.

3 Apl 1828   George Cloud and Mary Kellar. Min. Thomas Whitlock.

3 Apl 1828   George W. Cloud and Lucinda Walker. Sur. John A. Cloud.

9 Aug 1817   Martin Cloud and Polly Dickerson. Sur. and Min. Thomas Whitlock.

9 Oct 1834   John Cobb and D. Kennerly. Sur. Joseph Kennerly.

27 Nov 1837   Samuel E. Cobb and Jane F. Vah....Sur. H.H. Staples.

21 Sep 1842   Preston Cock of Carrol Co.,Va. son of John Cock,Sr., and Judith C. Hubbard, daughter of Joel C. Hubbard. Sur. Joel Hubbard. Wit. John Cock,Jr.

15 Jul 1838   Brice Cockram and Willy Lewis, daughter of Alvin Lewis. Sur. Joseph Cox.

20 Oct 1825   David Cockram and Anna Wood. Min. Stephen Hubbard.

7 Oct 1825   David Cockram and Anna Wood, daughter of Richard Wood. Wit. Isham Cockram and Jonathan Hale.

4 Nov 1806   Edward Cockram and Mary Rakes, daughter of Charles Rakes. Sur. Charles Rakes. Min. William H. Robertson.

28 Feb 1848   John Cockram and Mahala Cruise. Sur. John Cruise, who takes oath that John Cockram is over 21 years of age. Min. William Lawson. M.R. 9 Mar 1848.

23 Aug 1833   Marvel B. Cockram and Susanah(Lucinda) Edwards. Sur. Brice Edwards. Min. Jesse Jones.

12 Jan 1798   Nathan Cockram and Bathsheba Pedigo, daughter of Edward Pedigo. Sur. Elijah Pedigo. Min. John Pedigo.

13 Jun 1841   Nathan Cockram and Ruth Cockram (Ruth Brammer). Consent of S. Cockram. Sur. William Griffith. Min. William Lawson.

25 Jan 1847   Richard Cockram, son of David Cockram, and Judith Wood. Sur. Jeremiah Wood. Wit. A. Wood & Joel F. Wood. Min. G.W.Conner. M.R. 31 Jan 1847.

29 May 1817   Spencer Cockram and Nancy Boyd, daughter of Hugh Boyd. Sur. Nathan Cockram. Wit. Andrew Boyd. Min. Stephen Hubbard.

 8 Mar 1805   Charles Cole and Any Freeman. Sur. Richard Atkinson. Min. Thomas Whitlock. M.R. 18 Mar 1804.

21 Nov 1831   William C. Cole of Stokes Co.,N.C., and Elizabeth Murphy. Sur. Jesse Murphy. Min. Joseph Goodman.

 7 May 1805   Charles Collier, Jr. and Jane Parr. Sur. Smith Parr.

29 May 1834   David Collier and Elizabeth MacCraw. Sur. James W. Warshop.

29 Dec 1847   Absalom Collins and Elizabeth Nunn. Sur. Francis Collins. Min. Julius Terrell.

 6 Feb 1846   David C. Collins and Levinia Kimbell, daughter of John Kimbell. Sur. John Kimbell. Min. Julius Terrell. M.R. 17 Feb 1846.

 8 Apl 1847   David Collins and Ruth Vipperman. Sur. Daniel Vipperman. Min. Julius Terrell. M.R. 15 Apl 1847.

 6 May 1828   Edmond Collings and Eliza Tucker. Sur. George Gunter.

16 Jul 1836   Frances Collings,age 22 son of Edward Collings, and Sally F. Clark. Sur. Madison Clark. Min. Joshua Adams. M.R. 20 July 1836.

15 Jan 1834   George Collings and Martha Campbell, daughter of James Campbell. Sur. Edward Prindle. Wit. Elisha Collins. and William Shelton. Min. Julius Terrell.

24 Apl 1800 Isaac Collins and Nancy Blackburn. Sur. Thomas Blackburn.

17 Sep 1840 James Collins and Nancy Slate. Sur. Isham Slate.
Min. Joshua Adams.

7 Dec 1852 James Collins and Annis Flippen. M. Julius Terrell.

2 Jul 1829 Leaton Collins and Sarah N. Tucker. Min. Bird Lowe.

7 Apl 1827 William Collins and Martha Nunn. Sur. Alexander
Overby. Min. Bird Lowe.

17 Aug 1828 William Collins and Zady Fry. Sur. Brett Stovall.
Min. Joshua Adams.

5 Jan 1835 William Combs and Elizabeth Sayers. Sur. Harding
H. Moore.

22 Dec 1848 Peyton Connaway and Jane Robertson. Sur. Samuel
Staples. Min. Joshua Adams. M.R. 24 Dec 1848.

10 Feb 1815 Daniel Conner and Mary Hart. Sur. John Hurt and
Richard Hopkins. Min. Brett Stovall. M.R. 23 Apl 1815.

11 Dec 1828 Daniel Conner and Anna McAlexander, daughter of
William McAlexander. Sur. John Conner,Sr.
Min. John Conner.

24 Dec 1816 Daniel Conner and Mary Conner give consent for their
daughter to marry Edward Hilton.

16 Oct 1834 David Conner and Susanna Adams. Sur. John Conner.
Min.Joshua Adams.

29 Nov 1840 G. W. Conner and Nancy Bolling. Sur. B. Clark.

2 Apl 1835 George Washington Conner, son of Mary Conner, and
Nancy Dehart, daughter of Gabriel Dehart,Sr.
Sur. Stephen Dehart.

30 Nov 1826 James Conner and Keziah Ross, daughter of Daniel Ross.
Sur. John Conner. Wit. Isaac Adams.

16 Dec 1794 John Conner and Lucy Robertson, daughter of David
Robertson. Sur. Benjamin Morris. Wit. William
Roberson and David Roberson,Jr. Min. Robert Jones.

16 Nov 1826 John Conner, Jr. and Milly McAlexander, daughter of
William McAlexander. Sur. John Conner,Sr. Min.
John Conner,Sr.

5 Mar 1828 Peter Conner and Naomi Slaughter, daughter of John
Slaughter. Sur. John Conner. Min. John Conner.
M.R. 6 Mar 1828.

7 Apl 1804 William Conner and Susanah Kindle. Sur. Isaac Stinson.

14 Sep 1819   William Conner and Aney Ross. Sur. John Conner.
Min. Jesse Jones. M.R. 7 Sep 1819.

28 Jan 1822   Freeman Copland and Elizabeth East. Sur. William
East. Min. Thomas Whitlock.

2 Jan 1844   William Copland and Elizabeth T. Corn, daughter of
Jesse Corn. Sur. William H. Corn. Min. Joshua Adams.

15 Mar 1810   Jesse Corn, Jr. and Elizabeth Burnett. Sur. John
Burnett. Min. Lewis Foster.

13 Jul 1809   John Corn and Elizabeth Adams. Sur. John Adams.
Min. Brett Stovall. M.R. 22 Jul 1809.

20 Sep 1796   John Corn and Hannah Haile, daughter of James Hale.
Sur. George Corn. Wit. William Adams and Tyre Tatum,
Jr. M. Isaac Adams.

27 Nov 1806   John Adam Corn and Polly Ware (Mary Moore), daughter
of Berryman Moore. Sur. William Corn. Min. Lewis
Foster. M.R. 1 Nov 1806.

17 Feb 1848   Joshua C. Corn and Matilda Spencer. Sur. Martin
Spencer. M. Joshua Adams.

18 Oct 1827   Richard Corn and Jane Hightower. Sur. Thomas Hightower.
Min. Joshua Adams.

28 Nov 1816   Samuel Corn and Permelia Burnett. Sur. John Burnett.
Min. Stephen Hubbard.

13 May 1819   Samuel Corn and Susannah Slaughter, daughter of John
Slaughter, Sr., Wit. John Slaughter, Jr. Min. Stephen
Hubbard.

14 Feb 1814   William Corn and Jencey Carter. Sur. and Min. Thomas
Whitlock. M.R. 14 Nov 1814.

5 Jan 1812   William Corn and Phebey Adams, daughter of John Adams,
Sur. Joshua Adams. Wit. Sara Adams. Min Peter Frans.

27 Nov 1806   William Corn and Nancy Sharp, daughter of William
Sharp. Sur. John Adam Corn. Min. Lewis Foster.

28 Oct 1852   William H. Corn and Mary Ann Koger. Min. Joshua Adams.

25 Nov 1797   John Cotreh(Cotrete,Cotrell) and Sally Rowark.
Min. John Nunns.

11 Nov 1833   Joseph Covington and Elizabeth(Betsy) Hudnall, daughter
of Richard Hudnall. Sur. Richard N. Hudnall, Jr.
M. John Washburn. M.R. 5 Dec 1833.

2 Jan 1830   Andrew Cox and Anis Stegall. Sur. Peter Dickerson.
Min. Thomas Whitlock.

17 Sep 1813   Erskine Cox and Sally Walden, daughter of William
Walden. Wit. James Ingram and Francis Cox. Min.
Brett Stovall.

7 Feb 1809   Francis Cox and Perninah Walder. Min. Lewis Foster.
M.R. 8 Feb 1809.

13 Oct 1853   George W. Cox, son of Randall & Jane Cox, and Nancy M.
Craddock, daughter of Braxton & Sarah Craddock. Sur.
Abel Pedigoy. Min. Joshua Adams.

28 Oct 1828   James Cox and Elizabeth Belcher. Sur. Richard Maynor.
Min. John Turner.

13 Aug 1835   James Cox and Jane Lewis. Sur. Joseph Cox. Min.
Joshua Adams. M.R. 23 Aug 1835.

6 Oct 1847   John Cox and Elizabeth Harris. Sur. James Harris.
Min. Joshua Adams.

15 Apl 1830   Joseph Cox and Nancy Lewis. Sur. James Ingram, Jr.
Min. Stephen Hubbard. M.R. 27 Apl. 1830.

23 Mar 1826   Lewis Cox and Susannah Hollandsworth. Sur. Thomas
Hollandsworth. Min. Joshua Adams.

22 Oct 1842   Preston Cox and Judy Hubbard. Min. John Conner.

18 Oct 1804   Randolph Cox and Jane Bryant, daughter of Elias
Bryant. Sur. Joseph Cummings.

14 Jun 1832   Braxton Craddock and Sally Spencer. Sur. William
Spencer. Min. Joshua Adams. M.R. 26 Jun 1832.

15 Dec 1852   Ezekiel Craddock and Lucy R. Law, consent of William
Law. Wit. John H. Washburn. Min. Jeremiah Burnett.

4 Mar 1804   Isham Craddock and Sarah Hollandsworth. Sur. Joseph
Cummings. Min. Nathan Hall. M.R. Feb 1804

29 Apl 1813   James Craddock and Polly Purdy. Sur. Ezekiel Purdy.
Min. Lewis Foster. M.R. 19 May 1814.

7 Dec 1846   James Craddock and Lavicy Purdy. Sur. William Tudor.
Min. Joshua Adams.

16 Sep 1834   James Craddock and Delpha(Perdelpha) Martin. Sur.
Isaac Martin. Min. Joshua Adams.

3 Feb 1807   Nathaniel Craddock and Caty Handy. Sur. Isham Craddock.

18 Jul 1801   Thomas Craddock and Sarah Bryant, daughter of Elias
Bryant. Sur. Moses Godard. Min. Nathan Hall.
M.R. 28 July 1801.

1 Oct 1838   Thomas Craddock and Lucy Cruise. Sur. J. Craddock.

15 Feb 1853   Greensville Craig and Susanna Jane Rogers. Min.
Samuel J. Lackey.

16 Dec 1839   James J. Craig and Jane Woodall. Sur. Simeon Woodall.
Consent of Adam Craig. Wit. Daniel H. Woodall.

24 Oct 1843   Cary Crawford and Olive Hancock, daughter of Martha
Hancock. Sur. Daniel Smith.

16 Jun 1818   William Crawford and Martha Elizabeth Rowan. Sur.
Robert Rowan. Min. Jesse Jones.

27 Feb 1810   John Cresley and Hannah Harrel. Sur. Joseph Williams.
Min. Thomas Whitlock.

17 May 1831   Archelaus Critz and Luvinna Penn. Sur. Green Penn.
Min. John C. Traylor.

23 Jan 1812   Fredrick Critz and Nancy Frans. Sur. George Critz.

20 Oct 1814   George F. Critz and Polly Philpott. Sur. Thomas Adams.
Min. Peter Frans.

24 Sep 1849   Hamon Critz and Sarah E. Frasure. Sur. Peter A. Lee.
Min. Joshua Adams. M.R. 27 Sept. 1849.

6 Apl 1850   Hamon Critz, consent of William Critz, and Luvena
Shelton, daughter of Hubert Shelton. Sur. Samuel
G. Staples. Min. Joshua Adams. M.R. 11 Apl 1850.

30 Oct 1816   William Critz and Polly Harrison. Sur. George Carter.
Min. Peter Frans.

26 Jul 1847   William Critz, Jr and Susan Critz. Sur. Hamon Critz.
Min. Joshua Adams. M.R. 29 July 1847.

1 Feb 1822   John Cross and Abigail Edens. Min. John Conner.

13 Feb 1822   John Cross and Tabitha Edwards. Sur. John Tuggle.
Min. John Conner. M.R. 1 Feb 1822.

23 Dec 1824   David Cruise,Jr., son of David Cruise,Sr.,and Susannah
Craddock, daughter of Isham Craddock. Min. Joshua
Adams.

Cruise, Crews

29 Dec 1811 David Crews and Sally Martin. Sur. Isaac Martin.

13 Feb 1847 David Cruise and Zina Rakes. Sur. Chesley Rakes.
Min. G.W. Conner M.R. 14 Feb 1847.

15 Feb 1853 Greenville Cruise and Susanna Jane Rogers.
Min. Samuel J. Lackey.

23 Dec 1847 James Cruise, consent of guardian, Brice Edwards,
and Mary Ann Belcher, daughter of Benjamin Belcher.
Wit. Harden Belcher. Min. William Lawson.
Sur. Peter Cruise.

7 Jun 1812 John Cruise and Mazy Martin. Sur. Isaac Martin.
Min. Lewis Foster. M.R. 6 Jul 1812.

18 Mar 1832 Redman Cruise, son of David Cruise, and Lucinda
Craddock. Sur. Braxton Craddock. Wit. Jarman
Craddock. Min. Joshua Adams. M.R. 22 Mar 1832.

4 Dec 1849 William Cruise and Luvenia Daniel. Sur. Bailey
Daniel. Min. Joshua Adams.

22 Oct 1834 Anderson P. Crum and Latisha Akers, daughter of
Nathaniel Akers. Sur. Samuel Howell.

8 Jul 1819 Henry Crum and Polly Wright. Sur. William Crum.
Min. Stephen Hubbard.

5 Dec 1817 James Crumb and Penca Reynolds, daughter of Moses
Reynolds. Sur. Samuel Staples. Wit. Joseph Kennerly.
Min. Peter Frans. M.R. 7 Dec 1817.

17 Oct 1833 John Crum and Nancy Lawless, daughter of Sally
Lawless. Sur. Charles Wilson. Wit. Alexander H.
Spencer. Min. Joshua Adams. M.R. 18 Oct 1833.

13 Aug 1813 William Crum and Ruth Sharpe. Sur. John Sharp.

30 Oct 1846 William Crum and Matilda J. Harbour, daughter of
Martha Harbour. Sur. James Harbour. Min. Joshua
Adams. M.R. 20 Oct. 1846.

28 Aug 1806 Samuel Crutcher, Jr. and Nancy James. Sur. John James.

26 Oct 1807 Joseph Cummings and Susannah (Saran) Corn. Sur. Moses
Cummings. Min. Peter Frans.

27 Jan 1819 Moses Cummings and Polley Mayo. Sur. Caleb Purdy.

10 Nov 1853 Andrew J. Dalton, son of Coleman & Dolly Dalton, and
Sarah Gilbert, daughter of Fredrick & Jane Gilbert.
Min. Samuel J. Lackey.

21 Apl 1849 Fredrick Dalton and Martha Clifton, daughter of
William Clifton. Sur. Coleman Dalton. Min. Joshua
Adams. M.R. 25 Apl 1849.

4 Jun 1845 Hamon C. Dalton and Sarah Critz. Sur. John L. Anglin.
Min. Joshua Adams. M.R. 5 Jun 1845.

16 Aug 1820 James Dalton and Nancy Critz. Sur. Hamon Critz.
Min. Peter Frans.

4 Oct 1845 Leander H. Dalton and Matilda Stovall. Sur. Joseph
H. Hanby.

29 Jan 1807 Lewis Dalton and Elizabeth Phillips. Min. Thomas
Whitlock.

6 Dec 1848 Nicholas Dalton and Matilda A. Thomas, daughter of
Richard Thomas. Sur. Samuel D. Critz. Wit. James
H. Dalton. Min. Joshua Adams. M.R. 10 Dec 1848.

19 Oct 1826 Bailey Daniel and Phoeby Trent. Sur. Zachariah Trent.
Min. Joshua Adams.

24 Dec 1791 Edward Daniel and Polly Consolvent. Sur. Stephen Rennoe.

12 Jan 1847 James Daniel and Elizabeth Spencer. Min. Jeremiah
Burnett.

19 Jan 1826 Nehemiah Daniel and Kitty Mankin. Sur. & Min.
Thomas Whitlock.

13 Mar 1796 John Davenport and Nancey Burnett, daughter of
Jeremiah Burnett. Sur. Dandridge Slaughter. Wit.
Beveridge Hughes. Min. John Pedigo.

30 Nov 1826 Benjamin Davis and Nancy Packwood. Sur. John
Packwood. Wit. Grandason B. Lesueur. Min. John
Turner. M.R. <u>17 May 1827</u>.

14 Oct 1848 George Davis, lives with Gabriel Boling who gives
consent, and Elizabeth Palmer, daughter of Judy
Palmer. Sur. John W. Boling. Min. G. W. Conner.
M.R. 15 Oct 1848.

19 Apl 1828 George R. Davis and Nancy Akers, daughter of John
Akers. Sur. William Ayres. Wit. W. Akers.

6 Mar 1848 Jesse H. Davis and Susan Ann Koger, daughter of John
Koger. Sur. Jacob W. Koger. Min. Joshua Adams.
M.R. 14 Mar 1848.

17 Feb 1820 John Davis and Rhoda Harris. Sur. Samuel Harris.

9 Dec 1829 John Davis and Temperance Wright. Sur. Robert
Wright. Min. John Conner.

27 Dec 1812   Joseph Davis and Polley Blancett. Sur. Abraham Penn.
              Min. Thomas Whitlock.

17 Apl 1836   Joseph Davis and Sophia Watson. Sur. John Scott.
              Min. Thomas Whitlock.

 9 Dec 1795   Richardson Davis and Rachel Foley. Sur. John Ferrel.
              Min. Robert Jones.

 5 Jun 1799   James Deal and Molly Keaton. Sur. William Keaton.

 9 Jun 1810   Thomas Deal and Mary Clemmons. Sur. Leonard Owen.
              Min. Thomas Whitlock.

31 Oct 1800   William Deal and Lucy Spencer. Sur. Samuel Staples.

17 Mar 1816   Henry Dean and Rlurey Ayres. Sur. Thomas Whitlock.

18 Jun 1816   Hirem Dean and Nancy Jonson. Sur. Elkanah Ayres.
              Min. Thomas Whitlock.

21 Oct 1839   James Dean and Easter Hiatt, daughter of Josiah Hiatt.
              Sur. Samuel Thomas.

 2 Feb 1832   Aaron Dehart and Tamer McAlexander. Sur. James Reynolds.
              Min. Stephen Hubbard. M.R. 5 Feb 1832.

20 Sep 1822   Adam Dehart and Elizabeth Tune. Min. Thomas Whitlock.
              M.R. 20 Sep 1822.

13 Oct 1836   Charles Dehart and Nancy Conner. Sur. William Conner.
              Min. John Conner.

28 Jan 1797   Elijah Dehart and Mary Jordon. Sur. Thomas P. Jordon.
              Min. John Pedigo.

27 Mar 1843   Elijah Dehart and Eliza Ann Taylor, daughter of Polly
              Dehart. Sur. George N. Clark. Wit. Thomas Dehart.
              M.R. 30 Mar 1843.

 3 Oct 1842   Elijah J. Dehart, Jr. and Rebecca McAlexander. Sur.
              David McAlexander. Min. Jesse Jones. M.R. 4 Oct 1842.

28 Feb 1833   Gabriel Dehart and Martha Gates. Min. Stephen Hubbard.

 4 Jan 1797   James Deharc and Catherine Hubbard. Wit. Elijah Dehart
              and Thomas Tenison. Min. Jospeh Pedigo. M.R. 28 Jan 1797.

 3 Dec 1831   James Dehart and Delpha Martin, widow of Moses Martin.
              Sur. Stephen Hubbard. Wit. Elijah H. Dehart.
              Min. Stephen Hubbard. M.R. 14 Dec 1831.

22 Oct 1835   James W. Dehart and Rebecca Martin, daughter of Delpha
              Dehart. Sur. Elijah H. Deharc. Min. Jesse Jones.

24 Feb 1853   Jesse H. Dehart and Mentery Ayres. Min.G.W. Conner.

12 Mar 1835   Jesse P. Dehart and Deborah Thomas, daughter of
Charles Thomas. Sur. John S. Dehart. Wit. Nicholas P.
Thomas.

21 Oct 1827   John Dehart and Susanah Booth. Sur. John Johnson.
Min. Stephen Hubbard. M.R. 4 Oct 1827.

24 Feb 1840   John Dehart, son of Gabriel Dehart, and Sarah
Parmer, daughter of Chasloly Parmer. Sur. John D.
Cheatham. Wit. Madison Parmer. Min. John Conner.
M.R. 25 Feb 1840.

14 Feb 1853   John H. Dehart and Mentoric (?) Ayres, daughter of
Frances Ayres. Wit. Texas Ayres.

19 Feb 1824   Joshua Dehart and Sally James Stegall, consent of
George Stegall. Sur. Drinkard Stegall. Min. Stephen
Hubbard.

29 Dec 1831   Paul W. Dehart and Lucinda Dehart. Min. Stephen Hubbard.

21 Jan 1853   Robert Dehart, consent of guardian C. Ross, and Elizabeth
Taylor, daughter of James A. Taylor. Wit. William Dehart
Min. John Conner, Sr.

 2 Aug 1828   Stephen Dehart and Susanna Elgin. Sur. Paul Elgan.
Min. John Conner. M.R. 3 Aug 1828.

28 Oct 1819   Thomas Dehart and Martha Via, daughter of William Via.
Sur. Isham Harris. Min. Stephen Hubbard. M.R.
25 Nov 1819.

27 Feb 1843   Thomas Dehart and Mary Taylor. Sur. Samuel G. Staples.
Wit. John Tuggle.

22 Mar 1847   Thomas Dehart and Milly Conner. Sur. Daniel Conner.
Min. John Conner, Sr. M.R. 25 Mar 1847.

18 Mar 1849   William Dehart and Exony Timinda Taylor, daughter of
Mary Dehart. Sur. George N. Clark, who takes oath
that he believes William to be over 21 yrs of age.
Wit. John Akers and Elijah Dehart.

14 May 1800   Ezeriah Denny and Sally Blackburn, daughter of Thomas
Blackburn. Sur. Richard Pilson.

26 Oct 1798   Jeremiah Denny and Sally Harris. Sur. James Harris.
Min. Jesse Jones.

7 Mar 1815 William Dwege and Lacy Littrell, consent of Thomas
Littrell. Wit. J. Helms. Sur. Ezekiel Aldridge.
Min. John Conner. M.R. 8 Mar 1815.

14 Nov 1816 Leonard Dickerson and Susannah Hylton, consent of
Archelaus Hylton. Sur. E. Hylton. Min. Jesse Jones.
M.R. 21 Oct 1816.

8 Dec 1846 Leonard Dickerson, son of John & Mary Dickerson, and
Lucy Slaughter. Sur. Martin Slaughter. Wit. M.D.
Carter. Min. John Conner. M.R. 27 Dec 1846.

12 Jun 1813 Nathaniel Dickson and Priscilla Blackburn. Sur.
Jacob Blackburn. Min. Lewis Foster. M.R. 24 Jun 1814.

14 Sep 1799 William Dickson and Jemimah Mayor. Sur. Jeremiah
Maynor. Sur. George Clark and Gab Penn.

18 Aug 1814 Edward Dillard and Polly or Nelly Daniel. Sur.
Abraham Penn. Min. Thomas Whitlock. M.R. 12 Aug 1815.

 1 Dec 1815 James Dillard and Polly Smith. Sur. & Min. Thomas
Whitlock.

16 May 1816 John Dillard and Matilda Hughes. Sur. John P. Hill.
Min. Maning Hill. M.R. 23 May 1816.

26 Sep 1844 Abraham Dillon, son of Carrington Dillon, and Martha
Spencer. Sur. William Spencer. Min. Joshua Adams.
M.R. 25 Sep 1844.

 8 Jan 1818 Carrington Dillon and Polly Spencer, daughter of
John Spencer,Sr. Sur. Jerman Baker.

26 Oct 1841 Carrington J. Dillion, son of Sally Dillion, and
Elizabeth McAlexander, daughter of William McAlexander.
Sur. N.P. Adams. Wit. William Dillen.

* 1 Dec 1852 George Dillard and Frances Penn, daughter of P.P.Penn.

20 Mar 1804 Henry Dillon and Phebe Gussett. Sur. John Gussett.
M.R. 17 Mar 1804.

16 Mar 1837 James Dillon and Elizabeth Agee. Sur. John Agee.
Min. John Conner.

 2 Apl 1841 James Dillon and Lucy Brammer, daughter of John
Brammer. Sur. A. Staples. Wit. William Ayres. Min.
Jesse Jones. M.R. 13 May 1842.

21 Aug 1844 Jesse Dillon and Martha Tuder, daughter of Martha
Tuder. Sur. John Tuder. Min. Joshua Adams.

20 Apl 1822   Martin Dillon and Malinda Elliott. Sur. William Elliott.
               Min. Peter Frans.

16 Jul 1845   Peter Dillon and Lucinda Spencer, daughter of John
               Spencer. Sur. Martin Dillon. Min. Joshua Adams.
               M.R. 17 Jul 1845.

21 Jan 1808   William Dillon and Sally Pigg. Min. Peter Frans.

26 Feb 1838   William Dillon and Lucy Agee, daughter of John Agee.
               Sur. James Dillon.

22 Mar 1847   William Dillon and Susan (Ann) McArthur. Sur. Perry
               McArthur. Min. Joshua Adams. M.R. 25 Mar 1847.

 9 Apl 1812   Thomas Dinkins and Rhody Pennington. Sur. Leonard
               Owen. Min. Thomas Whitlock.

26 Apl 1798   William Dinkins and Mary Donathan. Sur. David Roark.
               Min. John Nunns.

26 Mpv 1849   Thomas M. Dobbins and Exony L. Conner. Sur. William
               Conner. M.R. 11 Dec 1849.

 7 Aug 1825   Eli Dodson, an orphan age 23, and Susannah Deal, age
               21, brother Elijah Deal states that her mother consents.
               Sur. Elijah Deal. Min. Joshua Adams.

20 Oct 1853   Elisha John Dodson, son of William and Judy Dodson, and
               Nancy Mariah Hollandsworth, daughter of William & Frances
               Hollandsworth. Min. Joshua Adams.

12 Mar 1792   George Dodson was ordained a Baptist Minister.
               Witness: John Flectcher & George Penn.

 1 Dec 1830   George C. Dodson and Lucinda Foster, daughter of
               Charles Foster. Sur. Thomas J. Penn. Min. John
               Washburn.

 8 Apl 1793   George Dodson, Jr and Martha Lockhart, daughter of
               Elizabeth Lockhart. Sur. George Dodson, Sr., Wit.
               Jesse Dodson. Min. George Dodson. M.R. 19 Apl 1793.

28 May 1805   Isaac Dodson and Eleanor Carter, daughter of George
               Carter. Sur. Benjamin W. Philpott.

14 Jul 1792   Leonard Dodson and Mary Randals, daughter of John
               Randals. Sur. Thomas Dodson. Min. George Dodson.
               M.R. 17 Jul 1792.

21 Apl 1831   Miller(Milton R) Dodson and Jane Philpott. Sur.
               Robert G. Aistrap. Min. Bird Lowe.

29 Mar 1794 Simon Dodson and Febey Hollandsworth, daughter of
Thomas Hollandsworth. Sur. Joseph Cummings.
Min. George Dodson.

11 Aug 1849 Thomas Dodson and Mary Keaton. Sur. Sampson Keaton.
Min. Joshua Adams. M.R. 21 Aug 1849.

 1 May 1802 James Dove and Avice Davidson. Sur. Richard Davidson.

 1 Sep 1803 Richard Dove and Elisabeth Taylor. Sur. Daniel
Martindale.

20 Oct 1829 Samuel Doyle and Nancy Fulkerson. Sur. Reuben Taylor.
Min. Maning Hill. M.R. 26 Mar 1828.

27 Jan 1834 Soloman Draper and Ruth Rogers. Sur. Robert Rogers.

 8 Jan 1835 Hiram Duncan and Lucinda Robertson. Sur. Robert
Dunkley.

 7 Oct 1826 James Duncan and Julia Duncan. Sur. Gilbert Bowman.
Min. Brett Stovall. M.R. 28 Oct 1826.

30 Nov 1828 John Duncan and Nancy Bowman. Sur. Gilbert Bowman.
Min. Brett Stovall. M.R. 5 Dec 1828.

10 Dec 1845 Wade Duncan and Mary Slate, daughter of Isham Slate.
Sur. Jackson Gregory.

23 Aug 1850 William Duncan and Jane Bowman. Sur. John W. Duncan
and Harden Beasly.

15 Aug 1815 William Dunford and Polly Haynes. Sur. Thomas Whitlock.
Min. Thomas Whitlock.

 4 May 1806 James Durnal and Diana Jinnons(Jennings?) Min. Thomas
Whitlock. Sur. James Dickenson.

26 Nov 1835 Daniel Duvall and Elizabeth Roberson. Sur. William
Robertson. Min. J. Adams.

 6 Oct 1825 James Duvall and Matilda Reynolds, daughter of Moses
Reynolds. Sur. Meeking Reynolds. Min. Joshua Adams.

21 Oct 1833 George W. Dyer and Mary Ann, daughter of Edward
Philpott. Sur. Christopher C. Mason. Min. Arnold
Walker. M.R. 7 Nov 1833.

12 Jan 1837 Jabez G. Dyer of Henry Co. Va., and Martha E. Ivie,
daughter of John W. Ivie. Sur. John D. Cheatham.
Wit. Joseph Dyer and Greenwood Jones.

Eadens, Edens

25 Nov 1852 Claborn Edens, consent of Elizabeth Edens, and
Bashabay Cockram daughter of S. Cockram. Wit.
H. H. Edens & Nathan Cockram. Min. William Lawson.

23 Sep 1813 David Edens and Elizabeth Harris, daughter of William
Harris. Sur. William Harris. Min. Jesse Jones.

27 Dec 1842 George W. Edens and Letha George, daughter of James
H. George. George W. Edens the son of David Edens.
Sur. Jesse Edens. Wit. Hugh George. Min. Jesse Jones.

25 Jan 1842 Jesse Edens and Martha George, daughter of James H.
George. Sur. Featherston Akers. Wit. William Canaday.

31 May 1832 Jesse Earls and Mary Boyd, daughter of William Boyd.
Sur. William Boyd. Wit. Nancy Boyd. Min. Nathaniel
Thompson. M.R. 5 Jun 1832.

21 Dec 1810 John East and Mary Simson. Sur. Ewel Moore.
Min. Thomas Whitlock. M.R. 27 Dec 1810.

13 Jun 1833 John East and Mary Kimbrough. Sur. Norman Staples.

15 Jun 1848 John East and Mary B. Abington, daughter of Elizabeth
Abington. Sur. William M. Abington.

14 Dec 1843 Thomas East and Jeston Cloud. Sur. Samuel G.Staples.
Min. Joshua Adams. M.R. 26 Dec 1843.

11 Mar 1813 George Eaton and Betsey Sisemore. Sur. Stephen McMilion.

15 Sep 1832 Newell Eaton and Matilda Sayers. Sur. Alexander Ayers.
Min. Thomas Whitlock.

20 Apl 1809 John Eaton and Frances Burress. Sur. Jessey Manikns.
Min. Thomas Whitlock.

20 Feb 1794 Aaron Ecton and Elisabeth Littrell. Sur. Robert Littrell
Min. George Dodson. M.R. 22 Feb 1794.

29 Dec 1811 Abraham Edds and Sarah East. Sur. Samuel Cannon.

19 Oct 1841 Abraham Edwards and Ruth Newman. Sur. George Rogers.
Min. Joshua Adams.

9 Feb 1811 Elisha Edwards and Nancy Ahart. Sur. Jacob Grigg.
Min. Thomas Whitlock.

30 Dec 1844 George J. Edwards and Sarah Arrington. Sur. Samuel
Arrington. Min. Joshua Adams.

8 Oct 1804 Isham Edwards and Patsey Witt, consent of William Witt.
Sur. Daniel Witt. Min Nathan Hall. M.R. 11 Oct 1804.

11 Feb 1809   James Edwards and Keziah Pedigo. Sur. John Pedigo.
              Min. Stephen Hubbard. M.R. 16 Feb 1809.

27 Nov 1840   Capt. Joseph Edwards and Martha Hancock, daughter
              of John Hancock. Sur. J.W. Hancock. Min. John Conner.
              M.R. 4 Dec 1840.

 7 Sept 1806 Thomas Edwards and Mary McDaniel. Sur. Joshua Haynes.
              Min. Thomas Whitlock. M.R. 27 Sep 1806.

10 Aug 1826   William Edwards and Keziah Walker. Sur. Tandy Walker.
              Min. John Washburn.

30 Aug 1833   William Edwards and Nancy Cox. Sur. Daniel R. Cox.
              Min. Stephen Hubbard. M.R. 1 Sep 1833.

 5 May 1849   William Edwards and Mary Ann Edwards (Shelton).
              Sur. Thomas Shelton. Min. Joshua Adams. M.R. 9 May 1849.

27 Dec 1837   Jonathan Eggelton and Elizabeth C. Clark. Sur. John
              Clark. Min. John Washburn.

20 Feb 1807   John Eldrick and Elizabeth Cook. Sur. Moses Freeman.
              Min. Thomas Whitlock.

10 Feb 1852   Alfred Elgin and America Houchens. Min. G. W. Conner.

21 Oct 1827   Hues Elgin and Elizabeth Tomson. Min. John Conner.

24 Feb 1822   Jonathan Elgin and Sally Terry. Sur. James Keath.
              Min. John Conner. M.R. 24 Feb 1822.

19 Oct 1827   Lewis Elgin and Elizabeth Thompson, daughter of
              Elizabeth Thompson. Sur. John Elgin. Wit. Jesse
              Hubbard & William Hubbard.

15 Oct 1832   Paul Elgin and Luvina Harris. Sur. Moses Burnett.
              Min. John Conner. M.R. 8 Oct 1832.

 8 Oct 1804   James Elkins,Jr. and Mary Layne. Sur. Samuel Layne.
              Min.Stephen Hubbard.

 5 Mar 1830   Amos Elliott,consent of William Elliott, and Malinda
              Hopkins. Sur. Daniel Pedigo. Wit. George R. Fulcher.

13 Aug 1792   Joseph Elliott and Anna Plymale. Sur. J. Henderson.

 6 Oct 1827   Lewis Elliott, son of William Elliott, and Jane (Jiney)
              Moore, daughter of Jesse Moore. Sur. James Moore.
              Min. Joshua Adams.

22 Aug 1826   William Elliott and Polly Fulcher. Sur. Thomas
              Reynolds. Min. John Washburn.

25 Dec 1809 William Elliott and Kitty Simkins. Sur. & Min.
            Thomas Whitlock.

12 Dec 1853 Jabez T. Emberson and Ruth Price.

 5 Jan 1853 Allerson W.Emerson and Febe Cox, father Randolph
            Cox consents. Sur. Banes Carter & George W. Cox.
            Min. Jeremiah Burnett.

20 Dec 1806 Yearlington Ennis and Margaret Going. Sur. John
            Bolt. Min. Thomas Whitlock.

15 Jun 1853 Jesse P. Epperly and Caroline Akers. Min.G.W. Conner.

21 Jan 1836 Daniel Epperson and Leatha Bowman. Sur. Fowlkes Smith.
            Min. Thomas Whitlock.

23 Oct 1803 Peter Epperson and Ellenor Finney, daughter of Margaret
            Finney. Sur. Alexander Finney.

25 Jan 1840 William Epperson, Jr. and Polly Hensley. Sur. Isham East.

 4 Dec 1791 Robert Euings(Ewing) and Peggy Brown, daughter of
            Susanah Brown. Sur. Joseph Elliott.
            M.R. lists Robert Evens and Peggy Brown. Min. Robt Jones.

 3 Jun 1837 Bernard Fain and Elizabeth Hylton. Sur. Jacob Hylton.
            Min. John Conner.

 7 Feb 1836 Daniel Fain and Sally Handy. Sur. James Handy.
            Min. John Conner.

 5 Feb 1846 Henry Fain and Nancy Hylton. Sur. Absalom Hylton.
            Min. G. W. Conner.

26 Mar 1816 Richard Fain and Jane Harris. Sur. Barnard Harris.
            Min. H. Fitzgerald.

11 Dec 1847 Richard Fain and Nancy Houchins. Sur. Richard Houchins.
            Min. John Conner. M.R. 21 Dec 1847.

24 Mar 1846 William Fain and Temperance Hylton, daughter of Joseph
            Hylton. Sur. Absalom Hylton. Wit. Nathaniel Hylton.
            Min. Austin Hylton.

25 Aug 1813 Micajah Falkner and Nancy Carter. Sur. Samuel Hanby.
            Min. Thomas Whitlock.

30 Dec 1805 Joshua Farrington and Nancy Critz. Sur. William Frans.
            M.R. 27 Dec 1805.

25 Mar 1813 George R. Farris and Frances Lee, daughter of Richard Lee. Sur. Samuel Staples. Min. Brett Stovall. M.R. 26 Mar 1813.

1825 Josiah Farris and Polly Penn. Min. Bird Lowe.

15 Jan 1852 King H. Farris and Malinda F. Jarrott, daughter of Wiatt Jarrott. Wit. Henry F. Jarrott. Min. Daniel G. Taylor.

27 Sep 1809 Alias Fendley and Sally Rickman. Sur. Peter Fendley.

30 Dec 1825 John Findley and Catherine Rickman. Sur. Thomas Rickman. Min. Joshua Adams.

20 Dec 1809 Joseph Fendley and Lucy Nicholds. Sur. Alexander Harris. Min. Brett Stovall. M.R. 31 Dec 1809.

21 Apl 1821 Paskell Findley and Matilda Stewart. Sur. Edward Fendley and John Stewart. Min. Peter Frans.

28 Sep 1797 Peter Fendley and Rebecca Going. Sur. John Cameron. Min. Isaac Adams.

26 Nov 1802 William Fendley and Susannah Rickman. Sur. John Going.

7 Dec 1846 Abner Ferguson and Temperance Martin, daughter of William Martin. Sur. William Martin. Min. Joshua Adams. M.R. 22 Dec 1846.

5 Dec 1853 Caleb Ferguson of Franklin Co.,Va., son of John & Sopha Ferguson, and Frances Shelton, daughter of William C. & Sara Shelton. Wit. Hiram Hazelwood. Min. Samuel L. Lackey.

20 Mar 1849 James P. Ferguson, son of Archibald Ferguson, and Ruth Spencer, daughter of John Spencer. Sur. John Spencer.

22 Jan 1849 Lewis E. Ferguson, son of Archiblad Ferguson, and Celia Martin, daughter of James Martin. Sur. James Martin. Min. Joshua Adams. M.R. 23 Jan 1849.

18 Dec 1838 Pleasant W. Ferguson and Jane Moore, daughter of H. H. & Ann Moore. Sur. Thomas Clark. Wit. Jacob M. Fergson.

27 Aug 1822 Christopher J. Terrell and Susannah Kennerly, daughter of Joseph Kennerly. Sur. John C. Staples.

13 May 1793 James Ferrell and Peggy Sharp. Sur. Brett Stovall. Min. George Dodson. M.R. 19 May 1793.

9 Dec 1793   John Fields and Elizabeth Collings, daughter of Roger Collings. Sur. Joseph Going. Wit. Sarah Collings and Nathaniel Collings.

25 Sep 1800   Stephen Fields and Elizabeth Davidson. Sur. Richard Davidson.

15 Oct 1793   William Fields and Nancy Eadins. Sur. George Rogers.

15 Apl 1823   Adam Finch and Jane Ruder. Sur. William Baker. Min. Peter Frans. M.R. 14 Apl 1823.

1823/1824   William Finch and Polly Purdy. Min. John C. Traylor.

4 Jan 1803   Alexander Finney and Elizabeth Carter, daughter of William Carter. Sur. Alexander Carter. Wit. Henry Frans.

5 Jan 1835   Peter Finney and Sally Cruise. Sur. John Cruise. Min. John Conner.

10 Aug 1833   Robert P. Finney and Mary B. Morris. Sur. William Morris.

1 Jan 1833   James Fitzgerald and Nancy Newman. Sur. David Smith.and Eliphas Shelton. Min. Joshua Adams. M.R. 3 Jan 1833.

2 Dec 1832   Leonard Fitzgerald and Nancy Smith. Sur. David W. Smith.

21 Dec 1829   Madison Fitzgerald and Luvenia Lacky, daughter of George Lacky. Sur. Jesse Aistrop. Min. Bird Lowe. M.R. 22 Dec 1829.

19 Feb 1822   Thomas Fitzgerald and Mary Hudson, daughter of John R. Hudson. Sur. John C. Staples. Wit. George Carter. Min. Brett Stovall M.R. 22 Feb 1822.

13 Feb 1795   William Fitzgerald and Mary Ann Smith. Sur. Harvy Fitzgerald. Min. Joshua Adams.

19 May 1825   William Fleming and Rossy Keller. Sur. Thomas Whitlock. Min. Thomas Whitlock.

6 Jul 1797   John Fletcher and Selyan Russell. Sur. William Barton. Min. Isaac Adams.

20 Oct 1823   Thomas Flynt and Susanah C. Fulkerson. Sur. Frederick Fulkerson. Min. Maning Hill. M.R. 6 Nov 1823.

17 Mar 1842   Jesse A. Flippen, of Stokes Co.,N.C.,James Flippen consents, and Ruth Adams. Sur. & Min. Joshua Adams.

18 Jan 1836   Raleigh W. Flippen and Ersley Newman. Sur. Winston
Newman. Min. Joshua Adams.

 3 Dec 1838   Samuel Flippen of Stokes Co. N.C., and Mildred
Fulkerson. Sur. Reuben Taylor. Min. Joshua
Adams. M.R. 4 Dec 1838.

25 May 1799   Henry Floyd and Ursly Nunn. Sur. John Hughes.

28 Aug 1802   Thomas Floyd and Polley Christian. Sur. James Taylor.

 5 Jun 1826   Charles Fodrell and Mary Nelson. Sur. & Min. Brett
Stovall. M.R. 2 June 1826.

21 Jan 1853   Alfred Foley and Sally Ann Wilkes, daughter of Tempy
J. Wilkes. Wit. Booker W. Smith.

20 Jan 1843   Andrew J. Foley and Lucinda Witt. Sur. Saunders Witt.
Min. Joshua Adams.

12 Apl 1803   Christopher Foley and Mary Whaling (Whalen). Sur.
John Whalen. Min. S. Hall.

29 Nov 1813   Gabriel Foley and Elizabeth Tuggle. Sur. John Elgin.

10 Dec 1833   James Foley and Nancy Foley. Min. John Conner.

19 Nov 1849   James A. Foley and Letitia Foley, daughter of James
Foley Sr. Wit. Charles T. Foley. Sur. Richard B.
Foley. Min. John Conner. M.R. 22 Nov 1849.

16 Jul 1847   James M. Foley, his guardian John H. Walker consents,
and Luncinda Clifton. Mim. Joshua Adams. M.R. 20 Jul
1847.

 2 Aug 1823   Jeremiah Foley and Nancy Foley. Sur. Namon Harbour.
Min. John Conner. M.R. 3 Aug 1823.

28 Feb 1848   Richard B.Foley and Parshandatha McAlexander.
Sur. Samuel McAlexander.

14 May 1850   Samuel J. Foley and Emeline Adeline Foley, daughter
of James Foley,Sr.,. Sur. Richard B. Foley. Wit.
Jeremiah A. Foley. Min. John Conner.

 5 Jan 1843   Wesley Foley, guardian John H. Walker consents, and
Matilda Boling. Sur. James Bowlen,Jr. Wit. Marvil
Bowlen. Min. G. W. Conner.

19 Dec 1838   Abram P. Foster and Mary Jane Critz. Sur. George C.
Dodson. Min. D. B. Nicholson. M.R. 19 Dec 1838.

8 Sep 1811   Charles Foster and Polly Penn. Min. Peter Frans.

20 Nov 1832   Charles Foster and Cerine Philpott,daughter of
              David Philpott. Sur. Charles G. Philpott. Min.
              Joshua Adams. M.R. 22 Nov 1832.

28 Jan 1826   George Foster and Nancy Martin, daughter of Moses
              Martin,Sr. Sur. Moses Martin. Wit. Lewis Turner.
              Min. Stephen Hubbard. M.R. 27 Jan 1826.

19 Apl 1832   Ignatious Foster and Elisabeth Hagood, consent of
              Gregory Hagood. Sur. Charles Foster. Min. Joshua
              Adams. M.R. 3 May 1832.

18 Dec 1814   John Foster and Joyce Lewis. Sur. John Jonson. Min.
              Thomas Whitlock.

 5 Nov 1807   Lewis Foster and Ginsey Simms. Sur. Isaac Adams.

20 Aug 1826   Lewis Foster, Jr. and Nancy Haynes. Sur. Charles
              Foster,Jr.. Min. Stephen Hubbard.

 1 Nov 1792   Henry France(Frans) and Sarah Carter. Sur. George
              Carter. Min. George Dodson.

12 Oct 1841   H.C. France and Martha A.C. Penn. Sur. C. Penn.

12 Jan 1816   Malakejah Francis and Polly Fitzgerald, daughter of
              Harvy Fitzgerald. Min. Brett Stovall. M.R. 23 Jan 1816.

25 Mar 1848   William M. Francis and Susan J. Hines. Sur. James H.
              Hines. Min. S.G. Hill.

27 Sep 1814   John Franklin and Nancy Stone. Sur. John Stone.

19 Jan 1797   Daniel Frans and Sophia Crutchen, daughter of Samuel
              Crutchen(Crutcher). Sur. Samuel Staples.
              Min. Isaac Adams.

26 Jan 1803   John Frans and Polly Jones. Sur. William Jones.

 7 Dec 1840   Joseph Frans and Matilda J. Spencer, daughter of Benjamin
              Spencer. John Frans gives consent for Joseph Frans. Sur.
              Reuben Ziglar. Min. Joshua Adams. M.R. 10 Oct 1840.

28 Feb 1811   William Frans and Harriet Harrison, daughter of Richard
              Harrison. Min. Peter Frans.

21 Feb 1832   William Frans and Ruth Clark,George Clark consents.
              Sur. Richard D. Stanley. Min. John Washburn.

12 Nov 1792   Alexander Frazer (Abraham Frazer) and Elisabeth Noe.
              Sur. Samuel Noe. Min. George Dodson. M.R.24 Feb 1793.

25 Nov 1824 Benjamin Frazor and Virginia Fulkerson. Sur. George
Carter.

11 Feb 1832 John Frazer and Angeline Hudnall. Sur. Thomas Hudnall.
Min. Joshua Adams. M.R. 15 Feb 1832.

10 Aug 1799 Thomas Frasure and Sarah Joyce. Sur. Arthur Parr.

15 Mar 1795 William Frazer and Arty Elkins, daughter of James
Elkins. Sur. Barnard M. Price. Min. John Pedigo.

30 Mar 1809 Larkin Freeman and Mary Daniel(Dowel). Sur. Charles
Cole. Min. Thomas Whitlock.

8 Aug 1826 Edmund Fulcher and Nancy Nowling. Sur. Clark Penn.
Min. Joshua Adams.

29 Oct 1811 George Fulcher and Elisabeth Roberson. Sur. Fredrick
Shelton. Min. Peter Frans.

28 Jan 1811 Henry Fulcher and Polly Boaz. Sur. James Boaz.
Min. Brett Stovall. M.R. 30 Jan 1811.

16 Oct 1832 James Fulcher and Polly Plaster. Sur. Conrad Plaster.
Min. Joshua Adams. M.R. 18 Oct. 1832.

2 Dec 1852 John Fulcher and Sarah Ann Taylor, daughter of
Jeremiah W. Taylor. Min. Joshua Adams.

5 Jan 1846 Phillip Fulcher and Jane Williams. Sur. James Fulcher.
Min. G. W. Conner. M.R. 14 Jan 1846.

15 Sep 1813 Abner Fulton and Rachel Jones, daughter of William
Jones. Sur. Nelson Philips. Min. Peter Frans.
M.R. 16 Sep 1813.

31 Dec 1811 James Fuson and Martha Sneed, daughter of William Sneed.
Sur. William Sneed. Min. Jesse Jones. M.R. 4 Jan 1812.

13 Oct 1816 Jeptha Fuson and Polly Sneed, daughter of William Sneed.
Sur. Isiah Fuson. Min. Stephen Hubbard. M.R.18 Oct 1816.

14 Dec 1805 Jesse Fuson and Sarah Eadens. Sur. William Fuson.
Jesse Fuson the son of William Fuson.

26 Sep 1803 Joel Fuson and Bethaniah Brammer, daughter of Mary
Brammer. Sur. John Brammer. Min. Jesse Jones.

1791 Thomas Fuson and Rachel Roberson. Min. Robert Jones.

28 Jul 1808 William Fuson,Jr. and Damy Lee. Sur. Joshua Haynes
and Joshua Adams.

3 Feb 1811   Washington Gaines and Sally Joyce. Sur. Frederick Shelton.

11 Oct 1812   Jacob Galandon and Martha Hiatt. Min. Thomas Whitlock.

8 Jun 1820   James Gardner and Lucy Howell. Sur. David Howell. Min. Jesse Jones.

14 Sep 1820   William Garner and Ony Martin. Sur. Giles Martin.

8 Oct 1792   William Garrett and Winifred Bolt. Sur. John Bolt.

14 Jul 1791   William Garrison and Elizabeth Dickerson. Sur. George Penn. M.R. 16 Jul 1791.

11 Oct 1839   John W. Gates and Jwanowni Ayres. Sur. William Ayres. Min. Jesse Jones.

25 Feb 1802   Valentine Gearhart and Exony Packwood. Sur. Samuel Packwood. Min. Samuel King. M.R. 11 Mar 1802.

4 Dec 1832   Leonard Gereat and Nancy Smith. Min. John Conner.

9 Feb 1819   Fredrick Gilbert and Jane Sharp. Sur. Samuel Gilbert. Min. Brett Stovall. M.R. 10 Feb 1819.

6 Jan 1853   George M. Gilbert and Milly Rogers. Min. Joshua Adams.

9 Jan 1838   John Gilbert and Jane Fulcher, daughter of Patsy Fulcher. Sur. W. A. Sandefer. Min. Joshua Adams.

10 Dec 1847   John R. Gilbert and Verlinka E. Rogers. Sur. Hiram Rogers. Min. Joshua Adams.

23 Nov 1848   Pendleton Gilbert and Polly Malinda Rakes. Sur. Chesley Rakes. Min. Joshua Adams.

11 Apl 1846   Robert Gilbert and Martha Jane Cassell, daughter of John Cassell. Sur. John Cassell. Min. Joshua Adams. M.R. 15 Apl 1846.

5 Mar 1823   Samuel Gilbert and Lucy Sharp. Sur. Samuel Sharp. Min. Peter Frans.

7 Jan 1845   Samuel Gilbert and Martha J. Potter. Sur. William Potter.

8 Jan 1794   Martin Giles and Nancy Ingram. Min. George Dodson.

4 Dec 1848   Samuel Gill and Rebecca Dehart. Sur. John T. Gill. Wit. Namon J. Short. Min. Owen Sumner. M.R. 5 Dec 1848.

22 May 1852   Founten Gilley and Jane Hopkins, daughter of Nancy Gilley. Min. Joshua Adams.

28 Sep 1852   William Gilley and Luvena Elliott, who lives at the
              home of Hardin Hopkins. Min. Joshua Adams.

 1 Sep 1803   James G. Gimnell and Jane Fitzgerald. Min.
              Reuben Short.

15 May 1839   James Jennings(Gennons) and Levina Barnard. Sur.
              Tinea Barnard.

 2 Feb 1815   William Jinnings and Anney Henson. Min. Thomas Whitlock.

11 Oct 1812   Jacob Glandon and Martha Hiett. Sur. William Slaughter.

21 Oct 1834   Berryman Glasgow and Ruth Anglin, daughter of Phillip
              Anglin. Sur. James Duvall. Min. Joshua Adams.
              M.R. 25 Oct 1834.

13 Feb 1840   Berryman Glasgow and Helen Slaughter, daughter of
              Dandridge Slaughter. Sur. Jesse Chaney. Min. John
              Conner. M.R. 16 Feb 1840.

19 Jul 1828   Robert Glasgow, Jr. and Polly Belcher. Sur. Obediah
              Belcher. Min. Bird Lowe.

 6 Jul 1792   Isham Goard and Nancy Reynolds. Sur. Bartlett and
              Charles Hibbert. Min. George Dodson. M.R. 7 Jul 1792.

21 Jan 1833   Jesse Goard and Elizabeth Martin, daughter of Isaac
              Martin. Sur. Marvel Spencer. Min. Joshua Adams.
              M.R. 22 Jan 1833.

12 Oct 1793   John Godard and Anny Hodges. Sur. Joseph Cummings.
              Min. George Dodoson. M.R. 17 Oct 1793.

10 Jan 1844   George W. Goggins and Frances A. Tate, daughter of
              Obediah Tate. Sur. Clemons Oyler. Wit. Pleasant M.
              Goggin. Min. Joshua Adams. M.R. 13 Jan 1844.

13 Apl 1792   Benjamin Going and Elizabeth Stevens, consent of
              Solman Stevens. Sur. Ezekiah Shelton. Wit. Rachel
              Mcgee and Holden McGee.

26 Jul 1810   Beveridge Going and Agnes Harris, daughter of James
              Harris. Sur. William Frans. Min. Peter Frans.
              M.R. 12 Aug 1810.

 9 Jun 1802   Caleb Goin and Polly Duncan, daughter of Martin
              Duncan. Sur. Harden Dunham.

11 Mar 1852   Ewell Going and Rosanah Horne. Min. Julius Ferrel.

12 Apl 1796   Isaac Going and Nancy Lizby, daughter of Mary Lizby.
              Sur. Eliphaz Shelton. Wit. Henry Lizby and William
              Moore. Min. John Nunns.

18 Jan 1792 Jacob Going and Nancy Smith, who is upwards of 22 yrs. Sur. John Canron. Wit. John Clark.

5 Mar 1812 John Going Jr. and Margaret Gregory. Sur. John Going, Sr. Wit. Eliphaz Shleton. Min. Brett Stovall. M.R. 26 Mar 1812.

7 Dec 1835 Norman Going and Polly Jones, daughter of Susanna Jones. Sur. Elisha Anglin. Wit. Charles Wilson. Min. John Washburn. M.R. 10 Dec 1835.

24 Feb 1807 Stephen Going and Nancy Going, daughter of John Going. Sur. Obediah Going. Wit. David Hanby and William Moore. Min. William H. Robertson.

26 Jul 1802 William Going and Elizabeth Pack, daughter of Mary Bowman. Sur. John Going. William Going, the son of John Going.

17 Feb 1802 William Going and Polly Overman. Sur. Thomas Beasley. Wit. Benjamin Haile.

7 Jan 1832 William Goodson and America H. Sandefur. Sur. M. Sandefur. Min. John Conner. M.R. 8 Jan 1837.

1 Jul 1830 Leonard Grady and Delilia Spencer, daughter of William Spencer. Wit. Jeremiah Taylor. Sur. James Nowland. Min. John Washburn.

4 Feb 1809 William Grady and Frances Grady. Sur. John Grady. Min. Peter Frans. M.R. 5 Feb 1809.

27 Dec 1841 Alexander Graham and Lucinda Hall. Sur. Thomas R. Hall. Min. Jesse Jones. M.R. 13 Jan 1842.

13 Mar 1806 Dunkin Graham and Bregit Foley. Min. William H. Robertson

16 Jun 1809 James Graham and Rebecca Dehart, daughter of Aaron Dehart Sur. Henry Tuggle. Min. Jesse Jones.

7 May 1842 Perry Graham and Sarah Reynolds, daughter of James Reynolds. Sur. Thomas Shelton. Wit. William Reynolds. Min. Jesse Jones. M.R. 21 May 1842.

12 Dec 1815 Elijah Gray and Malinda Frasure. Sur. Thomas Frasure. Min. Maning Hill.

6 Jul 1812 Joseph Gray and Rachel Fulkerson. Sur. James & Peter Fulkerson. Min. Maning Hill. M.R. 9 Jul 1812.

21 Jan 1827 Norman Gray and Mary Powell, daughter of Plolemy Powell. Mary Powell has been living at the home of Mrs. Mary Gray for three months. Min. Bird Lowe.

20 Nov 1823   Powell Gray and Denty M. Taylor. Sur. Washington Thomas.
              Min. Maning Hill.

13 Nov 1823   Samuel Gray and Phebe Booker. Sur. William Booker.
              Min. Bird Lowe.

10 Dec 1816   Isham Green and Ginsey(Jane) Hopkins. Sur. Cornelius
              Hopkins. Min. Peter Frans.

30 Jul 1801   Reynolds Green, son of William Green, and Frances
              Hall, daughter of John Hall.

25 Dec 1794   Robert Green and Selah Hammons, daughter of John
              Hammons. Sur. William Carter.

15 Jul 1828   Bartlett Greenwood,Jr. and Polly Poore. Sur. Smith
              Joyce. Min. Bird Lowe.

 3 Jan 1833   Thomas Greenwood and Lock(?) Conner. Sur. Martin
              Cloud. Min. Thomas Whitlock.

22 Sep 1834   Bluford Griffin and Sarah Sharp. Sur. William N.Sharp.

29 Jul 1829   Gilbert Griffin and Miley Haney. Min. John Washburn.
              Wit. Washington Thomas. Cosent for Jemly Coalson.

10 Jan 1799   Richard Griffin and Sarah Scruggs. Sur. John Phillips.

 2 Sep 1824   Thomas Griffin and Phebe Kington, daughter of John
              Kington, who refuses to give his consent; but the
              daughter was of age. Sur. Greenville Penn. Min.
              Maning Hill. Wit. Samuel Moore.

23 Feb 1842   Thomas Griffin and Frances Short, widow of Almond
              Short. Sur. John L. Anglin. Wit. James E. Ashley.
              Min. John Washburn. M.R. 24 Feb 1842.

16 Sep 1841   William Griffin and July Collins. Sur. Larkin Collins.

14 Aug 1828   Caleb Griffith and Ruth Witt. Sur. William Witt and
              Abram Koger and Willis Luttrell. Min. John Conner.
              M.R. 24 Aug 1828.

15 Feb 1831   David Griffith and Violet Plaster. Sur. Conrad Plaster.
              Min. Bird Lowe. M.R. 1 Mar 1831.

19 Jan 1839   David Griffith and Elizabeth Witt. Sur. William Griffith.
              Min. William Lawson. M.R. 24 Jan 1839.

 8 Mar 1829   Evan Griffith and Anna Thompson, daughter of Elizabeth
              Thompson. Sur. Charles Rakes. Min. Stephen Hubbard.
              M.R. 3 May 1829.

17 Mar 1839 John F. Griffith, son of Daniel Griffith, and Judy Rakes. Sur. Samuel Rakes. Wit. Sparrel H. Griffith.

22 Jun 1830 William Griffith and Susanah Reynolds. Sur. Micajah Martin. Min. Joshua Adams. M.R. 24 Jun 1830.

4 Jun 1807 Jacob Griggs and Nancy Dickinson. Sur. John A.Grigg. Min. Thomas Whitlock.

2 Sep 1812 Jacob Grimes and Martha Martin. Sur. Giles Martin. Min. Lewis Foster. M.R. 4 Sep 1812.

4 Dec 1798 John Grimes and Mary Pennington, daughter of Isaac Pennington, who is surety. Min. John Nunns. M.R. 5 Dec 1798.

9 Aug 1830 Josiah Grimmitt and Susanah Thomas. Sur. Cornelius Thomas. Min. Stephen Hubbard. M.R. 26 Aug 1830.

23 Aug 1803 Nicholas Grimmitt and Peggy Cox,daughter of James Cox. Sur. Randolph Cox. Wit. Ben Walden.

4 Oct 1837 William Grogan and Dicy Cradock, daughter of Thomas Craddock. Sur. Joseph Cox and Jerman Cradock.

3 May 1835 Austen Gunnell and Lucy Clark, daughter of Lucy Clark. Sur. James Bartlett. Min. John Conner.

9 Jan 1851 Beverly L. Gunter and Mary Joyce. Min. Joshua Adams.

15 Sep 1842 Daniel Gusler and Elizabeth Cox. Sur. Randolph Cox.

26 Feb 1838 Jacob Gusler and Maryann H. Ferguson, daughter of Archibald Ferguson. Sur. William Martin. Wit. Lewis E. Ferguson. Min. Joshua Adams.

26 Apl 1798 Abraham Gussett (Gossett) and Betsy Adams. Sur. John Gossett.

5 Dec 1808 John Gossett and Nancy Dillion. Sur. Jacob C. Koger. Min. Lewis Foster. M.R. 8 Dec 1808.

1853 Abner Hagen and Agnes Dotson, daughter of William.

30 Jul 1813 Anderson Hagood and Elizabeth Sims. Sur. Ignatious Sims.

24 Apl 1806 Gregory Hagwood and Polly Lessonby Sims. Sur. Ignatious Sims.

2 Jan 1853 Grisham Hagood and Virginia E. Nance, who signs own consent. Wit.Joiel C. Tate. Min. William M.Schoolfield.

23 Mar 1799 Benjamin Haile and Jane Barton. Sur. William Barton.

13 Dec 1802 Benjamin Hale and Polly Hollandsworth, daughter of James Hollandsworth. Sur. William Adams. Wit. Isaac Adams and David Tittle.

31 Dec 1832 Dennis Hale and Sally Thompson, daughter of David Thompson. Sur. S. Webb. Wit. William Thompson. Min. Nathaniel Thompson.

7 Dec 1846 Francis Hale and Latitia Martin. Sur. William Martin. Min. Joshua Adams. M.R. 22 Dec 1846.

21 Dec 1848 John P. Hale and Vely Ann Martin, daughter of William Martin. Sur. John M. Vest. Min. Joshua Adams.

2 Aug 1796 Moses Hale and Milly Poor. Sur. Hugh Poor. Min. Isaac Adams. M.R. 3 Aug 1796.

18 Nov 1834 Thomas Hale and Sarah Whalen. Sur. Jonas Plaster. Min. Joshua Adams.

26 May 1804 William Hale and Nancy Redman.

5 Nov 1833 John A. Hairston and Malinda Corn. Min. Stephen Hubbard.

28 Oct 1849 Peter W. Hairston and Columbia S. Stuart, daughter of Arch. Stuart. Min. John L. Prichard. M.R. 8 Nov 1849.

18 Dec 1826 Samuel Hairston and Elizabeth P. Hairston, consent of Harden Hairston. Sur. Peter Hairston.

26 Oct 1848 Samuel W. Hairston and Eliza Penn. Sur. Peter W. Watkins. Min. William M. Schoolfield.

12 Nov 1818 John Halbert and Elizabeth F. Booker. Sur. Samuel Staples. Min. Brett Stovall. M.R. 20 Nov 1818.

21 Jan 1827 Adam Hall and Martha Vaughters. Sur. & Min. Thomas Whitlock.

26 Mar 1841 Adam Hall, son of Henry Hall, and Sabrinah Hall, daughter of Russell Hall. Sur. Henry Hall.

11 Jan 1847 David Hall, son of Sarah Hall, and Jane Rakes, daughter of Samuel Rakes. Sur. Nathan Hall. Wit. William F.Hall.

24 Nov 1853 David Hall,age 21, of Terry Co,N.C.(?) the son of Oliver Hall, and Julina Hall, age 23, daughter of Jorden Hall. Min. Martin Cloud.

8 Oct 1828 Harden R. Hall and Martha Adams. Sur. Jefferson Taylor.

26 Jan 1815 Henry Hall and Betsy Turner. Sur. Adam Turner. Min. Jesse Jones. M.R. 16 Mar 1815.

15 Mar 1851　Henry Hall and Judah Hall, daughter of Russell Hall. Wit. William F. Hall & Adam Hall.

13 Oct 1845　Henry H. Hall and Exoney Turner, daughter of Lewis Turner. Sur. P. R. Ross.

22 Nov 1800　James Hall and Jane Burnett(Jinny), daughter of John Burnett. Sur. Robert Rowan. Min. Robert Jones. M.R. 27 Nov 1800.

28 Oct 1845　Jasper Hall and Vina(Levinah) Hall. Sur. Russell Hall. Min. Jesse Jones.

 7 Oct 1807　John Hall,Jr. and Sarah Harbour. Sur. Jesse Harbour. Min. Stephen Hubbard.

26 Sep 1811　John Hall and Judith Hall, Thomas R. Hall gives consent. Sur. Nathan Hall.

 2 Sep 1847　John Hall and Elizabeth Cox. Sur. James Cox. Min. Jeremiah Burnett. M.R. 3 Sep 1847.

21 Sep 1842　John Hall and Nancy Hall. Sur. Joseph Hall. Min. John Conner. M.R. 22 Sept 1842.

12 Jul 1843　John Hall and Letha Massey. Min. Jesse Jones.

27 Feb 1821　Jordon Hall and Sally Vaughter. Sur. Tyre Bowman.

14 Nov 1839　Joseph Hall and Anna Midkiff. Sur. Conrad Plaster.

28 Apl 1814　Joshua Hall and Anna Rakes. Sur. Charles Rakes.

28 Jan 1808　Nathan Hall and Elisabeth Hancock. Sur. William Hancock.

16 Feb 1837　Nathan Hall,Jr. and Deborah McAlexander. Sur. David McAlexander. Min. John Conner. M.R. 7 Mar 1837.

14 Feb 1822　Parker Hall and Ruth McMilion. Sur. Tyre Bowman. Min. Thomas Whitlock. M.R. 14 Feb 1822.

15 Jan 1826　Randolph Hall and Polly Canaday, daughter of William Canaday. Sur. Harden R. Hall. Min. Stephen Hubbard.

 2 Dec 1815　Russell Hall and Sally Turner. Sur. Adam Turner. Min. Jesse Jones. M.R. 16 1815.

27 Sep 1804　Shadrack Hall alias Sloan and Caty Reynolds. Min. Jesse Jones.

21 Jul 1808　Thomas R. Hall and Sally Fuson. Min. Lewis Foster.

27 Sep 1847　Thomas R. Hall and Sarah Ann Burnett, daughter of Jeremiah Burnett. Sur. Jeremiah F. Burnett. Min. John Conner. M.R. 30 Sep 1847.

1 Feb 1810   William Hall and Polly Shelton. Sur. William N.
             Sharp and Hudson Hall. Min. Peter Frans.

12 Jan 1835 William Hall and Celia Harris, daughter of
             Samuel Harris. Sur. Samuel Terry. Min. John Conner.

15 Aug 1837 William Hall and Sally (Sara) Hatcher. Sur. James
             Hatcher. Min. Jesse Jones. M.R. 5 Sep 1836.

 4 Jul 1844 William W. Hall and Frances Bolling. Sur. James
             Bolling.

15 Feb 1811 Zadoe Hall and Elizabeth Boman. Sur. Peter Beller.
             Min. Thomas Whitlock.

13 Sep 1827 James Hambleton and Celia Hancock. Sur. Absalom
             Hancock. Min. Stephen Hubbard.

16 Dec 1817 George Hammons and Polly Gruin(Green?). Sur. and
             Min. Thomas Whitlock.

 7 Apl 1827 George Hammons and Elizabeth Lewis.
             Min. Nathaniel Thompson.

30 Jan 1800 Leroy Hammons and Nancy Green, daughter of William
             and Juda Green. Sur. Robert Green.

19 Jan 1846 Harden H. Hanby and Ann Martin, daughter of James
             Martin. Sur. Joseph H. Hanby. Min. Joshua Adams.
             M.R. 28 Jan 1846.

11 Aug 1848 Harden H. Hanby and Mary C. King. Sur. John A.
             Hanby. Min. Joshua Adams. M.R. 15 Aug 1848.

 8 Nov 1800 John Hanby and Elizabeth Tatum. Sur. Samuel Staples.

10 Mar 1852 John A. Hanby and Mary Clark. Min. Joshua Adams.

22 Jan 1834 John M. Hanby and Nancy Gaines. Sur. Thomas Waller.

26 Feb 1805 Samuel Hanby and Polly Koger. Sur. G. Hanby.

 7 Jan 1813 Samuel Hanby and Sally Carter. Sur. Gabriel Hanby.

15 Dec 1806 Absalom Hancock and Martha Graham. Sur. Silas
             Ratliff. Wit. Susanah Perkins. Min. William H.
             Robertson.

13 Jan 1840 Benjamin Hancock and Lucy Harris. Sur. William Hall.
             Min. John Conner.

 9 Jan 1830 Charles Hancock and Nancy A. Koger. Sur. John Hancock.
             Min. John Turner. M.R. 14 Jan 1830.

13 Dec 1838 Greensville Hancock and Elizabeth Stegall. Sur. Richard Stegall. Min. John Washburn. M.R. 23 Dec 1838.

9 Feb 1804 John Hancock and Elizabeth Witt. Sur. Isaac Dodson.

13 Aug 1845 John Hancock and Mary Joyce, daughter of James Joyce. Sur. Thomas Hancock. Min. Joshua Adams. M.R. 9 Sep 1845.

9 Oct 1841 John W. Hancock and Jane Edwards, daughter of Brice and Jane Edwards. Sur. Joseph H. Edwards. Min. William Lawson. M.R. 14 Oct 1841.

13 Dec 1793 Major Hancock and Jeaney Perry Morrow, daughter of Thomas Morrow. Sur. William J. Mayo. Min. George Dodson. M.R. 2 Jan 1794.

29 Aug 1814 Major Hancock and Elizabeth Fuson Adams(widow of Joshua Adams, daughter of William Fuson). Sur. Benjamin Hancock.

24 Dec 1839 Peter G. Hancock and Elizabeth Edwards. Sur. Brice Edwards. Min. John Conner.

12 Apl 1821 Thomas Hancock and Sally Washburn. Sur. John A. Hairston. Min. Stephen Hubbard. M.R. 14 Apl 1820.

22 Nov 1852 Thomas Hancock and Penelope Taylor.

23 Mar 1830 Henry Handy and Elizabeth Harris, daughter of Samuel Harris. Sur. Marvel Bolling. Wit. C.D. Harris. Min. Jesse Jones. M.R. 28 Mar 1830.

30 Aug 1853 Henry J. Handy, age 23 son of James Handy, and Levina Ann Williams age 16 daughter of John B. Williams. Min. Austin J. Cassell.

26 Aug 1853 Jackson Handy and Ann Williams, daughter of J.B. Williams Wit. James Branch amd Sparel Williams.

18 Jan 1814 James Handy and Nancy Hughes, daughter of Nancy Hughes. Sur. John Boling. Wit. Dandridge Slaughter. Min. Joshua Adams. M.R. 20 Jan 1814.

30 Dec 1817 John Handy and Sally Harris, daughter of Samuel Harris. Sur. E. Harris. Min. Jesse Jones. M.R. 7 Nov 1817.

12 Feb 1849 John Handy, Jr. and Hannah Handy. Sur. Peter Handy. Min. John Conner. M.R. 22 Feb 1849.

1822 Joseph Handy and Cueda Morris. Min. John C. Traylor.

15 Sep 1822   Nicholas Handy and Polly Dehart. Sur. James Dehart.
Min. Stephen Hubbard.

15 Feb 1825   Peter Handy and Elizabeth Plaster. Min. John Conner.
Sur. Conrad Plaster. M.R. 17 Feb 1825.

22 Nov 1852   Peter Handy, son of Peter Handy, and Serenor Stovall,
daughter of Mary T. Stovall.

24 Aug 1841   Samuel H. Handy and Nancy Williams, daughter of
J.B. Williams. Sur. Edward Duggin. M.R. 26 Aug 1841.

14 Sep 1841   William Handy and Mary Ann Witt. Sur. Sanders Witt.

14 Sep 1815   John Haney and Lucinda Ellyson. Sur. Thomas Reives.

26 Mar 1808   George Hanigear and Rebecca Daniel. Sur. Abram Penn.
Min. Thomas Whitlock. M.R. 23 Mar 1808.

William Hankins - bond with this name only.

2 Nov 1812   Abner Harbour and Mary Hall. Sur. Thomas R. Hall.
Min. Jesse Jones. M.R. 12 Nov 1812.

30 Mar 1809   Benjamin Harbour and Elizabeth Reynolds, daughter of
Moses Reynolds. Sur. Thomas Morrison.
Min. William H. Robertson. M.R. 11 Apl 1809.

28 May 1795   Elisha Harbour and Jane Morrison. Sur. Samuel Staples.
Min. Isaac Adams.

20 May 1819   James Harbour and Hannah Nowling. Sur. Frances Nowlen.
Min. Peter Frans.

13 Mar 1817   Jared Harbour and Ruth Reynolds. Sur. Moses Reynolds
and Thomas Sharp. Min. Brett Stovall. M.R. 14 Mar 1817.

12 Oct 1810   Jesse Harbour and Jinny Hall, daughter of John Hall.
Sur. John Hall. Wit. Randolph Hall.
Min. Stephen Hubbard. M.R. 16 Oct 1810.

3 Mar 1836   Jesse Harbour and Elizabeth Thomas, daughter of
Charles Thomas. Sur. Nathan Hall. Wit. Nicolas Thomas.

11 Oct 1831   Joshua Harbour and Sally Williams. Min. Joshua Adams.

Bond with signatures of Moses Harbour and Alexander
McAlexander. Not dated.

2 Dec 1827   Naman Harbour and Polly Thomas, consent of Pleasant
Thomas. Sur. William Edwards. Min. Stephen Hubbard.

28 Apl 1808   Noah Harbour and Mary Burnett. Sur. William Burnett.

17 Aug 1820   Thomas Harbour and Martha Slaughter. Sur. John J.
Slaughter. Min. Stephen Hubbard. M.R. 24 Aug 1820.

30 Dec 1821   Joseph Hardy and Lucinda Morris, consent of
Samuel C. Morris. Sur. John T. Arrington.
Wit. Deverau Jarrett.

27 Nov 1845   Joseph Hardy and Ann E. Varner, alias Poindexter;
daughter of Peggy Varner. Sur. Joseph Varner.
Min. Joshua Adams. M.R. 28 Nov 1845.

9 May 1819   Spencer Hardy and Elizabeth Packwood. Sur.
Elisha Packwood.

5 Dec 1826   William Hardy and Jane Edmonds, consent of Esom and
Sofiee Edmonds. Sur. Preston Edmonds.
Min. Maning Hill.

22 Apl 1797   Stephen Harper and Susanah Salmons, daughter of
Roland Salmons. Wit. James Hall. Sur. William
Sneed. Min. Jesse Jones.

13 Nov 1811   Jesse Harrell and Marey East. Min. Thomas Whitlock.

19 Oct 1809   Jonathan Harrel and Frances East. Sur. William
Russey. Min. Thomas Whitlock.

14 Nov 1811   Alexander Harris and Elvia Clark. Sur. Absalom
Rickman. Min. Peter Frans.

3 Jan 1807   Alexander Harris and Judith Fendley. Sur. Thomas
Rickman.

2 Sep 1844   Burrel (Burr) Harris and Kizia Nowlen. Sur.
John H. Dillard. Min. Joshua Adams. M.R. 21 Sep 1844.

15 Apl 1806   Burress Harris and Elizabeth Bolt. Sur. Charles Bolt.

17 Oct 1835   Caleb Harris and Mildred Trent, sister of Ferreby
Daniel. Caleb Harris is the son of Elizabeth Harris.
Sur. Madison Hollandsworth. Min. John Washburn.
M.R. 18 Nov 1835.

23 Dec 1819   Calbourn Harris and Elizabeth Blanks. Sur.
Thomas Blanks. Min. Brett Stovall.

23 Oct 1829   Daniel Harris and Nancy Trent. Sur. Thomas Harris.
Wit. Carrington Dillen. Min. Joshua Adams.

3 Oct 1816   Elijah Harris and Levinah Terry, daughter of Mary
Terry. Sur. William Hancock. Min. Joshua Adams.

5 Mar 1824   Fleming Harris, son of Reubin Harris and Nancy Lyon.
Sur. William Lyon. Min. Jesse Jones. M.R. 7 Mar 1824.

13 Jan 1852   Greenville Harris and Rhoda Davis, consent is given
by Rhoda's grandfather Samuel Harris. Min. G.W. Conner.

25 Jun 1793   Henry Harris and Mary Garrison, daughter of Thomas
and Comfort Garrison. Sur. William Woody.
Min. Robert Jones.

6 Jun 1808   Henry Harris and Barberry King. Sur. Samuel Harris.

13 Jan 1808   Isham Harris and Elizabeth Jordon. Sur. Elijah Dehart.

23 Feb 1826   James Harris and Nancy Craddock. Sur. David Cruise.
Min. Joshua Adams.

6 May 1830   James Harris and Lockey Bowman. Sur. John Staples.

2 Mar 1843   James Harris and Polly Cole. Sur. Joseph Harris.
Min. Brett Stovall. M.R. 5 Mar 1843.

15 Nov 1846   James Harris and Elizabeth Blendia Terry, daughter
of Henry B. Terry. Sur. William Harris.

16 Jun 1812   Jacob Harris and Sarah Weddle. Min. Jesse Jones.

17 Nov 1837   John Harris, son of William Harris, and Lydia Edens,
daughter of David Edens. Sur. William Lawson.

9 Dec 1834   Joseph Harris, son of Elijah Harris and Nancy
Morefield, daughter of William Morefield. Sur.
Allen Morefield and Alex Murphey. Min. Bird Lowe.

28 Dec 1818   Moses Harris and Justine Ayres. Sur. Murphy Ayres.
Min. Peter Frans. M.R. 30 Dec 1818.

23 Jun 1846   Murphy Harris and Martha Ayres, daughter of
Thomas Ayres. Sur. Moses Harris. Min. Joshua Adams.
M.R. 2 Jul 1846.

27 Mar 1813   Nathaniel Harris and Peggy Bishop. Sur. and Min.
Thomas Whitlock.

13 Jan 1831   Nathaniel N. Harris,Jr. and Belinda Palmer, daughter
of Charlotte Palmer. Sur. Samuel Harris.

13 Feb 1828   Robert Harris and Elizabeth Vaughan. Sur. Samuel
Harris. Min. John Conner. M.R. 17 Feb 1828.

11 Nov 1793   Reuben Harris and Margaret McAlexander. Sur.
William McAlexander. Wit. William McPeek.

10 Sep 1792   Samuel Harris and Martha Hylton, daughter of Numan
and Elizabeth Hylton. Sur. William McPeek. Wit.
Thomas Barton & Thomas Mitchell. Min. Robert Jones.

14 May 1793 Samuel Harris and Betsey Hollandsworth. Sur.
Thomas Hollandsworth. Min. George Dodson.
M.R. 10 Oct 1794.

8 Jan 1817 Samuel Harris and Nancy Clay. Sur. Jordon Clay.
Min. John Conner. M.R. 9 Jan 1817.

18 Aug 1817 William Harris and Rhoda Burnett. Sur. Isham
Burnett. Min. Jesse Jones. M.R. 21 Aug 1817.

28 Jul 1809 William Harris and Sarah Tuggle, daughter of
Joshua Tuggle. Sur. Elijah Hylton. Min.
Jesse Jones. M.R. 20 Jul 1809.

7 Nov 1814 William Harris and Elizabeth Hilton, consent of
Numan Hylton. Sur. Elijah Hylton.

4 May 1823 William Harris and Ann(Anna) Hodges. Sur. Samuel
Midkiff. Wit. B.W. Philpott. Min. Peter Frans.

15 Dec 1847 William Harris,Jr and Mary E. Slaughter, daughter
of Martin Slaughter. Sur. William Harris,Sr.
Min. John Conner. M.R. 19 Dec 1847.

27 Apl 1848 William Harris and Tempy Jane Ayers, daughter of
Thomas Ayers. Sur. Moses Harris. Min. Joshua Adams.
M.R. 11 May 1848.

4 Nov 1841 William Harris, Jr., and Angeline Booth. Sur.
Jesse Chaney. Wit. Claiborne Thompson.
Min. G.W. Conner.

8 Mar 1803 Francis B. Harrison, of Amherst Co.Va., and
Franky Crutcher, daughter of Samuel Crutcher.
Sur. Samuel Crutcher.

24 Mar 1809 Joseph Haskins and Winney Simson. Sur. William
Moore. Min. Thomas Whitlock.

10 Nov 1803 William Haskins and Nancy Johnson. Min. Thomas
Whitlock.

28 Dec 1836 Wyatt Hart of Stokes Co.N.C., and Sally M. New.
Sur. Woody Burge. Min. Joshua Adams.

6 Jun 1812 Jacob Harter and Sarah Weddle, daughter of Mary
Weddle. Sur. Benjamin Howell.

3 Apl 1837 Ammon Hatcher and Temperance Massey. Sur. John
Massey.

30 Oct 1830 Austin Hatcher and Sarah Lyon, daughter of Elisha
Lyon, of Franklin Co. Va., Min. Jesse Jones.
M.R. 1 Nov 1830.

13 Nov 1845   James C. Hatcher and Lucy Hubbard. Sur. Benjamin
Hubbard. Min. John Conner.

1 Jan 1846   John B. Hatcher, son of Agnes Hatcher, and Kizziah
Hubbard, daughter of John Hubbard. Sur. William F.
Hall. Wit. Richard H. Hatcher and Benjamin Hubbard,Jr.
Min. John Conner. M.R, 15 Apl 1847.

22 Nov 1847   Richard Hatcher,son of Agnes Hatcher, and Delila Wood.
Sur. John R. Wood. Wit. John Hatcher and Benjamin
Hubbard. Min. John Conner. M.R. 16 Dec 1847.

9 Dec 1825   William Hatcher, son of A. Hatcher, and Lucy G. Wells.
Sur. Jennings Moore. Wit. Dolley A. Moore
Min. John Washburn.

6 Oct 1842   William Hatcher and Judith Turner. Sur. Francis Turner.
Min. Jesse Jones. M.R. 14 Oct 1842.

20 Nov 1832   Anderson Haten and Mary Chandler. Sur. Martin Cloud.

8 Oct 1792   John Hawks and Winney Falkner. Sur. David Rowark.
Wit. Jacob Adams.

21 Dec 1800   John Hayse and Elizabeth Morris. Sur. Ezekiel
Morris.

18 Jul 1803   John Hayse and Fanny Sharp. Sur. Richard Sharp.

13 Aug 1813   Phillip T. or J. Hay and Elizabeth Scales.
Sur. Pleasant Scales. Min. John Conner.
M.R. 17 Aug 1817.

26 Oct 1791   James Haywood and Frances Turman. Sur. George Tittle
and John Turman.

Hanes, Haynes

15 Mar 1812   Archelus Hanes and Sally McMillon. Sur. Henry
McMillon. Min. Thomas Whitlock.

5 Jan 1826   Greensberry Hanes and Nancy Bingham. Sur. and Min.
Thomas Whitlock. M.R. 5 Feb 1826.

26 Mar 1808   Joshua Haines and Clarey Daniel. Sur. J. Snow.
Min. Thomas Whitlock. M.R. 23 Mar 1808.

10 Jan 1811   Luster Hains and Mary Branson. Sur. William Cox.
Min. Thomas Whitlock.

20 Oct 1835   Preston Hanes and Morning Green. Sur. Richard Hanes.
Min. Thomas Whitlock.

23 Sep 1843   William G. Haynes and Susan Martin. Sur. A.H.Carter.
              Min. John Jones. M.R. 18 Oct 1843.

21 Jul 1808   William Haynes and Nancy Smith. Sur. Joshua Haynes.
              Min. Thomas Whitlock. M.R. 20 July 1808.

26 Oct 1791   James Haywood and Frances Turner. Sur. George Tittle,
              John Turman and Abram Penn.

 3 Nov 1829   Edward Hazelwood and Elizabeth(Betsy) Rogers.
              Sur. Hiram Rogers. Min. Bird Lowe.

13 Dec 1846   Hiram Hazelwood and Elizabeth Shelton.
              Min. Joshua Adams.

16 Dec 1852   Josiah Hazelwood and Ruth Rogers. Min. Joshua Adams.

 8 Apl 1823   Joshua Hazelwood and Lucy Rogers. Sur. Josiah Rogers.
              Min. Peter Frans. M.R. 3 Apl 1823.

17 Dec 1822   Jacob Helms and Becky Williams. Sur. John B.Williams.

 1 Oct 1847   John Helms, son of Thomas Helms, and Luvenia
              Alexander, daughter of Anny Alexander. Sur.
              Benjamin Helms.

19 Feb 1848   Peter Helms, son of Thomas Helms, and Dianah(Dianna)
              Booth, consent of Anna McAlexander, who is the sister
              of D. Booth's father). Sur. John Helms.

 6 Mar 1847   Thomas Helms and Sinai Turner, daughter of Obadiah
              Turner. Sur. Tazwell Turner.

 5 Sep 1829   Washington Helms, consent given by Jacob Helms, and
              Ruth Mayo Burnett, daughter of Martha Burnett.
              Sur. Jonas Plaster. Wit. Thomas Hopkins and William
              Watson. Min. John Conner. M.R. 10 Sep 1829.

                   Helton, Hilton, Hylton

21 Jul 1837   Absalom Hylton and Martha Fain. Sur. Richard Fain.
              Min. Nathaniel Thompson. M.R. 30 July 1837.

19 Jan 1822   Austen Hylton and Rachel Booth, consent of Abijah
              Booth. Sur. John Agee. Min. Nathaniel Thompson.
              M.R. 24 Feb 1822.

16 Dec 1852   Davis Hylton and Mary Ann Wood, daughter of Peter
              Wood. Min. G. W. Conner.

 3 Sep 1819   Elijah Hylton and Eava(Eve) Smith, daughter of
              Catharine Smith, formerly of Montgomery Co.,Va.
              Sur. Henry Smith. Min. Jesse Jones. M.R.14 Sep 1819.

7 Sep 1807   Elijah Hylton and Rachel Tuggle, daughter of
             Sashersay Tuggle. Min. Jesse Jones.
             Sur. P. Pendleton. M.R. 10 Sep 1807.

26 Dec 1816 Edward Hylton and Sally Hart, daughter of Daniel
             and Mary Conner, who give consent. Sur. John
             Hart. Min. Jesse Jones.

 1 Jan 1816 George Hylton and Milly Wade. Sur. Elijah Hylton.
             Min. John Conner. M.R. 12 Jan 1816.

22 Oct 1846 George W. Hylton and Nancy Handy, daughter of
             James Handy. Sur. Richard Fain. Min. G.W. Conner.

13 Jan 1851 George Hylton,Jr. and Leony F. Bowling, daughter
             of Mary Bowling.

22 Jan 1852 Harden Hylton and Charity Wood. Min. G.W. Conner.

12 Jul 1815 Jacob Hylton and Jenny Manning(Mannon) daughter
             of Davis Manning. Sur. Adin Hickman.
             Min. John Conner.

20 Dec 1822 Jacob Helton and _____Williams. Min. John Conner.

16 Dec 1819 Jeremiah Hylton and Nancy Jones, consent of Ann
             Jones. Wit. Sally Jones. Sur. John Jones.
             Min. Peter Frans.

16 Feb 1830 Jeremiah W. Hylton and Jane P. Clark, consent of
             George Clark. Sur. John Jones. Min. John Jones.

13 Mar 1807 John Helton and Sarah Wade. Sur. William McPeek.
             Min. John Conner.

11 Feb 1845 Moses Hylton and Elizabeth Cruise. Sur. Jacob
             Hylton. Min. William Lawson.

31 Dec 1802 Nathaniel Helton and Polly Pedigo, consent of
             Joseph Pedigo. Sur. John Agee. Wit. James Edwards.

16 Mar 1797 Samuel Hylton and Elizabeth Harris, daughter of
             Sary Harris. Sur. John Hoff. Wit. William Stone
             and Henry Harris. Min. Jesse Jones. M.R. 22 Sep 1797.

 4 Oct 1848 Edward Hemenes(his signature appears to be Jimens)
             and Lucinda C. Elkins. Sur. George Penn.

12 Oct 1839 Alfred Hendrick and Frances Young. Sur. Henry Young.

14 Nov 1791 John Henry and Margaret Pilson, consent given by
             her brother Richard Pilson. Sur. Richard Pilson.
             Wit. John Wingo and Adam Turner.

13 Oct 1808 Francis Henson and Elizabeth Hancock. Sur. Thomas
Reeves. Min. Lewis Foster. M.R. 27 Oct 1808.

Josiah Hereford and Martha Staples. Min. John C.
Traylor. Minister's List dated 14 Jan 1824.

26 Mar 1792 James Heron and Elizabeth Limings. Sur. John
Lemings. Min. George Dodson.

24 Oct 1810 John Hickman and Nancy Adams. Sur. Brett Stovall.
Min. Peter Frans. M.R. 9 Nov 1810.

21 Aug 1806 William Hickman and Anney Morgan. Sur. William
Cloud. Min. Thomas Whitlock.

14 Jan 1836 Hugh Hicks and Susanah Staley. Sur. Clem Bowman.
Min. Thomas Whitlock.

15 Aug 1811 John Hicks and Mary Bowman. Sur. Dudley McMilion.

27 Oct 1811 Azarah Hiett and Sarah Freeman. Sur. James Landreth.

10 Jul 1819 Josiah Hiatt and Alesley White. Sur. Jesse Mankin.
Min. Thomas Whitlock.

16 Dec 1829 Allen Hightower and Nancy Jane Burress, daughter of
Nancy Burress. Sur. Jeremiah Hylton. Wit. William
T. Burress. Min. Joshua Adams. M.R. 17 Dec 1829.

 3 Jun 1840 John Hightower and Mary J. Pendleton. Sur. Harrison
C. France. Min. Thomas Campbell. M.R. 4 Jun 1840.
(There is a letter attached to this bond, apparently
from her brother, telling her that he will be unable
to attend the wedding and other news).

28 Oct 1845 Benjamin Hill and Mary Martin. Sur. Stokley Martin.
Min. Joshua Adams.

18 Apl 1809 Charles Hill and Rebecca Robertson. Sur. John Gussett.
Min. Stephen Hubbard. M.R. 20 Apl 1809.

 2 Jan 1827 Charles Hill and Milly Mase(Mays). Sur. brother,
William Hill. Wit. John Purdy. Min. Joshua Adams.
M.R. 5 Jan 1827.

 8 Mar 1830 Daniel C. Hill and Susanah Hanes. Sur. James Mankin.
Min. Thomas Whitlock.

19 Nov 1815 John Hill,Jr. and Sally Robertson, consent of the
Widow Roberson. Sur. Charles Hill. Min. Stephen
Hubbard. M.R. 21 Nov 1815.

15 Mar 1817 John P. Hill and Eliza H. Morris, consent of J. Morris
of Lynchburg,Va., Eliza was living at the home of
Madison Hughes. Sur. John Hill. Min. John C. Traylor.

Oct 1846   Maning D. Hill and Louisa Shephard. Sur. James
            Shepherd.

28 Sep 1828 William Hill and Charity Richardson. Sur. P.C.
             Ingram. Min. Joshua Adams. M.R. 2 Oct 1828.

26 Jul 1819 Henry Hines and Lucinda Carter. Sur. George
             Carter. Min. Peter Frans.

18 Apl 1795 Isham Hodges and Elender Godard. Sur. Joseph
             Cummings.

29 Dec 1809 Ruben Hodson, consent of Richard Hodson and
             Elizabeth McPeek. Sur. William McPeek.

12 May 1823 Samuel Hoff or Hoof, and Polly Houchins. Sur.
             James Houchins. Min. Jesse Jones.

31 Oct 1814 Daniel Hogan and Milly Crusinbury, daughter of
             Moses Crusinbury. Sur. Edward Branham and William
             Adams. Wit. Edward Parmer and David Hogan.
             Min. John Conner.

14 Oct 1808 Thomas Holems and Charlotte Swiggett. Sur. Cameron
             Holems. Min. Peter Frans. M.R. 20 Oct 1808.

26 Jan 1809 Daniel Hollandsworth and Elizabeth Godard. Sur.
             Moses Godard. Wit. William Adams. Min. Lewis Foster.

31 Nov 1830 Daniel Hollandsworth and Ruth Purdy. Sur. Ezekiel
             Purdy. Min. Joshua Adams. M.R. 2 Dec 1830.

30 Oct 1838 James Hollandsworth and Catharine Purdy. Sur.
             Ezekiel Purdy. Min. Joshua Adams.

 5 Feb 1796 James Hollandsworth,Jr. and Nancy Smallman.
             Min. Isaac Adams.

18 Sep 1828 Jesse Hollandsworth and Dianah Alexander, daughter
             of Mary Alexander. Sur. Thomas Hollandsworth.
             Wit. Thomas Hollandsworth,Jr., and William
             Hollandsworth. Min. Joshua Adams.

20 May 1845 John Hollandsworth,Jr. and Lucy Carter. Sur.
             Benjamin Hill. Min. Joshua Adams.

23 Jan 1832 Madison Hollandsworth and Susanah Hollandsworth.
             Sur. William Hollandsworth and Jerman Hollandworth.
             Min. Joshua Adams. M.R. 24 Jan 1832.

28 Jan 1848 Peter Hollandsworth, son of William Hollandsworth,
             and Mary Hollandsworth, daughter of James Hollands-
             worth. Sur. Madison Hollandsworth. Wit. Ann G.
             Hollandsworth. Min. Joshua Adams.

27 Feb 1802 Thomas Hollandsworth, Jr. and Patsy Craddock, consent of guardian William Baker. Sur. David Baker.

22 Feb 1829 William Hollandsworth and Frances Spencer. William, the son of Thomas Hollandsworth Jr. Sur. William Spencer. Wit. Daniel Hollandsworth. Min. Joshua Adams.

4 Sep 1812 William Hollandsworth and Milly Corn. Sur. Joseph Cummings. Min. Lewis Foster. M.R. 5 Jul 1812.

18 May 1846 William Holly and Catherine Gusler. Sur. John Gusler.

17 Dec 1842 David Holt and Ruth Lawson. Sur. Francis Collins. Min. William W. Turner. M.R. 18 Dec 1842.

17 Mar 1807 Hugh Holt and Elizabeth Harris, daughter of Sherod Harris. Sur. Sherod Harris. Min. William H. Robertson.

8 Feb 1806 Newton Holt and Matilda Hall. Sur. Hudson Hall.

4 Jan 1852 Samuel Holt and Mary Hudson.

29 Jun 1812 Cornelious Hopkins and Darkis Thacker. Sur. Reuben Thacker. Min. Peter Frans.

20 Aug 1813 Daniel Hopkins and Nancy Hickman. Sur. Nicholas Murry. Min. John Conner. M.R. 22 Aug 1813.

15 Feb 1853 David Hopkins and Sarah Hollandsworth. Min. Joshua Adams.

15 Oct 1839 Harden Hopkins and Elizabeth Murphy. Sur. James Roe. Min. John Washburn.

20 Dec 1819 James Hopkins and Jane Gilbert. Sur. Samuel Gilbert. Min. Brett Stovall.

23 Aug 1812 James Hopkins and Elizabeth Spencer. Sur. John Spencer. Min. Peter Frans. M.R. 25 Aug 1812.

27 Oct 1853 Joseph Hopkins, son of James & Elizabeth Hopkins, and Susan Adeline Keaton, daughter of Joshua & Perlina Keaton. Min. Jeremiah Burnett.

4 Mar 1838 Richard Hopkins, Jr. and Charlotte F. Frans. Sur. William Critz. Min. John Washburn.

22 Mar 1816 Richard Hopkins and Betsy Burnett. Sur. John Carrell. Min. H. Fitzgerald.

11 Mar 1813   William Hopkins and Elizabeth Barrott. Sur.
              Francis Wilks. Min. Peter Frans.

7 Apl 1814   William Hopkins and Philida Thacker, daughter of
              Joseph Thacker. Sur. Hamon Critz, Jr.
              Min. Peter Frans.

16 Dec 1819   William Hopkins and Elizabeth Meredith. Sur.
              Susanah Meredith. Min. Brett Stovall.

27 Jan 1824   William Hopkins and Sally Snider. Sur. Alexander
              Murphy. Wit. John G. Lee. Min. Joshua Adams.
              M.R. 27 Jan 1824.

31 Dec 1819   Esam Hooker and J--- Blancett. Sur. John Going.

22 Aug 1827   Gabriel Hooker and Nancy Pack, daughter of Elizabeth
              Pack. Sur. Samuel Hooker. Wit. Greenville Pack.
              Min. Brett Stovall. M.R. 16 Aug 1827.

1 Oct 1830   Isham Hooker and Lavina Yeates. Sur. Samuel Hooker.
              Min. Brett Stovall. M.R. 16 Nov 1830.

23 Nov 1833   Jesse Hooker and Elizabeth Arrington. Sur. John
              Arrington. Min. Joshua Adams. M.R. 24 Nov 1833.

27 Jun 1849   Samuel Hooker and Letha Beasly, daughter of Polly
              Beasly. Sur. James Mize. Wit. Gabriel Hooker.

3 Aug 1849   Abraham W. Houchins, son of John Houchins, and
              Martha Sneed, daughter of Samuel Sneed. Sur.
              Richard B. Foley. Wit. Adam H. Witt.

23 Dec 1798   Bennett Houchins and Margaret Pilson. Sur.
              Adam Turner. Min. Jesse Jones.

2 Jun 1829   James Houchins and Sarah Hughes, consent of
              Nancy Hughes. Sur. Benjamin Terry.
              Min. Jesse Jones.

15 Sep 1825   James Houchins and Polly Terry. Sur. Moses Burnett.

15 Mar 1827   John Houchins and Esther Harbour. Sur. Naman Harbour.
              Min. Joshua Adams.

3 Mar 1817   Richard Houchins and Sally Kith (Keath). Consent of
              Richard Houchins. Min. Jesse Jones.

23 Jul 1849   Richard Houchins and Sarah Boling. Sur. D.W. Smyth.
              Min. G. W. Conner. M.R. 26 July 1849.

16 Nov 1826   William Houchins and Joyce Harbour. Sur. Isaac
              Adams. Min. Jesse Jones. M.R. 22 Nov 1826.

 5 Dec 1839   John Howe and Elizabeth Christian. Sur. Joseph T.
              Flippen. Min. Joshua Adams. M.R. 8 Dec 1839.

11 Dec 1823   Andrew Howell and Caroline Taylor. Sur. Jefferson
              Taylor. Min. Stephen Hubbard. M.R. 18 Dec 1823.

19 Jul 1821   Daniel Howell and Elizabeth Russell, consent of
              JoRiel & Martha Russell. Sur. Daniel Howell.
              Min. Jesse Jones. M.R. 16 Jul 1821.

13 Sep 1821   Daniel Howell and Franky Barrlett(Bartlett).
              Sur. Henry P. Clark. Min. Jesse Jones.
              M.R. 20 Sep 1821.

 6 Aug 1838   Fountain Howell and Nancy Dehart, daughter of
              Elijah Dehart,Sr.. Sur. William Houchins.
              M.R. 4 Sep 1838. Min. Jesse Jones.

 5 May 1825   Isaac Howell and Catharine Thomas. Min. Stephen
              Hubbard.

28 Feb 1812   James Howell and Hester Witt. Sur. Brett Stovall.
              M.R. 29 Feb 1812.

 8 Jul 1844   John D. Howell and Letha Massey. Sur. James J.
              Massey.

16 Feb 1837   Mark A. Howell and Elizabeth Dehart. Sur. Thomas
              Dehart. Min. John Turner. M.R. 23 Feb 1837.

30 Jan 1845   Pleasant Howell and Adaline J. Akers of Franklin
              Co. Va., daughter of Daniel Akers, deceased.
              Sur. William B. Beach. Min. Jesse Jones.

 8 Feb 1810   Samuel Howell and Lucy Witt. Sur. William Witt.
              Min. Peter Frans.

26 Oct 1819   Benjamin Hubbard and Emilia (Milly) Conner, daughter
              of John Conner. Sur. Jonathan Hubbard. Wit. Joel
              Hubbard. Min. John Conner. M.R. 28 Oct 1819.

29 Dec 1845   Benjamin Hubbard, Jr. and Agnes Hatcher, daughter of
              James Hatcher. Sur. John Hubbard. Min. John Conner.
              M.R. 1 Jan 1846.

29 Dec 1803   Eli Hubbard and Lucy Burnett. Sur. Stephen Hubbard.
              Min. Stephen Hubbard.

27 Jan 1834   Jesse Hubbard and Mary Bennett. Min. Stephen Hubbard.

5 Jan 1813   Joel Hubbard and Judith Conner, daughter of John Conner. Sur. Jesse Hubbard. Min. John Conner. M.R. 15 Jan 1813.

14 Sep 1791   Joel Hubbard and Mary Noe, daughter of Samuel Noe. Sur. William Fuson.

6 Jan 1816   John Hubbard and Mary Brammer, daughter of John Brammer. Sur. Jonathan Hubbard. Wit. James Brammer. Min. Stephen Hubbard. M.R. 9 Jan 1816.

23 Jan 1844   John C. Hubbard and Anna Wood, daughter of John R. Wood. Sur. Benjamin Hubbard. Wit. E. H. Dehart and James Dehart.

9 Sep 1821   Jonathan Hubbard and Mary Brammer, daughter of Mary Brammer. Sur. John Hubbard. Min. Stephen Hubbard. M.R. 9 Sep 1821.

13 Dec 1807   Jonathan Hubbard and Lucy Hylton, daughter of Nathaniel N. Hilton. Sur. Elijah Hilton. Min. Jesse Jones.

19 Jan 1842   Jonathan Hubbard, Jr., and Frances Cruise. Sur. John Cruise. Min. William Lawson. M.R. 20 Jan 1842.

11 Oct 1830   Samuel Hubbard and Elizabeth Pendleton. Sur. Pryor Pendleton.

31 Jul 1827   Stephen Hubbard, Jr., and Nancy Elgin. Sur. Jesse Hubbard. Min. Stephen Hubbard. M.R. 2 Aug 1827.

28 Dec 1826   William Hubbard, son of Jesse Hubbard, and Milly Elgin. Sur. John Hubbard. Min. Stephen Hubbard.

25 Jan 1825   John H. Hudson and Mary Wilson. Sur. Thomas Wilson. Min. John Conner.

21 Nov 1830   Joseph Henry Hudson and Nancy Clark. Sur. Moses Clark. Min. Bird Lowe. M.R. 25 Nov 1830.

14 Jan 1793   John Huff and Fanney Thomson, daughter of James Thomson. Sur. John Breeden, Jr. Min. Robert Jones.

13 Jan 1797   Archelaus Hughes and Nancy Martin. Sur. David Hanby.

18 Feb 1835   Beverage A. Hughes and Mary P. Wright. Sur. Robert Wright. Min. John Conner.

15 Apl 1824   Blackmor Hughes and Charlotte Vaughan. Sur. William Hancock.

27 Feb 1849   John J. Hughes and Barbara Branch. Sur. W. J. Robertson. Min. G.W. Conner. M.R. 1 Mar 1849.

21 Dec 1852   Thomas J. Hughes and Bettie F. Penn. Min.
Joshua Bethel.

24 Nov 1853   Claiborne Hundley and Elmira R. Clark, daughter of
Richard Hudnell,Sr.. Min. D.G. Taylor.

16 Sep 1830   John Hunget and Susanah Dehart. Min. Stephen
Hubbard.

10 Dec 1838   Owen E. Hunt and Jane Turner. Sur. William Turner.

22 Apl 1830   Robert Hunter and Elizabeth C. Sandefer.
Min. Stephen Hubbard.

 9 Sep 1852   Stephen Hurd and Jayne High. Min. G.W. Conner.

28 Jul 1797   Joseph Hurt and Milley Burnett. Sur. Moses Hurt.
Min. Jesse Jones. M.R. 22 Sep 1797.

15 Feb 1825   Roland Hurt and Elizabeth Lawson, daughter of
Dicy Lawson. Sur. William Lawson. Min. Nathaniel
Thomson. M.R. 3 Mar 1825.

25 Mar 1852   James M. Huse and Nancy W. Tatum. Min. J. Adams.

 2 Sep 1791   Alexander Huston and Jemimah Turner. Sur.
Nicholas Long. Wit. John W. Hunter.

13 Mar 1848   Leonard Hutts and Sarah Ayers, a grand-daughter of
old Murphey Ayers. James M. Ayers attests to her
being of age. Sur. Robert M. Clark. Wit. George
Hylton. Min. Joshua Adams. M.R. 18 May 1848.

29 Aug 1853   Alexander Ingram, son of James & Elizabeth Ingram
of Franklin Co. Va., and Harriet E. Young, daughter
of William D. Young and Tarmesia Young.
Min. Joshua Adams.

21 Sep 1842   Alexander Ingram,Jr and Martha Akers. Sur.
Nathaniel Akers. Min. Joshua Adams.

29 Nov 1847   Harden Ingram and Mary Ann Akers. Sur. Nathaniel
Akers. Min. Joshua Adams. M.R. 30 Dec 1847.

17 Aug 1850   Isaac Ingram,of Franklin Co,Va., and Jane Adams.
Sur. Joshua Adams. Min. Joshua Adams.
M.R. 29 Aug 1850.

27 Jun 1797   James Ingram and Rozinah Hall. Sur. John Hall.
Min. John Pedigo. M.R. 29 Jun 1797.

14 Nov 1816   James Ingram,Jr., and Elizabech Hall. Sur. John
Hall. Min. Stephen Hubbard. M.R. 21 Nov 1816.

1 Feb 1847   James A. Ingram and Martha J. Smart. Sur. Thomas J.
            Reynolds. Min. G.W. Conner. M.R. 4 Feb 1847.

12 May 1808 Paul C. Ingram and Sally Ingram. Min. Lewis Foster.

19 Jul 1809 Rowland Ingram and Nancy Corn. Sur. James Ingram,Jr.
            Min. Brett Stovall. M.R. 22 Jul 1809.

5 Dec 1835   Samuel C. Ingram, son of Rowland Ingram, and Sally
            N. Clark, daughter of John Clark. Sur. Thomas
            Morefield. Wit. Archilbald Ferguson.
            Min. Joshua Adams. M.R. 22 Dec 1835.

24 Apl 1846 Soloman Ingram and Elizabeth Joyce. Sur. John D.
            Cheatham. Min. Joshua Adams.

23 Jun 1851 William P. Ingram of Franklin Co.Va., and Maryan
            Koger. Min. Joshua Adams.

15 Apl 1797 James Innes and Patty Sublett. Sur. William J.
            Mayo. Min. Isaac Adams.

25 Jan 1812 John Iron or Jron and Mary Brown. Sur. John
            Brown. M.R. 2 Feb 1812.

15 Jan 1844 John H. Ivie and Nancy Stegall, daughter of Nathe (?)
            P. Stegall. Sur. Wiley B. Hix. Min. Joshua Adams.
            M.R. 18 Jan 1844.

20 Dec 1848 Peter W. Ivie and Jane Gray, daughter of Powell
            Gray. Sur. Samuel Martin. Min. John Robertson.
            M.R. 24 Dec 1848.

8 Jun 1809   Jacob Jackson and Susanna Gaines. Sur. James Gaines.
            Min. William H. Robertson.

1 Mar 1842   John Jackson and Nancy Bowman. Sur. John Bowman,Jr.

14 Jan 1841 Foster James and Nancy Arrington. Sur. Absolem
            Arrington.

28 Dec 1835 Franklin James and Tabithia Brown. Sur. Thomas Irion.
            Min. John Washburn. M.R. 10 Jan 1836.

13 Mar 1817 James James and Mary Foster. Sur. Charles Foster.
            Min. Lewis Foster.

3 Apl 1817   John Janney, son of Isaac Janney, and Ann Martin.
            Sur. James Martin. Wit. Stephen Thomas.

3 Jan 1804   Devereau Jarrett and Polly Morris, consent of
            Samuel C. Morris. Sur. John Morris.

25 Mar 1806 Robert Jarrott and Susannah Tommas. Min. Lewis
            Foster.

23 Dec 1840   Robert Jarrett and Sarah J.Clark, daughter of James
               Clark. Sur. William Craig. Min. Lewis Foster.

 8 Jan 1825   Thomas Jefferson Jarvis and Lucinda Atkinson, daughter
               of William Atkinson. Sur. John D. Atkinson.

15 Oct 1829   Edward F. Jefferson and Malinda Ross. Sur. Daniel Ross.
               Min. Joshua Adams. M.R. 20 Oct 1829.

17 Feb 1831   James Jefferson and Elizabeth Pilson. Sur. Thomas B.
               Jefferson. Min. John Conner. M.R. 24 Feb 1831.

14 Mar 1831   Peyton G. Jefferson and Nancy Pilson, daughter of
               Richard Pilson. Min. Joshua Adams. M.R. 15 Jan 1831.

21 May 1839   James Jennings and Lemina Barnard. Min. Nathaniel
               Thompson.

 2 Feb 1815   William Jennings and Aney Henson. Sur. Thomas Whitlock.

 1 May 1806   Eli Jessop and Jency Smith. Sur. Elijah Jessop.
               Min. Thomas Whitlock. M.R. 7 Apl 1806.

15 Dec 1801   Elijah Jessop and Becky Smith. Sur. Samuel Staples.

29 Sep 1853   Elijah S. Jessop, son of Martin Jessop of Surry Co.
               N.C., and Delila P. Smith, daughter of Bartlett
               Smith. Min. Martin Cloud.

19 May 1808   Elisha Jessop and Sally R. Robertson. Sur. William
               H. Robertson. Min. Wm. H. Robertson.
               M.R. 26 May 1808.

 3 Dec 1795   Benjamin Johnson and Sally Franklin.
               Sur. Roderick Shelton.

11 Sep 1813   Dabney Johnson and Eilzabeth Burnett. Sur. Isham
               Burnett. Min. Jesse Jones. M.R. 23 Sep 1813.

 2 Feb 1825   Fleming Johnson and Mary (Polly) Thompson.
               Sur. Jonathan Hubbard. Min. Stephen Hubbard.
               M.R. 30 Jan 1825.

26 Apl 1807   John Johnson and Jinsey Lewis. Sur. John A. Grigg.
               Min. Thomas Whitlock.

14 Sep 1820   John Johnston and Sarah Thomas. Sur. Richard Thomas.

22 Jan 1827   Josiah Jonson and Hannah Dehart, daughter of Gabriel
               Dehart. Sur. John Dehart. Wit. Stephen Dehart.
               Min. Stephen Hubbard. M.R. 24 Jan 1827.

16 Dec 1817   Larkin Johnson and Sally Harris, daughter of Reuben
               Harris. Sur. William McAlexander. Wit. Flemmon
               Harris. Min. Jesse Jones. M.R. 26 Jan 1818.

31 Aug 1820   Michah (Michael) Johnson and Judah Burnett. Sur.
              Jeremiah Burnett,Sr., Min. Jesse Jones.
              M.R. 5 Oct 1820.

15 Nov 1791   Perry Green Johnson and Mary Sanders, daughter of
              Benjamin Sanders, who gives consent. Sur. Lewis
              Johnston.

11 Mar 1841   Ambrose W. Jones and Louisa Wells. Sur. Gabriel
              Bolling.

16 Feb 1809   Daniel Jones and Elizabeth Kane. Sur. Jabez
              Johnson. Min. Thomas Whitlock.

19 Aug 1831   Gabriel Jones and Susanah Thomas, daughter of
              Washington Thomas. Sur. Adderson Philpott.

 4 Feb 1841   James A. Jones and Elizabeth Frans. Min. John
              Jones. Sur. John Frans.

23 Feb 1797   Jesse Jones and Sally Tuggle. Sur. John Tuggle.
              Min. Robert Jones. M.R. 22 Sept 1797.

27 May 1805   Jonathan Jones and Darkes(Dorcas) Howell. Sur.
              David Howell. Min. Robert Jones. M.R. 3 Jun 1805.

25 Nov 1852   Peter D. Jones and Nancy Joyce. Min. Joshua Adams.

17 Sep 1806   Samuel Jones and Mary Hammons. Sur. John A. Grigg.
              Min. Thomas Whitlock.

 4 Jul 1851   Thomas Jones and Sarah F. Smith, age 18, daughter of
              Martha W. Smith. Wit. George Sprouse. Min. Joshua
              Adams. M.R. 13 Jul 1851.

19 Mar 1806   Robert Jordon and Susanah Thomas, daughter of
              Charles Thomas.

11 Dec 1822   Alexander Joyce and Lucy R. Hudson. Sur. Jacob
              Hudson. Min. Brett Stovall. M.R. 12 Dec 1822.

26 Nov 1828   Allen Joyce and Sally Poore. Sur. Bartlett
              Greenwood. Min. Bird Lowe.

 9 Feb 1838   Calvin Joyce, son of Elizabeth Joyce, and Sarah
              Corn, daughter of John Corn. Sur. Livingston Joyce.
              Wit. Hamilton Joyce & Perrin Joyce. Calvin Joyce of
              Stokes Co. N.C.. Min. Joshua Adams. M.R. 15 Feb 1838.

22 Sep 1830   Elijah Joyce, of Stokes Co. N.C., and Catherine
              Moorman. Sur. Jacob Moorman. Min. Maning Hill.
              M.R. 23 Sep 1830.

16 Mar 1843   Franklin Joyce, of Stokes Co. N.C., and Martha
              Adams. Sur. A.B. Clark. Min. Joshua Adams.

14 Dec 1820   James Joyce and Susanah Corn. Sur. Samuel Corn.
Min. Maning Hill. M.R. 17 Dec 1820.

20 Dec 1827   John Joyce and Mary Norman. Sur. Joseph Norman.
Min. Bird Lowe.

16 Jan 1846   Lemuel G. Joyce and Martha Jane Spencer, daughter
of Thomas Spencer. Sur. Thomas Spencer. Min.
Joshua Adams. M.R. 22 Jan 1846.

1 Dec 1838   Livingston Joyce of Stokes Co. N.C., and Sally Nowlin.
Sur. Francis Nowlin. Min. Joshua Adams.
M.R. 6 Dec 1838.

4 Dec 1843   Richard Joyce and Mary Spencer. Sur. Abraham Spencer.
Min. Joshua Adams. M.R. 9 Nov 1843.

12 Dec 1827   Smith Joyce and Mariannah Poor. Sur. John Turner.
Min. Bird Lowe.

26 Nov 1795   Thomas Joyce and Polly Poor. Sur. George Poore.

15 Feb 1821   Thomas Joyce and Esther Joyce. Sur. Samuel Staples.

25 Jul 1843   Thomas Joyce and Malinda Turner. Sur. John D.
Cheatham. Min. Martin Cloud.

4 Feb 1804   William Joyce and Lidia Flood. Sur. Noah Parr.

1827   William Joyce and Nancy D. Hanby. Sur. Samuel Hanby.
Min. Bird Lowe.

11 Jul 1828   William Joyce and Betsy Bostick. Nancy James states
that Betsy is over 21 years of age. Sur. Samuel
Hughes. Min. Bird Lowe.

14 Jan 1841   William Joyce and Nancy Hudson, daughter of John B.
Hudson. Sur. William Martin. Min. Joshua Adams.
M.R. 17 Jan 1841.

20 Jan 1808   James Keath and Anney Morrison. Sur. James Morrison,Jr.
M.R. 23 Jan 1808.

27 Dec 1835   William J. Keath and Ann Clark, daughter of Lucy
Clark. Sur. James Houchens. Min. John Conner.
M.R. 31 Dec 1835.

8 Jun 1795   Cliffen Keaton and Sarah Parr. Sur. William Keaton.
Min. Isaac Adams.

12 Nov 1793   Cornelius Keaton and Sarah Adams. Sur. Jacob Adams,Sr.
Min. George Dodson.

7 Sep 1816   Cornelius Keaton and Mary Harris, daughter of
Samuel Harris. Sur. Larkin Keaton.

22 Dec 1797   Daniel Keaton and Mary Dovity. Sur. Henry Koger.

13 Jun 1839   Hansford Keaton and Malinda Hopkins. Sur. Jordon
              Keaton & James Roe. Min. John Washburn.
              M.R. 16 Jun 1839.

15 Feb 1844   Hiram Keaton and Susanah Keaton. Sur. Mekins
              Reynolds. Min. Joshua Adams.

13 Sep 1802   John Keaton and Susanah Epperson. Sur. James
              Epperson.

21 Nov 1835   Joshua Keaton and Perlina Keaton age 20, cousins.
              Sur. Jordon Keaton. Joshua Keaton, the son of
              Soloman Keaton. Wit. James Taylor.
              Min. Joshua Adams. M.R. 22 Nov 1835.

 8 Jan 1835   Jourdon Keaton and Kiziah Martin. Sur. Micajah
              Martin. Min. Joshua Adams.

 2 Feb 1839   Madison Keaton and Jestin Ayers, daughter of
              Hugh Ayers, deceased, and grand-daughter of
              Joseph M. Ayers. Sur. Anders Simmons.
              Wit. Leonard Ayers. Min. Joshua Adams.
              M.R. 3 Feb 1839.

15 May 1849   Madison Keaton and Sarah Ann Hutts, daughter of
              Leonard Hutts. Min. Joshua Adams. M.R. 17 May 1849.

       1816   Mr. Keaton and Miss Harris. Min. John Traylor.

 3 Apl 1833   Peter A. Keaton and Jane Keaton. Sur. Soloman
              Keaton. Min. Joshua Adams. M.R. 4 Apl 1833.

29 May 1841   Sampson Keaton and Mary Morefield, daughter of
              Rebecca Morefield. Sur. Wright Morefield. Wit.
              Meekins Reynolds. Min. John Washburn.
        **   M.R. 3 Jun 1841.

12 Dec 1824   Tazwell Keaton, son of William Keaton, and Sarah
              Keaton, daughter of Soloman Keaton. Sur. Soloman
              Keaton. Min. Joshua Adams. M.R. 14 Dec 1824.

14 May 1807   William Keaton and Susannah Hollandsworth.
              Sur. James Keaton.

18 Dec 1804   William Keaton, Jr. and Anna Haile.

17 Jan 1833   Mason Keller and Nancy Fleming.

17 Jan 1840   George W. Kelly and Hannah C. Carter, daughter of
              Elijah Carter. Sur. George Sprouse. Min.
              Joshua Adams. M.R. 28 Jan 1840.

** 7 Apl 1806 Soloman Keaton and Nancy Deal. Sur. William Keaton.

19 Nov 1815   Joseph Kelly and Jane Hill, daughter of John Hill.
Sur. Charles Hill.

29 May 1832   James Kendrick and Elizabeth Tuggle. Sur. William
Tuggle. Min. John Washburn. M.R. 30 May 1832.

13 Aug 1833   Osborn Kendrick and Esa Stewart. Sur. James Kendrick.

26 Mar 1838   William J. Kemp of Wilks Co. Ga., and Mary Thomas.
Sur. A. B. Thomas. Wit. Edward Thomas.

28 Dec 1840   John Kennerly and Martha Ross, daughter of David
Ross. Sur. H. Critz.

24 Dec 1828   James Kerks and Nancy Haslip. Sur. Henry Haslip.
Min. Joshua Adams.

29 Feb 1836   Benjamin L. King of Henry Co., and Mary A. Jones,
daughter of Augustine Jones. John King gives
consent for Benjamin King. Wit. James Trent.

 3 Sep 1838   Camellus King of Henry Co., and Sally Hylton,
daughter of J.W. Hylton. Sur. A. A. Morris.
Wit. Valentine Hylton & Elizabeth King.
Min. Joshua Adams. M.R. 17 Sept 1838.

20 Aug 1830   John King and Catherine Epperson. Sur. Joshua
Roberts. Min. Thomas Whitlock.

26 Apl 1850   John S. King and Sarah Ann Ivie, daughter of
John W. Ivie. Sur. Peter W. Ivie. Min. Daniel G.
Taylor. M.R. 28 Apl 1850.

15 Sep 1849   Lafayette King and Sarah C. Clark. Sur. John A.
Hanby. Min. Joshua Adams. M.R. 18 Sep 1849.

 6 Nov 1797   William King and J---Gussett. Sur. Field Trent.

26 Dec 1823   George Kington and Polly Stephens. Sur.
John Stephens. Min. Peter Frans.

17 Oct 1826   Micajah T. Kington and Ann B. Ivie, daughter of
Gilbert P. Ivie. Sur. Greensville Penn. Wit.
W. C. Moore & Benjamin Frazer. Min. John
Washburn.

21 Mar 1845   A. J. Kirby and Nancy Tuggle. Sur. John Tuggle.
Min. Joshua Adams. M.R. 30 Mar 1845.

 2 Mar 1850   David P. Knowles and Elizabeth Hill, daughter of
John Hill. Sur. James Cruise.

1 Apl 1815   Joshua Knowles and Jane Harbour. Sur. Richard Harbour.
Min. Jesse Jones. M.R. 6 Apl 1815.

1 Jan 1850   John Knowlin and Judith Sneed, daughter of Samuel
Sneed. Sur. Abram Houchins.

12 Jan 1850   Augustine L. Koger and Nancy Webb, daughter of
Sylvester Webb. Sur. Sylvester Webb.
Min. J.D. Wade. M.R. 17 Jan 1850.

23 Apl 1821   Henry Koger and Lucinda(Susan) Thomas. Sur. Middleton
Thomas. Min. John C. Traylor.

17 Aug 1826   Jacob Koger and Sinai Philpott, daughter of Edward
Philpott. Sur. Clark Penn. Min. Joshua Adams.
M.R. 22 Aug 1826.

15 Sep 1807   John Koger and Mary Anderson. Sur. Charles Foster.
Wit. William Adams. Min. Lewis Foster.
M.R. 19 Sep 1807.

18 Dec 1849   John S. Koger and Susan J. Reynolds, daughter of
Thomas Reynolds. Sur. William A. Reynolds.
Min. Joshua Adams. M.R. 19 Dec 1849.

17 Aug 1826   Joseph Koger and Ruth Slaughter. Sur. John Slaughter.
Min. John Conner. M.R. 22 Aug 1826.

22 Jun 1826   William Koger and Matilda Anglin, daughter of Phillip
Anglin. Sur. George C. Dodson. Wit. John Koger.

10 Mar 1798   Alexander Lackey and Mary Morgan, daughter of David
Morgan. Sur. William Slone. Min. Jesse Jones.

8 Oct 1795   George Lackey and Lucy Sharp. Sur. John Sharp.
Min. John Pedigo. M.R. 9 Oct 1795.

2 Dec 1799   James Lackey and Esther McAlexander, daughter of
William McAlexander. Sur. John Turman. Wit. James
McAlexander.

19 Dec 1810   James Lackey and Polly Anglin. Sur. Crawford Burnett.
Min. Stpehen Hubbard. M.R. 20 Dec 1810.

16 Feb 1830   John Lackey and Ruth Turner, daughter of John Turner.
Sur. P. Penn. Min. Stephen Hubbard.

7 Sep 1835   Samuel J. Lackey, consent of Lucy Lackey, and
Drucilla Corn, daughter of John Corn. Wit. John
Lackey. Min. Joshua Adams. M.R. 8 Sep 1835.

11 Jan 1836   William A. Lacky and Martha George, ward of William
Graves. Sur. Richard Turner. Min. John Turner.
M.R. 12 Jan 1836.

14 Dec 1839   Thomas Lambert and Malinda Thompson. Sur. John D.
              Cheatham. Min. William Lawson. M.R. 19 Dec 1839.

7 Feb 1815   Benjamin Landreth and Nancy Ballard (Bellar). Sur.
              Leonard Owen. Min. Thomas Whitlock. M.R. 15 Feb 1815.

6 Oct 1803   Jonathan Landreth and Catharine Vancel. Sur.
              Peter Bellar.
                                Priscilla
8 Dec 1848   William Law and Ruth Spencer. Sur. Lewis Spencer.
              Min. Joshua Adams. M.R. 14 Dec 1848.

30 Jan 1851   Zachariah Law and Martha Ann Hollandsworth, daughter
              of Daniel Hollandsworth. Min. Jeremiah Burnett.

22 Aug 1826   Augustine Lawless and Tempy Elliott, whose sister,
              Elizabeth Redman made oath that Tempy was 21 years
              of age. Sur. James Redman. Min. John Washburn.
              M.R. 23 Aug 1826.

25 Dec 1814   Thomas Lawless and Polly Spencer. Sur. Greensville
              Spencer. Min. Peter Frans. M.R. 26 Dec 1814

7 Oct 1826   Thomas Lawless and Zinia Keaton. Sur. William
              Nowland. Min. John Washburn. M.R. 10 Oct 1826.

29 Mar 1832   Thomas Lawless and Polly Frans, daughter of John
              Frans. Sur. David W. Smith.

2 Apl 1832   Thomas Lawless and Frances Reynolds. Sur. Elisha
              Anglin. Min. Joshua Adams.

2 Jan 1838   Andrew Lawson and Martha Beasley. Sur. Austin Collings.

21 Jun 1801   Elisha Lawson and Mary Lawson. Sur. Joshua Lawson.

4 May 1836   Elisha Lawson, of Stokes Co., N.C., and Nancy Willard.
              Sur. Allen Willard. Min. Julius Ferrell.
              M.R. 5 May 1836.

15 Nov 1847   Hiram Lawson and Ann Eliza Burnett. Sur. Obediah Burnett.
              Min. G. W. Conner. M.R. 16 Nov 1847.

19 May 1838   Isham Lawson and Charlotte Hughes. Sur. Rowland Hurt.
              Min. William Lawson. M.R. 5 Jun 1838.

12 Jul 1843   James Lawson and Sarah Strange. Sur. Henry Parker.

24 Dec 1818   James Lawson,Jr. and Nancy Hurt. Sur. James Lawson.
              Min. Jesse Jones. M.R. 3 Jan 1819.

23 Sep 1842   John Lawson and Kiziah Cockran, daughter of S. Cockran.
              Sur. George W. King. Min. William Lawson.
              M.R. 15 Oct 1842.

8 Nov 1847   Powell Lawson and Emily Hanby. Sur. Reuben Collings.
Min. Julius Terrell.

13 Jun 1791   Randolph Lawson and Susannah Cross. Sur. Jacob Lawson.

5 Nov 1847   Thornton Lawson and Nancy Puckett. Sur. ---New.
Min. Julius Terrell. M.R. 8 Nov 1847.

26 Apl 1826   William Lawson and Anny Thompson, daughter of Henry
Thompson. Sur. Rowland Hurt. Min. Nathaniel Thompson.
M.R. 30 Apl 1826.

              Layman - Lemmons - Limmons all seem to be the same.

12 Nov 1835   Christian Laymen and Kiziah Brammer. Sur. James Brammer.
Min. Jesse Jones. M.R. 3 Dec 1835.

5 Dec 1845   David Layman and Sarah Burnett, daughter of Agnes
Burnett. Sur. Beverage Burnett. M.R. 12 Dec 1844.
(The consent slip is date 5 Dec 1844).

21 May 1821   John Lemons and Phebey Stegall. Sur. John Tuggle.
Min. Jesse Jones. M.R. 22 May 1821.

5 Oct 1802   George Layne and Sarah Walden. Sur. Aaron Loe.

11 Dec 1817   Peter Leake and Elizabeth Rea. Sur. Andrew Rea.
Min. Maning Hill. M.R. 16 Dec 1817.

26 Jan 1836   Peter G. Leake, son of Josiah Leake, and Elizabeth
Gunter, daughter of George Gunter. Sur. John Gunter.
Min. Julius Terrell. M.R. 28 Jan 1836. Peter G. Leake
was of Stokes Co., N.C.

3 Apl 1804   Abel Lee and Polly Thompson, daughter of James Thompson.
Wit. William Lee and Jois McBride. Min. Jesse Jones.

12 Dec 1807   Abel Lee and Ursly Hilton. Sur. Edward Helton and Henry
Tuggle. Min. Stephen Hubbard.

28 Dec 1791   John Lee and Frances Ward, daughter of Thomas Ward.
Sur. William Fuson. Wit. John Ward.

21 Sep 1847   John Lee and Elizabeth A. Adams. Sur. Notley P. Adams.
Min. G. W. Conner. M.R. 23 Sep 1847.

28 Oct 1852   John A. Lee and Elvira G. Philpott; consent of John J.
Philpott. Min. Arnold Walker.

13 Jan 1823   John G. Lee and Susan Frans, daughter of
John Frans. Sur. Hamon Critz. Min. Peter Frans.
M.R. 16 Jan 1823.

Sep 1841   John G. Lee and Nancy Frans, daughter of John
Frans. Sur. Clark Penn. Min. Joshua Adams. M.R.
22 Sep 1841.

16 Nov 1811   Joseph Lee and Ona Newman. Sur. Edward J. Brickell. Min. Brett Stovall. M.R. 20 Nov 1811.

11 Aug 1845   Capt. Peter A. Lee and Ann Mariah Frashure. Sur. H. Critz. Min. Joshua Adams. M.R. 14 Aug 1845.

5 Feb 1797   Roland Lee and Kiziah Brammer, daughter of Mary Brammer. Sur. William Fuson. Wit. Andrew McBride. Min. Robert Jones.

4 Apl 1805   William Lee and Polly Tuggle. Min. Robert Jones.

29 Dec 1811   George LeNew and Mary Gray. Sur. Joseph Gray. M.R. 27 Feb 1812.

12 Mar 1835   Champ Lester and Rachel McAlexander, daughter of Thamer McAlexander. Sur. Samuel McAlexander. Min. Jesse Jones. M.R. 8 Mar 1835.

30 Sep 1806   Alven More Lewis and Sally Massey, daughter of Richard Massey, who is surety. Min. William H. Robertson. M.R. 7 Oct 1806.

16 Oct 1816   Andrew Lewis and Peggy Ayers. Sur. Elijah Hylton and Elijah Dehart. Min. Jesse Jones. M.R. 24 Oct 1816.

23 Dec 1848   Charles Lewis and Nancy A.F. Moles. Sur. John B. Moles. Min. Jeremiah Burnett. M.R. 4 Jan 1849.

15 Dec 1819   Edward Lewis and Polly Cruise. Sur. John Cruise.

27 Dec 1812   Felding Lewis and Charlotte Hanes. Sur. Abraham Penn. Min. Thomas Whitlock. M.R. lists Elizabeth Hanes.

6 May 1830   George W. Lewis and Frances Hall. Min. Stephen Hubbard.

22 May 1793   James Lewis and Sarah Price. Sur. Edward Lewis. Wit. William Price. Min. George Dodson.

16 Dec 1852   Samuel Lewis and Susan Emerson. Min. Jeremiah Burnett.

17 Sep 1840   James Light and Lucinda Hall. Sur. Joseph Hall. Min. John Conner.

11 Oct 1842   John G. Light and Lucinda Rickman. Sur. John Rickman. Min. Joshua Adams.

5 Oct 1842   Lazarus Light and Elizabeth Cassell, daughter of William Cassell. Sur. John G. Light. Wit. Jonas Plaster & William S. Cassell. Min. Joshua Adams.

24 Jul 1842 Franklin Lisk and Elizabeth Corn. Sur. John Corn.
Min. Joshua Adams.

9 Jul 1838 Hamilton J. Lisk and Phoebe Corn. Sur. John Corn.
Min. Joshua Adams. M.R. 10 Jul 1838.

3 Apl 1815 Thomas Lockhart and Sarah Rusk. Sur. Thomas Harbour.
Min. Stephen Hubbard.

21 Feb 1792 William Lockhart and Elizabeth Fletcher, daughter of
John Fletcher. Sur. John Fletcher. Wit. George Penn.

13 Nov 1817 Calm Loggin and Nancy Harris. Sur. M.R. Hughes.
Min. Brett Stovall. M.R. 11 Jan 1818.

27 Sep 1809 Tilman Logins and Prudence Fendley. Min. Brett Stovall.

12 Feb 1830 John Lovell of Montgomery Co.Va., and Mary Austin. Sur.
David Austin. Min. Nathaniel Thompson.

18 Apl 1850 William W. Lovell and Frances Cockram, daughter of
Robert Cockram. Sur. Robert Cockram.

3 Oct 1801 Aaron Low or Law and ----Frazer. Sur. William Frazer.

29 Jul 1828 Harrison R. Lowe and Jane Stone, daughter of
Eusebious Stone. Stephen Stone affirms that she is
of age. Sur. Tandy Stone. Wit. Susan Stone. Min.
John Turner. M.R. 4 Aug 1828.

5 Jun 1851 Isaac Lowell and Nancy Wade. Min.Jesse Jones.

13 Aug 1825 Joseph Loyd and Rachel Deal. Sur. Jesse Reynolds.
Min. Joshua Adams. M.R. 18 Aug. 1825.

3 Jan 1852 James D. Lyon and Sarah Pendleton. Min. G.W. Conner.

16 Dec 1830 John Lyon and Sarah F. Philpott. Sur. Samuel Sharp.
Min. Bird Lowe.

3 Nov 1838 Elias Lundy and Jane Ross, daughter of David Ross,Sr.
Sur. W. Ross.

26 Dec 1845 Abner Mabe, son of Abner Mabe, and Liddy Martin.
Sur. Masten Mabe. Min. Joshua Adams.
M.R. 29 Jan 1846.

14 Apl 1849 Jospeh Mabe, son of Abner Mabe and Aney(Oney) Martin.
Sur. Masten Mabe. Min. Joshua Adams.
M.R. 19 Apl 1849.

29 Nov 1838 Masten Mabe of Stokes Co. N.C., and Lucretia Martin.
Sur. Isaac Martin. Min. Joshua Adams.

2 Nov 1841 Matthew Mabe,age 21 son of Abner Mabe, and Elizabeth
Washburn. Sur. John Washburn. Wit. Lewis Bhoman &
William Shelton. Min. John Washburn. M.R. 4 Nov 1841.

8 Aug 1816 Joshua Mabery and Polly Huff. Sur. Thomas Whitlock.
Min. Thomas Whitlock.

16 Jan 1815 John Mabs and Mincey Bolling. Min. John Conner.

16 Jan 1808 Micajah Mahone and Nancy Hornsbay, daughter of
Thomas Hornsbay. Sur. John Fields.

17 Oct 1823 William Major and Elizabeth Nichols, consent of
Bazdel Nichols. Sur. Simeon Nichols.

25 May 1831 William Mankin and Harriet Smith. Sur. James
Mankin. Min. Thomas Whitlock.

4 Jul 1847 Joseph H. Mans, a free man of color of Henry Co.,Va.
and Catherine Loggin, daughter of Polly Loggin, a
free woman of colour. Catherine Loggin is a bound
girl to J.G. Lee. Sur. Isiah Loggin. Min. Joshua
Adams. M.R. 11 Aug 1847.

3 Jul 1802 Richard Manes and Anne Lawson.

19 Mar 1839 Elijah Manning and Catherine Hall.
Min. John Conner.

11 Jan 1822 Richard Manor and Nancy Belcher. Sur. Benjamin Belcher.

18 Sep 1814 John Marrow and Mary Lockhart. Min. Stephen Hubbard.

9 Sep 1845 Hamilton Marshall, son of Joseph D. Marshall and
Sarah Bowman, daughter of Margaret Bowman. Wit.
Henry Sutphin & Stephen H. Bolt. Min. William Lawson.
M.R. 13 Oct 1845.

29 May 1837 Robert M. Marshall and C. Bream. Sur. Joseph Bream.

10 Dec 1850 Berryman J. Martin and Susan Edwards. Min. Joshua
Adams.

16 Nov 1840 Daniel Martin and America Price, consent of B.M.Price,Sr.
and James Martin. Wit. B.M.Price,Jr. and John Martin.

4 Oct 1849 Ewell Martin and Sarah Gray, daughter of Powell Gray.
Sur. Samuel Martin. Min. D.G. Taylor.
M.R. 9 Oct 1849.

4 Mar 1834 George Martin and Nancy Hill, daughter of Charles Hill.
Sur. William Hill. Wit. Valencine Napier. Min.
Joshua Adams. M.R. 13 Mar 1834.

14 Dec 1849   George Martin and Malinda J. Allen, daughter of
              Lucy Allen of Floyd Co.Va.. Sur. James Moran.

 9 Jan 1794   Giles Martin and Nancy Ingram, daughter of John &
              Elizabeth Ingram. Sur. Thomas Bristow.

22 Oct 1844   Giles Martin and Sarah Arnold, daughter of John
              Arnold. Sur. Samuel C. Ingram.

11 Oct 1827   Isaac Martin,Sr. and Susanna Rogers. Sur. Zachariah H.
              Taylor. Min. Joshua Adams. M.R. 21 Oct 1827.

28 May 1818   James Martin and Hannah Carter. Sur. Samuel Hanby.
              Min. Thomas Whitlock.

18 Dec 1818   James Martin and Willy Massey. Sur. Obediah Massey.

 2 Sep 1843   James Martin and Mary Roberson. Sur. William Martin.
              Min. Joshua Adams. M.R. 7 Sep 1843.

 3 Oct 1838   James Martin and Rebecca T. Ferguson, daughter of
              Archibald & Frances Ferguson. Sur. William Martin.

28 Jan 1850   James J. Martin and Letha Brammer. Sur. John
              Brammer. Min. G.W. Conner. M.R. 7 Feb 1850.

 3 Jan 1846   James P. Martin and Ruth Wright. Sur. Jabel Wright.

22 May 1836   John Martin and Eliza Hooker. Sur. James Bryant.
              Wit. William D. Young. Min. Joshua Adams.

29 Mar 1846   John Martin and Elizabeth Proffit. Sur. Austen
              Proffit. Min. Jesse Jones.

13 Nov 1847   John Martin and Matilda Gray, daughter of Powell
              Gray. Sur. Mark A. Howell. Min. Daniel G. Taylor.
              M.R. 23 Nov 1847.

 5 Oct 1849   John Martin and Elizabeth A. Fulcher. Sur. Edmund
              Fulcher. Min. Joshua Adams. M.R. 16 Oct 1849.

27 Jun 1848   John Martin and Letha Smith. Sur. H. H. Hanby.
              Min. Joshua Adams.

24 Nov 1853   John H. Martin, son of Charles T. and Mary E. Martin,
              and Martha W. King, daughter of George & Mary C.King.
              Min. Joshua Adams.

27 Apl 1810   Joseph Martin and Sally Hughes. Sur. Fleming Saunders.
              Min. Brett Stovall. M.R. 28 Apl 1810.

11 Nov 1837   Joseph Martin and Martha J. Gray. Sur. Daniel Gray.
              Joseph Martin of Rockingham Co. N.C.

12 Nov 1850   Joseph J. Martin and Mary Jane Greer. Min.
              Jeremiah Burnett.

 7 Dec 1834   Lewis Martin and Roxy Clark,daughter of John Clark.
              Sur. Reuben Wright. Wit. Lewis Lancaster.

11 May 1848   Lewis Martin and Martha(Martey) Moorfield, daughter
              of Rebecca Moorefield. Sur. Isaac Martin.
              Min. Joshua Adams.

11 Jan 1838   Lindsy Haden Martin and Anna Midkiff. Sur. Samuel
              Midkiff. Min. William Lawson.

12 Jan 1807   Micajah Martin and Celey Reynolds. Sur. Abraham
              Reynolds.

17 Mar 1831   Moses Martin and Sally Moles. Sur. John Moles.

25 Aug 1825   Samuel Martin and Ruth Penn. Sur. Clark Penn.
              Min. Peter Frans. M.R. 26 Aug 1821.

 5 Mar 1845   Samuel Martin and Elizabeth Gray, daughter of Powell
              Gray. Sur. John D. Cheatham. Wit. Thomas Martin.
              Min. John Robertson. M.R. 11 Mar 1845.

25 Jun 1833   Sparks Martin and Sarah Guilliam. Sur. James Ferguson.
              Min. Stephen Hubbard. M.R. 4 Jul 1833.

10 Jan 1839   Stokley Martin and Mahaley Hollandsworth. Sur.
              William Hollandsworth. Min. Joshua Adams.
              M.R. 17 Jan 1839.

 6 Nov 1834   Thomas Martin and Rachel Mize, daughter of John &
              Frances Mize. Sur. James Nowlin. Wit. Ingram Stone.
              Min. Joshua Adams. M.R. 11 Nov 1834.

27 Jun 1820   William Martin and Sarah Harris. Sur. James Bartlett.
              Min. Stephen Hubbard. M.R. 29 Jun 1820.

11 Oct 1832   William Martin and Nancy Adams. Sur. Joshua Adams.
              Min. Joshua Adams.

27 Oct 1846   William Martin and Elizabeth Hollandsworth, daughter of
              Milly Hollandsworth. Sur. John Hollandsworth.
              Min. Jeremiah Burnett.

29 Nov 1798   Daniel Martindale and Barbary Danger. Sur. Ralph Danger.
              Min. John Nunns. M.R. 5 Dec 1798.

12 Oct 1820   Daniel Martindale and Elizabeth Puckett. Sur. Anthy
              Overby. Min. Peter Frans.

21 Oct 1833   Christopher C. Mason and Ruth Philpott, daughter of
              Edward Philpott. Sur. George W. Dyer.
              Min. John Turner.

8 Nov 1842   Abel Massey and Nancy Sprouse, daughter of George Sprouse. Sur. Hamon Critz. Min. Joshua Adams.

10 Sep 1827   Ancil Massey and Elizabeth Via, daughter of William Via. Sur. Thomas Dehart. Min. Stephen Hubbard.

4 Jan 1819   Charles Massey and Priscilla Hollandsworth. Sur. Lewis Bryant.

14 Mar 1848   James Madison Massey, consent of Obediah Massey, and Frances Elizabeth Fitzgerald, daughter of Madison Fitzgerald. Sur. William Parker. Min. Jeremiah Burnett.

16 Feb 1810   John Massey and Nancy Bartlett. Sur. James Bartlett. Min. Stephen Hubbard. M.R. 19 Feb 1810.

5 Jan 1819   Jubal Massey and Elizabeth Gravitt Philpott, daughter of B.W. Philpott. Sur. Adison Philpott. Min. Peter Frans. M.R. 6 Jan 1819.

28 Apl 1813   Obediah Massey and Nancy Bryant. Sur. Elias Bryant. Min. Lewis Foster.

7 Jun 1803   Warren Massey and Susanna Bartlett. Sur. James Bartlett.

14 Jul 1831   Warren Massey and Selah(Celia) Handy. Sur. Paul C. Ingram. Min. John Turner. M.R. 18 Aug 1831.

15 Dec 1836   Robert Matthews of Stokes Co. N.C., and Mary Critz. Sur. F. Critz. Min. Joshua Adams. M.R. 22 Dec 1836.

13 Jul 1847   Robert T. Matthews and Sarah E. Abington, daughter of Elizabeth Abington. Sur. Austen B. Thomas. Min. William Schoolfield.

1 Nov 1794   Valentine Mayo and Judith Hancock. Sur. John Hancock. Min. Isaac Adams.

15 May 1828   Pryer Mays and Sarah Puckett. Sur. Gilbert Bowman. Min. Joshua Adams. M.R. 18 May 1828.

1 Nov 1853   Thomas Mays and Elizabeth L. Harris. Min. J. G. Taylor.

1 Jun 1805   Samuel Medley and Elizabeth Hunt. Sur. Thomas Bolling.

3 Aug 1801   Richard Medley and Susanah Allen. Sur. John Allen.

24 Dec 1844   George C. Menefee and Elizabeth Burnett, daughter of Mary Ann Burnett. Sur. Jacob Prillaman. Wit. William Ross.

2 Aug 1838   Allen N. Meredith, son of John Meredith, and Permelia
             Wilson. Sur. James Reynolds. Wit. H.R. Hall.
             Min. Jesse Jones. M.R. 6 Aug 1838.

27 Jan 1807 Martin Miller and Sophea Banks. Sur. Thomas Banks.
             Min. Brett Stovall.

12 Dec 1813 Willeby Miller and Nancy Edwards. Sur. Thomas Edwards.
             Min. Thomas Whitlock.

13 Oct 1849 Benjamin F.Mitchell and Nancy F. Abington, daughter of
             Elizabeth Abington. Sur. William M. Abington.

16 Jan 1797 Thomas Mitchell and Nancy Hanby. Sur. Jonathan Hanby.
             Min. John Nunns.

25 Feb 1830 William Mitchell and Ann Hagood. Sur. Gregory Hagood.
             William Mitchell of Franklin Co. Va.
             Min. Joshua Adams.

21 Apl 1834 Fleming Mize and Polly Anglin. Sur. John Mize.
             Min. Joshua Adams. M.R. 4 May 1834.

 1 Oct 1828 James Mize and Lydia Anglin, daughter of Elizabeth
             Anglin. Sur. Horiato Penn. Wit. Elisha Anglin &
             John Mize. Min. Joshua Adams. M.R. 2 Oct 1828.

20 Sep 1800 John Mize and Franky Ingram. Sur. John Ingram.
             Min. Robert Jones. M.R. 25 Sep 1800.

 7 Sep 1840 John M. Mize and Martha Ann Anglin. Sur. John Anglin.
             Min. Joshua Adams. M.R. 10 Sep 1840.

18 Apl 1824 Joshua Mize and Rebecca Thomas. Sur. Charles Thomas.
             Min. Stephen Hubbard.

 4 Jan 1809 Isaac Mize and Ruth Ingram. Sur. John Mize.
             Min. Lewis Foster. M.R. 8 Jan 1809.

15 Jan 1815 John Mobbs and Mincey Bolling. Sur. Gabriel Bolling
             and Thomas Harbour.

19 Nov 1849 James C. Moir and Louisa E. Carter, daughter of John
             P. Carter. Sur. Phillip Anglin. Min. J. H. Jefferson.
             M.R. 20 Nov 1849.

30 Jul 1838 Allen Monday and Permela Taylor, daughter of Alford
             and Rachel Taylor.

14 Jul 1836 Isaac Monday and Lucy F. Hines. Sur. Henry Hines.
             Min. Joshua Adams.

11 Mar 1830 John Monday and Margaret Scott. Sur. Thomas Scott.
             Min. Nathaniel Thompson. M.R. 23 Mar 1830.

5 Aug 1830   Robert Monday and Catherine Stanley. Sur. Martin
              Cloud. Min. Thomas Whitlock.

24 Apl 1801   James Moles and Nancy (Nanny) Foley, daughter of
              Mary Foley. Sur. Richardson Davis.
              Min. Nathaniel Hall. M.R. 11 May 1801.

19 Apl 1832   James Moles and Elizabeth Keaton. Sur. Peter A.
              Keaton. Min. John Washburn.

10 Jan 1809   Jeremiah Moles,Jr. and Milley Reynolds. Sur.
              Jeremiah Moles,Sr. Min. John Conner. M.R. 12 Jan
              1809.

18 Nov 1805   John Moles and Nancy Bridges. Sur. Moses Harbour.
              Min. William H. Robertson. M.R. 21 Nov 1805.

26 Oct 1842   Samuel Moles and Mary Parker, daughter of John
              Parker. Sur. John Lackey. Min. Joshua Adams.
              M.R. 27 Oct 1842.

21 Feb 1831   William Moles and Elizabeth Lewis. Sur. James
              Martin. Min. John Turner.

10 Mar 1839   Elijah Moran and C. Hall. Sur. G. W. Lewis.

 7 Nov 1835   John Moran and Martha Cannaday, daughter of William
              Canaday. Sur. William Canaday. Min. Jesse Jones.
              M.R. 10 Dec 1835.

 9 Sep 1839   Nelson Moran and Nancy Brammer. Sur. Jonathan Brammer.
              Min. Jesse Jones. M.R. 11 Sep 1839.

27 Dec 1834   William Moran and Maryan Owen. Sur. David Owen.
              Min. Joshua Adams. M.R. 28 Dec 1834.

 2 Mar 1825   Allen Morefield and Martha Harris. Sur. Elijah Harris.
              Min. Bird Lowe.

 8 Mar 1830   Josiah Morefield, son of Rebecca Morefield, and Ruth
              Keaton. Sur. Allen Morefield. Min. Joshua Adams.

28 Oct 1853   Josiah Morefield, son of Allen & Martha Morefield,and
              Lethy Mays, daughter of Dury S. and Sena Mays.
              Min. Samuel J. Lackey.

11 Mar 1847   William Morefield and Maryann Winston Kasey, daughter
              of John N. Kasey. Sur. Wright Morefield.
              Min. Joshua Adams.

23 Dec 1831   Wright Morefield, son of Rebecca Morefield, and Jane
              Martin, daughter of Micajah Martin. Sur. George
              Reynolds. Min. Joshua Adams. M.R. 26 Dec 1831.

12 Aug 1844   Henry J. Moore and Caroline Moore, daughter of Ann
              Moore. Sur. James D. Cloud. Min. John B. Corn.
              M.R. 15 Aug 1844.

26 Dec 1805   Jesse Moore and Mary(Polly)Corn. Sur. Brett Stovall.

27 Oct 1845   Noah B. Moore of Floyd Co.Va., and Arteminca (A.E.)
              Hall. Sur. Isaac Adams. Min. Owen Sumner.
              M.R. 20 Nov 1845.

23 Sep 1820   Robert Moore and Elizabeth Chambers. Sur. John Chambers.
              Min. Stephen Hubbard. M.R. 17 Oct 1820.

11 Dec 1798   William Moore and Jane Hanby. Sur. Samuel Staples.
              Min. John Nunns. M.R. 13 Dec 1798.

 2 Sep 1824   William C. Moore and Dolly A. Wells, daughter of
              Reuben Wells. Sur. Jesse Wells. Min. Thomas
              Whitlock. M.R. 24 Sep 1824.

 9 Feb 1805   Archibald Morris and Martha Cheatham.

16 Dec 1794   Benjamin Morris and Janey McAlexander, daughter of
              William McAlexander. Sur. John Conner.
              Min. Robert Jones.

29 Apl 1835   Benjamin Morris and Nancy Hagood, daughter of
              Gregory Hagood. Sur. William R. Sims.
              Min. Joshua Adams. M.R. 4 May 1835.

24 Nov 1853   Coleman Morris and Locky Pack. Min. Julius Terrell.

31 Dec 1793   Jacob Morris and Nancy Ryall. Sur. Jacob Lawson.

18 Nov 1837   John Morrisand Lydia Edens. Min. William Lawson.

14 Jul 1836   S. Morris and Martha Wray. Sur. William Wray.

17 Jan 1797   Samuel J. Morris and Maria Brewer, daughter of
              Lackville Brewer. Sur. Lackvill Brewer.

12 Jan 1826   Samuel C. Morris,Jr. and Susannah D. Baker.
              Sur. Charles Foster, Jr.

28 Sep 1819   William Morris and Elizabeth Harris, daughter of
              James Harris. Sur. William Ayers. Min. Jesse Jones.

 3 Sep 1816   Zachariah Morris and Clare Haynes.
              Sur. Joel Blansett.

13 Apl 1820   James Morrison and Rebecca Nevells. Sur. Samuel
              Staples. Lewis Foster states that James Morrison
              lives with him.

16 Jun 1842   John T. Morrison and Mary E. Rorer. Sur. David Rorrer.
              Min. John Conner. .R. 5 Jul 1842.

28 Nov 1839   Joseph Morrison and Mary Harbour. Sur. Thomas Morris.
              Min. Joshua Adams. M.R. 1 Dec 1839.

 2 Feb 1852   Joseph Morrison and Exoney Balisle, daughter of
              Barnabas Balisle,Sr.. Min. Joshua Adams.

31 Dec 1806   Lawrence Morrison and Elizabeth Clay. Sur. Archibald
              Barnard. Min. Stephen Hubbard. M.R. 1 Jan 1807.

18 Jul 1824   Lawrence Morrison and Polly Midkiff. Sur. Thomas
              Morrison. Min. John Conner. M.R. 19 Jul 1824.

27 Aug 1795   Nathan Morrison and Mary Hancock. Sur. George Corn
              and John Hancock.

 6 Jun 1809   Thomas Morrison and Jenny(Jean) Reynolds. Sur.
              James Morris. Jenny, daughter of Gessy Reynolds.
              Min. William H. Robertson.

13 Oct 1853   Thomas Morrison, son of James & Nancy Morrison, and
              Sarah Cox, daughter of James and Sarah Cox.
              Min. Joshua Adams.

25 Oct 1798   William Morrison and Nancy(Anna) Morrow, daughter of
              Thomas Morrow. Sur. Nathan Morrison. Min. John Nunns.
              M.R. 3 Oct 1798.

16 Sep 1814   John Morrow and Mary Lockhart. Sur. Thomas Lockhart.

10 Jul 1834   Robert Moss, consent of William Moss, and Jane Collins,
              daughter of Edward & Frances Collins. Sur. Edmund
              Collins. Min. Julius Terrell.

27 Oct 1836   James Mouning and Delila Canaday, daughter of William
              Canaday. Sur. David Owens.

12 Aug 1828   Edward Murphy and Harriett Frans. Sur. William Frans.
              Min. John Conner. M.R. 14 Aug 1828.

 5 Oct 1832   Jesse Murphy and Anstis W.F. Mills, daughter of
              Richard Mills. Sur. Edward Murphy. Min. John
              Washburn. M.R. 18 Oct 1832.

 4 Jun 1844   Joshua Murrow (Murry) and Elizabeth Hancock, daughter
              of Thomas Hancock. Sur. Asa Wood. Min. William
              Anderson. M.R. 11 Jun 1844.

              Alexander McAlexander --bond with only this signature.

11 Dec 1817   David McAlexander, son of John McAlexander, and Jane
              Thomas, daughter of Squire Charles Thomas. Sur.
              Charles Thomas,Jr. Wit. Samuel McAlexander. Min.
              Stephen Hubbard. M.R. 30 Dec 1817.

8 Feb 1801   James McAlexander and Charlotte Hall, daughter of John Hall. Sur. William McAlexander. Min. N.Hall. M.R. 5 Mar 1801.

27 Nov 1818   John McAlexander and Ruthy Kidd. Sur. James Mc Alexander. Min. Stephen Hubbard. M.R. 30 Nov 1818.

17 Jan 1828   John McAlexander and Margaret Brammer, daughter of Jeremiah Brammer. Sur. Edmund McAlexander.

25 Dec 1848   Peter McAlexander and Cynthia Massey. Sur. David McAlexander. Wit. Burwell Akers. Min. Jesse Jones.

27 Dec 1798   William McAlexander and Tamer Booth, daughter of George Sr. & Milly Booth.   Sur. Beveridge Hughes. Wit. George Booth,Jr., Sarah Booth & Daniel Booth.

26 Nov 1835   William McAlexander and Lucy Hubbard. Sur. William McAlexander,Sr. Min. John Conner.

9 May 1807   William McAlexander and Anna Booth. Sur. Isaac Bolt. Min.Jesse Jones.

26 Dec 1812   William McAlexander and Nancy Harris, daughter of Rueben Harris. Min.Jesse Jones. M.R. 30 Dec 1817.

15 May 1820   David G. McArthur and Susannah Trent. Sur. Field Trent.

30 Dec 1847   Perry McArthur and Elizabeth Akers. Sur. Nathaniel Aker. Min. Joshua Adams.

31 Oct 1807   Andrew McBride and Sally Fuson. Sur. Abel Lee. Min. Jesse Jones. M.R. - Nov 1807.

27 Jul 1802   Joseph McBride and Elizabeth Brammer, daughter of Mary Brammer.

28 Aug 1845   Thomas McCabe and Mary M. Staples. Sur. Asa S. Howard. Min. Nathaniel Thompson. M.R. 25 Aug 1845.

16 Nov 1804   John McCoy and Sally Hopkins, consent of William and Peggy Hopkins.

18 Mar 1836   Jacob McCraw and Eliza Daulton. Sur. James Daulton. Min. Joshua Adams. M.R. 31 Mar 1836.

13 Jan 1816   William McCraw and Sabrina Ahart. Sur. Jonson Snow. Min. Thomas Whitlock.

18 Aug 1807   William McCraw and Sally Hanby, daughter of Jonathan Hanby. Sur. Samuel Hanby.

20 Aug 1814   George McCutchen and Necey Chitwood, daughter of Joel Chitwood. Sur, Charles Rowe.

10 Feb 1813   John McCutchen and Eady Packwood, daughter of Samuel
              Packwood. Sur. George McCutchen. Min. Lewis Foster.

 8 Nov 1808   William McCutchen, son of James McCutchen, and Nancy
              Roberson, daughter of Nancy Roberson. Sur. James
              McCutchen. Wit. Rebecca Robisson.

 6 Jul 1820   Ezekiah(Hezekiah) McDaniel and Polly Gillenwaters,
              daughter of Joshua Gillenwaters. Sur. Henry Wood.
              Wit. Nathan Jones. Henry Wood states that Hezekiah
              is 21 years of age and has resided in Patrick Co.
              for 6 months. Min. Stephen Hubbard. M.R. 10 Feb 1820.

13 May 1793   Thomas McDaniel and Seley Tuggle. Sur. George Mabry.
              Min. Robert Jones.

 1 Oct 1797   Jonas McDonald and Elizabeth Foster, daughter of
              Charles Foster. Sur. William Adams.
              Min. John Pedigo. M.R. 3 Oct 1797.

16 Jan 1823   George McGhee and Elizabeth Terry, daughter of
              Joseph & Mary Terry. Sur. Henry B. Terry. Min.
              Stephen Hubbard. M.R. 29 Jan 1823.

 5 Aug 1824   Harmon McGhee and Leeanna Ayers, daughter of Leonard
              Ayers. Sur. Peter Critz. Min. Peter Frans.
              M.R. 6 Aug 1824.

21 Sep 1834   John McGhee and Nancy Keith. Sur. James Houchins.
              Min. John Conner.

 9 Jun 1836   Lewis McGhee and Agga Wood, daughter of John Wood,Sr.
              Sur. Andrew Boyd. Wit. Elijah Dehart.

 6 Jan 1831   William McGhee and Nancy Branch. Min. Joshua Adams.

 7 Jan 1839   Joseph C. McGuffin and Adaline Haynes, daughter of
              Hampton Haynes. Sur. Isaac N. Haynes. Wit. Asa
              Fitzgerald & Nancy W. Fitzgerald.

27 Feb 1794   Henry McGuffey,Jr. and Lidda Mannin, daughter of
              Samuel Mannin. Sur. Henry McGuffey,Sr.

 9 Nov 1822   James McGuffey and Lucy Barnard. Sur. Isham Barnard.
              Min. Brett Stovall. M.R. 9 Nov 1822.

22 May 1793   John S. McGuffey and Elizabeth Blevins. Sur. Henry
              McGuffey. Min. Robert Jones.

25 Feb 1830   John McIntosh and Lucinda B. Dodson, daughter of
              Ellenor Dodson. Sur. Henry Aistrop. Min. Bird Lowe.

22 Jan 1811   Mark McKinney and Nancy Sands. Sur. William Sands.
              Min. Brett Stovall. M.R.25 Jan 1811.

14 Nov 1825   Thomas McKinzey and Elizabeth Hill. Sur. William Hill. Min. Joshua Adams. M.R. 17 Nov 1825.

14 Feb 1843   Aaron McMillion and Jane Willis. Sur. William McMillon.

6 Jul 1828   Abijah McMillion and Sally Chandler. Sur. James Dillard. Min. Thomas Whitlock.

4 Jul 1805   Dudley McMillion and Elizabeth Hicks. Sur. Thomas Puckett. Min. Thomas Whitlock.

8 Oct 1828   Henry McMillion and Fanney Archer. Sur. Joshua Haynes. Min. Thomas Whitlock.

17 Dec 1812   Henry McMillion and Sally Daniel. Sur. James Russey. Min. Thomas Whitlock. M.R. 27 Dec 1812.

18 Feb 1837   Isham McMillion and Catherine Hart, daughter of Mary Hart. Sur. A.B. Clark. Wit. Martin Cloud and James Hubbard.

14 Oct 1840   Reynolds McMillion and Lyda Scott. Sur. Eli Hiatt. Wit. Palen Chappell. Lyda, the daughter of John Scott.

1 Jun 1839   Samuel McMillion and Nancy Hiatt, daughter of Josiah Hiatt. Sur. Joseph Bream. Wit. Nathan Hiatt.

13 Dec 1810   Stephen McMillion and Martha Blansett. Sur. Phillip Anglin. Min. Thomas Whitlock.

8 Sep 1832   William McMillion and Amendey Snow. Sur. Parker Hall. Min. Thomas Whitlock.

12 Aug 1793   Ezekiel McPeek and Maggy McBride, daughter of James McBride. Sur. William McPeek.

22 Aug 1817   Edmond Nance and Anna Simms, daughter of Ignatious Sims. Sur. Peyton Nance. Min. Lewis Foster. M.R. 25 Aug 1817.

6 Jan 1823   Lissonby Nance and Oney D. Simms, daughter of Jinnet Sims. Sur. Edmund Nance.

20 Dec 1816   Peyton Nance and Ellenor Simms. Sur. Lewis Foster. Min. Lewis Foster. M.R. 31 Dec 1816.

14 Jan 1840   George W. Napier and Mary Finney, daughter of John Finney. Sur. John Koger.

11 Feb 1836   Moses C. Napier and Emily Poindexter, daughter of John Poindexter. Sur. William E. Price and Richard Poindexter. Wit. James Poindexter.

12 Feb 1847   Thomas L. Napier and Sinai P. Turner, daughter of William Turner. Sur. Josiah H. Turner. Min. Joshua Adams. M.R. 4 Feb 1847.

28 Jan 1806 Jerdin Nelson and Sarah Owen. Sur. Thomas Ayres.
Min. Thomas Whitlock.

15 Jan 1818 Stephen Nelson and Anny Adams. Sur. John Adams and
Isaac Martin. Min. Joshua Adams. M.R. 29 Jan 1817.

4 Oct 1834 William H. Nelson and Sarah Midkiff. Sur. John W.
Davis. Min. John Conner.

1 Jan 1812 Allen Newman and Anna Boaz. Sur. James Boaz.
Min. Brett Stovall. M.R. 25 Jan 1812.

9 Jan 1837 Armstead W. Newman and Frances Sharp. Sur. Samuel
Gilbert. Min. Joshua Adams. M.R. 10 Jan 1837.

16 Feb 1804 Elam Newman and Elizabeth Shelton. Sur. Frederick
Shelton. Min. Peter Frans. M.R. 20 Sep 1813.

11 Feb 1852 Hamon Newman and Ruth Hazelwood. Min. Samuel J.Lackey.

12 Dec 1817 James Newman and Charlotte Shelton. Sur. John Tatum.
Min. Peter Frans. M.R. 15 Dec 1817.

7 Feb 1832 James Newman Jr. and Sally Flippen. Sur. John Flippen.

8 Nov 1852 John Newman and Milly Pack daughter of Isham Pack.
Wit. William Barnard.and John Lawson. Min.
William Lawson.

10 Dec 1847 Joseph Newman and Sarah R. Rogers. Sur. Hiram Rogers.
Min. Joshua Adams.

1 Apl 1833 Ralph Newman and Polly L. Edwards. Sur. William Edwards.
Min. Julius Terrell.

11 Feb 1807 Winston Newman and Conah Nolen. Sur. Samuel Nolen.
Min. William H. Robertson. M.R. 17 Feb 1807.

14 May 1825 Christopher Nichols and Elizabeth Midkiff, daughter of
John Midkiff,Sr. Sur. John Midkiff.

9 Dec 1833 Nehemiah Nichols and Mary Harris. Sur. Christopher
Nichols. Min. John Conner.

30 May 1792 Gideon Noe and Lucy Price. Min. George Dodson.
M.R. 1 June 1792.

6 Aug 1832 Alexander Nowlin and Mary Ann Turner. Sur. Shadrack
Turner. Min. Jesse Jones. M.R. 16 Aug 1832.

2 Dec 1834 Charles P. Nolen and Nancy Adams, daughter of Isaac
Adams. Sur. William Houchins. Wit. Marvel Bowlen.

19 Feb 1801 Francis Nowlin and Sally Shelton. Sur. Archibald Shelton.

21 Mar 1818 Francis Nowlin and Polly Harbour. Sur. Elum Newman.

17 Oct 1821 James Nowland and Nancy Shelton. Sur. Robert Boaz.
             Min. Peter Frans. M.R. 18 Nov 1821.

23 Feb 1799 John Nowlin and Polly Thomas, daughter of Charles
             Thomas,Sr. Sur. Richard Thomas.

22 Jan 1823 John Nowlan and Elizabeth Nowland. Sur. Francis
             Nowland. Min. Jesse Jones. M.R. 20 Feb 1823.

 5 Jan 1850 John Nowlen and Judith Sneed. Min. Jesse Jones.

17 Sep 1827 Pleasant Nowland and Elizabeth Nowlin.
             Sur. Richard Nowlin.

30 Jun 1796 Richard Nowland and Polley Burnett, daughter of
             Jeremiah Burnett,Sr. Sur. William Sloan.
             Min. Robert Jones.

19 Jan 1809 Samuel Nolen and Olive Shelton, daughter of Eliphaz
             Shelton. Sur. Frederick Shelton.
             Min. William H. Robertson.

23 Nov 1834 Spencer F. Nowlin and Elizabeth Shelton. Sur. James
             Shelton. Min. Joshua Adams.

 1 Jun 1826 William Nowlin and Ruth Nowlin. Min. Joshua Adams.

 1 Sep 1840 Wilson Nowlen and Mary Sneed, daughter of Samuel
             Sneed. Sur. John D. Cheatham.

21 Feb 1826 Joseph Norman and Polly Joyce. Sur. A. Joyce.
             Min. Bird Lowe.

20 Dec 1809 Elisha Nunn and Delilah Hurst. Sur. Pierce Green.
             Min. Thomas Whitlock.

18 May 1826 James Nunn and Ursley East. Sur. William East.
             Min. Thomas Whitlock.

25 Feb 1850 James Madison Nunn and Martha W. Spencer. Sur.
             William R. Spencer. Min. Joshua Adams.
             M.R. 29 Feb 1850.

30 Dec 1794 John Nunn and Sara Detherage. Sur. Harvy Fitzgerald.

12 Feb 1814 John Nunn and Leviny Reynolds. Sur. Jesse Reynolds.

 5 Feb 1834 Majer Nunn and Eleanor Collings. Sur. Edward Collings.
             Min. Julius Terrell.

25 Jan 1844 Richard Nunn and Frances Carter. Sur.Walker Carter.

27 Sep 1834   Squire Nunn and Nancy N. Carter. Sur. Walker Carter.
Min. Julius Terrell. M.R. 28 Sep 1834.

20 Jul 1813   Henry Oakley and Sarah Trent. Sur. Alexander Trent.
Min. Peter Frans. M.R. 26 Jul 1813.

23 Sep 1851   James M. Oakley and Amanda Scruggs, daughter of
John G. Scruggs. Sur. William M.Abington.

3 Aug 1813   Samuel Oakley and Elizabeth Gossett, daughter of
John Gossett. Sur. Thomas Hollandsworth,Jr.

2 Oct 1851   William Madison Oakley and Amanda Scruggs.
Min. William M. Schoolfield.(Must be same as James
M. Oakley).

6 Dec 1845   William Harrison O'Bryan, of Floyd Co. Va., and
Ann,Washington, daughter of Soloman Washington.
Sur. William Dillon. Wit. Susana Washington and
Winney Bond. Min. Owen Sumner.M.R. 9 Dec 1845.

28 Oct 1841   Jonathan Ogden and Nancy Durham. Sur. Henry Durham.

7 Sep 1823   Thomas Ogel and Edney P. Lewis. Sur. Levi Johnston.
Min. Thomas Whitlock.

1834   Frederick Oldeman and Roxey Watson.

11 Nov 1847   William Oldham and Sarah McArthur, daughter of
Susanah McArthur. Sur. Perry McArthur.
Min. Joshua Adams. M.R. 4 Nov 1847.

10 Apl 1851   John H. Oneal, son of A.M. Oneal, and Milly (Amelia)
Reynolds. Min. Nathaniel Thompson.

23 Mar 1807   Samuel Oneal and Anney Perkins. Sur. Joseph Jonson.
Min. Thomas Whitlock.

26 Oct 1852   William Oreander and Barbara Ann Gilbert, daughter of
Lethe Gilbert. Sur. Martin Cloud. Wit. J.H. Brown.

1 Sep 1821   Allen T. Overby and Dida Collings. Sur. Isham Slate.

12 Jan 1826   Alexander Overby and Sarah Nunn. Sur. Brett Stovall.
Min. Brett Stovall. M.R. 19 Jan 1826.

10 Aug 1819   George Overstreet and Sophia Hylton. Sur. Brett Stovall.
Min. Peter Frans.

13 Mar 1814   Jason Owen and Betsy Thompson. Sur. Mitchell Thompson.
Min. Thomas Whitlock.

16 Aug 1803   Leonard Owen and Jane Qualls. Sur. Elisha Ayers.
Min. Thomas Whitlock.

26 Oct 1805   Leonard Owen and Nancey Hampton. Sur. Archibald
Bryson. Min. Thomas Whitlock.

15 Aug 1811   Leonard Owen and -----------.Sur. McKinley Landreth.

10 Mar 1810   Thomas Owen and Jane Sprowil. Sur. John A. Grigg.
Min. Thomas Whitlock.

27 Apl 1815   James Owing and Tabithia Harris. Sur. Elijah Harris.
Min. Brett Stovall. M.R. 2 May 1815.

9 Jan 1823   Greenville Pack and Nancy Hooker, consent of William
Hooker. Sur. William Hooker & Gabriel Hooker.
Min. Brett Stovall. M.R. 10 Jan 1823.

5 Apl 1853   James Pack, son of Isham ˏPack, and Martha Hooker,
daughter of Gabriel Hooker. Wit. Samuel Hooker and
William Barnard. Min. Julius Terrell.

27 Sep 1850   Tyree Pack and Penai Going. Min. Julius Terrell.

25 Jan 1798   Elisha Packwood and Polly Burnett. Sur. John Burnett.
Min. John Pedigo. M.R. 26 Jan 1798.

15 Dec 1803   Richard Packwood and Nancy Spaldin. Sur. John Spauldin.
Min. Reuben Short.

27 Feb 1836   James Padget of Stokes Co. N.C., and Jane Brown.
Sur. Thomas Irion.

Palmer, Parmer

22 Jul 1805   Edward Parmer and Charlotte Harris, daughter of Sherwood
Harris. Sur. Claibourne Harris.

22 Jan 1840   James Parmer and Martha Handy. Sur. John Handy.
Min. G.W. Conner. M.R. 30 Jan 1840.

1 Dec 1843   Madison Palmer and Elizabeth Jane Vaughan.
Sur. Robert Harris. M.R. 5 Dec 1843.

1798   Noah Parr and Rhodah Poor. Sur. Hugh Poor.

13 Oct 1802   Noah Parr and Polly Deal. Sur. Arthur Parr.

12 Mar 1803   Thomas Parr and Perscilla Sitton. Sur. Thomas Penn.

4 Nov 1842   Lewis Parker and Martha Hopkins. Sur.Hamon Critz.
Min.John Washburn. M.R. 10 Nov 1842.

7 Nov 1850   William Parker and Mary Dodson. Min. Jeremiah Burnett.

10 Feb 1853   William Parker and Evaline Turner, daughter of
O. or P. Turner. Wit. T. P. Turner & Creed O. Turner.
Min. Jeremiah Burnett.

19 May 1812   Joseph Parson and Mary Cox. Min. Lewis Foster.

Pedigo, Pedigoy

13 Jan 1845   A. G. Pedigo and S. J. Harbour. Sur. Richard Harbour.

19 Feb 1851   Bluford Pedigo and Lucy Hancock. Min. Joshua Adams.

22 Jan 1824   Daniel Pedigo and Agnes Boaz. Sur. John B. Hudson.
              Min. Bird Lowe.

31 Jan 1805   Elijah Pedigoy and Sally Hall. Sur. John Hall.
              Min. Jesse Jones.

12 Mar 1835   Elijah Pedigo and Nancy S. Price. Sur. Bernard M.
              Price. Min. John Conner.

20 Sep 1805   Elkin Pedigo and Patsy Harris, daughter of William
              Harris. Min. Robert Jones. M.R. 24 Sep 1805.

14 Dec 1797   Levi Pedigo and Mary Edens, daughter of John Edens.
              Sur. William Roberson. Min. John Pedigo.
              M.R. 15 Dec 1797.

 6 Apl 1819   Lewis R. Pedigo and Sarah Harbour, daughter of
              David Harbour. Sur. Richard Harbour. Min. Jesse Jones.

22 Nov 1802   Jacob Peery and Keziah Hale. Wit. Benjamin Hale and
              William Adams.

22 Nov 1815   Joseph Pelly and Zanly Hill. Min. Stephen Hubbard.

20 Oct 1836   Hardin Pendleton, son of Prier Pendleton, and Ruth
              Burnett. Sur. Valentine Burnett. Min. John Conner.

20 Nov 1833   John Pendleton and Anna Hubbard. Sur. Joel Hubbard.
              Min. John Conner.

 7 Sep 1807   Prier Pendleton and Mary Tuggle, daughter of
              Tasherway Tuggle. Sur. Elijah Hylton. Min. Jesse Jones.

15 Jan 1832   William Pendleton and Elizabeth Hubbard.
              Min. John Conner.

21 Dec 1805   Abraham Penn, Jr. and Elizabeth Chitwood.
              Sur. William Penn.

20 Jun 1831   Clark Penn and Barbara Ann Penn, daughter of James
              Penn. Sur. Arch. Critz.

 7 Oct 1848   Clark Penn and Susan Clark. Sur. Abram Penn.

11 Jun 1816   Edmond Penn and Polly Farris. Sur. A. Staples.
              Min. Peter Frans.

18 May 1831 Edmund Penn and Mary Ann Reid. Sur. Clark Penn.

20 Dec 1794 Gabriel Penn and Charlotte Crutcher, daughter of
Samuel Crutcher. Sur. Samuel Staples.

16 Feb 1797 Gabriel Penn and Jinsey Clark. Sur. Greensville
Penn.

19 Sep 1833 Gabriel Penn and Susan Frans. Sur. G. W. Penn.
Min. John Washburn. M.R. 25 Sep 1833.

25 Jul 1850 George W. Penn and Mary A. Penn. Sur. Henry Lane.
Min. John Rich. M.R. 30 Jul 1850.

 5 May 1803 Greensville Penn and Nancy Leath. Sur. Samuel Staples.

13 Jul 1807 Horatio Penn and Nancy Parr. Sur. Samuel Hurt and
James Penn. Min. Brett Stovall. M.R. 7 Jul 1807.

 1 Oct 1832 Jackson Penn and Martha Ann Kennerly, daughter of
Joseph Kennerly. Sur. Thomas J. Penn.

10 May 1808 James Penn and Catherine Leath, consent of G.W. Penn.
Sur. Frederick Critz. Min. Brett Stovall.
M.R. 14 May 1808.

25 Dec 1810 Joseph Penn and Polly Chitwood, daughter of Joel
Chitwood. Sur. Benjamin Harrison. Min. Peter Frans.
M.R. 27 Dec 1810.

14 Sep 1832 Peter P. Penn and Frances J. Penn. Sur. John C.Staples.

24 Nov 1805 Thomas Penn and Patsy Leath. Sur. John Norton.

 7 Nov 1839 Thomas J. Penn and Lucinda Catherine Penn.
Min. L. B. Nicholson.

28 Dec 1796 Wilson Penn and Sally Chitwood, daughter of Joel
Chitwood. Sur. Edmon Chitwood. Min. Isaac Adams.

 5 Feb 1829 Jefferson Pennington and Eady Redford.
Sur. Jesse Redford.

 8 Nov 1804 David Perkins and Amelia Banks. Sur. Elijah Banks.

28 Dec 1816 David Perkins and Polly Banks. Sur. Elijah Banks.
Min. Peter Frans.

13 Sep 1845 Jared Perkins and Catharine R. Robertson. Sur. John S.
Robertson. Min. John Conner. M.R. 18 Sep 1845.

24 Nov 1833   William Perkins and Malinda Carter. Sur. M.D. Carter.
              Min. Stephen Hubbard.

18 May 1813   Joseph Persons and Mary Cox, consent of James Cox.
              Sur. Erskine Cox. Min. Lewis Foster.

28 Sep 1848   Frederick Peters and Juliann Jones, daughter of
              John Jones. Sur. William P. Scott.

 6 Sep 1849   Robert Pettis(Pettite) and Martha Dillion. Sur.
              Henry B. Dillion. Min. Joshua Adams.

 5 Dec 1845   Archibald Phariss and Mary Webb, daughter of
              Silvester Webb. Sur. John D. Cheatham. Min. Joshua
              Adams. M.R. 14 Dec 1845.

31 Apl 1811   Elijah Phillips and Nancy Stephens. Sur. Greensville
              Penn. Min. Brett Stovall. M.R. 20 Jun 1811.

27 Feb 1806   Stephen Phillips and Elizabeth Fitzpatrick. Sur.
              John Talbot. Min. Thomas Whitlock. M.R. 6 Mar 1806.

13 Oct 1812   William Phillips and Patience Bons. Sur. John Vancel.
              Min. Thomas Whitlock.

21 Dec 1817   Adison Philpott and Lucy Jones, daughter of William
              Jones. Sur. Charles Philpott. Min. Maning Hill.

10 Dec 1807   Alexander Philpott and Patsy Penn. Sur. David Taylor.
              Min. Peter Frans. M.R. 22 Dec 1807.

 9 Jan 1841   Edward Philpott, son of Edward Philpott of Henry Co.,
              and Nancy Turner. Sur. John Turner. Min. Joshua
              Adams. M.R. 14 Jan 1841.

 3 Feb 1834   Reuben B. Philpott and Sally(Sarah) Koger. Sur.
              Joseph Koger. Min. John Conner.

 2 Apl 1816   James Pigg and Sally Holliday. Sur. Abraham Reynolds.
              Min. Stephen Hubbard. M.R. 30 Apl 1816.

17 Dec 1796   John Pigg and Delilah Chitwood, daughter of Joel
              Chitwood. Sur. William Willis. Min. Isaac Adams.
              M.R. 21 Dec 1796.

25 Feb 1808   Benjamin Pike and Polly Hooker, daughter of William
              Hooker. Sur. William Hooker.

23 Oct 1851   Benjamin Pikes of Stokes Co. N.C., and Nancy Collins.
              Min. Julius Terrell.

27 Oct 1853   Gabriel Pike and Sarah F. Fry. Min. Julius Terrell.

6 Jan 1838   Moses Pilson and Becky Kelly. Sur. Richard Pilson. Min. John Conner. M.R. 7 Jan 1838.

30 Jul 1807   Richard Pilson and Rachel Harbour. Sur. Moses Harbour. Min. Jesse Jones. M.R. 5 Aug 1807.

25 Dec 1794   Richard Pilson, Jr. and Frances Denny, daughter of James Denny. Sur. Adam Turner. Min. Robert Jones.

15 Aug 1852   Richard Pilson and Elizabeth Lewis. Min. John Conner.

6 Nov 1851   Richard T. Pilson and Nancy Jane Joyce. Min. Joshua Adams.

11 Aug 1842   William Pilson and Elizabeth Harbour. Sur. Richard Pilson. Min. G. W. Conner. M.R. 1 Sep 1842.

19 Nov 1831   Claiborn Plaster and Elusha Griffith. Sur. Owen Griffith. Min. John Conner.

6 Oct 1840   Conrad Plaster and Jane Griffith. Sur. A. Staples. Wit. J. M. Griffith.

31 Mar 1825   John Plaster and Sally Bowling(Bowen), daughter of Marvel Bowling. Sur. John Keath. Min. John Conner.

17 Oct 1833   Jonas Plaster and Sally Cassell. Sur. William Cassell. Min. Joshua Adams.

13 Sep 1836   Mark Plaster and Louvenia Sharp, daughter of Philipeanah Sharp. Sur. Jonas Plaster. Min. Joshua Adams.

20 Nov 1837   Joseph S.Poindexter and Martha Frasure. Sur. H. B. Cockram. Min. Joshua Adams.

6 Dec 1798   Hugh Poor and Martha Hutchings. Sur. William Burress.

3 Sep 1829   Levi Poor and Peggy Whitlock. Min. Stephen Hubbard.

25 Jan 1828   James B. Porter and Fanny Baker, daughter of Mildred Baker, also of Henry Co., Va. Jeremiah Baker consents. Min. Arnold Walker. M.R. 31 Jan 1828.

18 Jun 1816   Archelus Prater and Sally Huet. Min. Thomas Whitlock. M.R. 9 Aug 1816.

25 Mar 1850   Joel H. Preston and Amanda P. Ferguson. Sur. Notley P. Adams. Wit. John L. Adams. Min. G. W. Conner. M.R. 2 Apl 1850.

18 Nov 1839   William Ballard Preston, of Montgomery Co, Va., and Lucinda S. Redd. Sur. John C. Staples. Min. Richard Buckingham. M.R. 28 Nov 1839.

12 Jan 1805   Bernard M. Price and Elizabeth Manor. Sur. Charles Foster,Jr. Min. Jesse Jones.

16 May 1839   Barnard M. Price and Louisa Ayres. Sur. William Ayres. Min. John T. St.Clair.

10 Aug 1833   Daniel Price, consent of Samuel Price, and Ellender Morris. Sur. William Morris. Wit. Robert P. Finney.

22 Feb 1843   George Price, of Henry Co. Va. consent of Samuel Price, and Martha Weaver, daughter of John Weaver. Sur. Robert Jarrott. Wit. James M. Wells. Min. William Schoolfied. M.R. 23 Feb 1843.

24 Oct 1840   James N. Price and Nancy D. Stuart, daughter of Archibald Stuart. Sur. A. Stuart. Wit. David P. Short and Mary F. Stuart.

15 Sep 1841   Jeremiah Price and Jane Dillion. Sur. Thomas Dehart. Min. Jesse Jones. M.R. 12 Sep 1841.

4 Dec 1820   Abraham Prillaman and Elizabeth Packwood. Sur. Samuel Packwood.

24 Jan 1826   George Prillaman, son of Jacob Prillaman of Franklin Co, Va., and Dicey Ross. Sur. Daniel Ross. Min. Stephen Hubbard. M.R. 2 Feb 1826.

16 Feb 1829   Samuel Prillaman, son of Jacob Prillaman, and Permela C. Harbour. Sur. John Harbour.

30 Jan 1851   William Prillaman and Maryan M. Spencer. Min. Jeremiah Burnett.

15 Dec 1842   Lewis Proffit, consent of Austin Profit, and Eliza George, consent of James H. George. Sur. Jesse Edens. Wit. Hugh George. M.R. 27 Dec 1842.

24 Feb 1834   Olive B. Pringle.and Lydia Collings. Sur. Allen Prindle.

16 Jan 1833   Anthony Puckett and Hannah Hoelt. Sur. Seaton Chandler. Min. Julius Terrell.

8 Feb 1811   Ephrim Puckett and Martha Hix. Sur. Thomas Dunn. Min. Thomas Whitlock.

6 Jan 1816   James Puckett and Susanah Sayers. Sur. Thomas Whitlock. Min. Thomas Whitlock.

28 Dec 1812   Lewis Puckett and Morning Spence. Sur. James Puckett. Min. Thomas Whitlock. M.R. 27 Dec 1812.

3 Mar 1830   Richard Puckett and Rebecca Clevor. Sur. Samuel
              Clever. Min. Julius Terrell.

12 Mar 1835   Braxton Purdy and Mary Ann Hopkins. Sur. James
              Hopkins. Min. Joshua Adams.

22 Apl 1820   Caleb Purdy and Satire Jones, daughter of Nancy
              Jones. Sur. Robert Akers. Wit. James Craddock.

20 Jan 1806   Ezekiel Purdy and Nancy Spencer. Sur. John Spencer.

8 Dec 1849   James Purdy and Julia Hollandsworth. Sur. Jermon
              Hollandsworth. Min. Joshua Adams. M.R. 12 Dec 1849.

4 Jan 1800   John Purdy and Mary Hollandsworth, daughter of
              Thomas Hollandsworth. Sur. John Gossett.

3 Oct 1840   John A Purdy, son of Caleb Purdy, and Martha Custer,
              daughter of Abraham Custer. Sur. Ezekiel Purdy.
              Wit. Tandy Stone and M. Fitzgerald.
              Min. Joshua Adams.

26 Oct 1848   John James Purdy and Peggy Susanna Spencer, daughter
              of Lewis Spencer. Sur. Ezekiel Purdy. Min. Joshua Adams.

27 Apl 1850   Joshua Purdy and Martha Ann Susan Hollandsworth.
              Sur. William Hollandsworth. Wit. Ezekiel Purdy.
              Min. Jeremiah Burnett. M.R. 2 May 1850.

1 Apl 1852   William Quisenberry of Carrol Co.,Va., and
              Judah Conner. Min. John Conner,Sr.

13 Oct 1807   Thomas Rabon and Mildred Thompson. Sur. Joshua Haynes.

24 Nov 1845   Jesse Radford, son of Robert Radford, and Dorothy R.
              Thomas, daughter of Richard Thomas. Sur. Stephen
              Thomas. Wit. Harden Cockram.

21 Nov 1845   William R. Radford, son of Robert Radford, and
              Arta Cockram, daughter of Edward Cockram. Sur.
              Stephen Thomas. Wit. Lewis A. Radford.

24 Jun 1843   Aaron Rakes and Lucinda Cruise. Sur. John Cruise.
              M.R. 29 Jun 1843.

22 May 1827   Charles Rakes and Nancy Hubbard. Sur. Harden R. Hall.
              Min. Stephen Hubbard.

22 Sep 1851   Charles J. Rakes and Delila Cockram. Min.G.W. Conner.

3 Dec 1821   Chesley Rakes and Sally Dehart. Sur. Gabriel Dehart.
              Min. Stephen Hubbard. M.R. 6 Dec 1821.

6 Mar 1853   David Rakes, son of Chesley Rakes, and Rocksana Rakes.
              Wit. Levi Rakes. Min. Austin J. Cassell.

13 Jan 1829   Rubin Rakes and Elizabeth Canaday. Sur. William
               Canaday. Min. Stephen Hubbard.

13 Oct 1807   Thomas Rakmen and Mildred Thompson.
               Min. Thomas Whitlock.

12 Sep 1853   Alexander Ratliff, son of Lewis & Matilda Ratliff,
               and Milly C. Stegill, consent of guardian John G.
               Lee. Min. Joshua Adams. Married at the home of
               Ezekiel Purdy.

26 Jun 1822   Benjamin Ratliff, son of Ralph Ratliff, and Elizabeth
               Stickleman. Sur. Valentine Ratliff. Min. Stephen
               Hubbard. M.R. 27 Jun 1822.

30 Dec 1850   Elias Ratliff and Susan Jemima Smart.
               Min. William Lawson.

26 Nov 1835   James Ratliff and Nancy S. Vest. Sur. John D. Vest.
               Min. Jesse Jones.

 1 Jan 1833   Jeremiah Ratliff and Sally Via. Min. Jesse Jones.

15 Oct 1835   John R. Ratliff and Agnes Clemmons. Sur. Ezekiel
               Purdy. Min. John Conner.

27 Nov 1850   John W. Ratliff and Cathan Moles. Min. Joshua Adams.

29 Mar 1803   Joseph Ratliff and ----Godard. Sur. Joseph Cummings.

 6 Jan 1822   Lewis Ratliff and Matilda Purdy. Sur. Ezekiel Purdy.

23 Dec 1853   Lewis Ratliff and Elizabeth Kelly.

12 Apl 1826   Milton Ratliff and Nancy Ratliff. Sur. Thomas Tenerson.
               Min. Stephen Hubbard. M.R. 15 Apl 1826.

11 Jul 1792   Ralph Ratliff and Charity Sumner, consent of Kiah
               Sumner. Sur. James Bartlett. Wit. Silas Ratliff and
               John Sharp. Min. Robert Jones.

15 Jul 1829   Roland(Robert) Ratliff, son of Usley Ratliff, and
               Zelpha Keaton, daughter of William Keaton. Sur.
               John Spencer. Wit. Paul C. Ingram.

27 Dec 1838   Rowland Ratliff, of Wythe Co.,Va.,and Charlotte
               Salmons, daughter of John Salmons. Sur. Robert Boaz.
               Wit. Alford Salmons. Min. Joshua Adams.M.R. 28 Dec 1838.

25 May 1825   John L. Rausseau and Nancy Shelton, daughter of
               Abslam & Polley Shelton. Sur. Robert Glasgow.
               Min. Bird Lowe.

14 Dec 1831   Abner Rea and Susannah Stone. Sur. Eusebus Stone.
               Min. John Turner.

29 Jan 1795   John Rea and Mildred Fulkerson, daughter of Mildred Fulkerson. Sur. William Rea. Min. Isaac Adams.

16 Jul 1851   Willis Reed and Louisa Wade. Min. Jesse Jones.

30 Oct 1825   James M. Redd and Ruth P. Staples. Min. Bird Lowe.

29 Dec 1816   W. Redd and Keziah C. Staples. Min. Peter Frans.

9 Aug 1810   Anthony Redley and Elizabeth Going. Sur. John Johnson. Min. Thomas Whitlock. M.R. 9 Apl 1809.

21 Dec 1817   James Redman and Betsy(Elizabeth) Elliott, daughter of William Elliott. Sur. Thomas Penn. Min. Peter Frans. M. R. 25 Dec 1817.

3 Feb 1818   John Redman and Caty Brown. Sur. John Brown. Min. Maning Hill. M.R. 5 Feb 1818.

16 Oct 1816   Charles Reeves and Elizabeth Lackey, daughter of George Lackey. Sur. Thomas Reeves.

27 Oct 1807   John Reeves and Hannah Pedigo. Sur. Lewis Hancock. Min. Lewis Foster. M.R. 29 Oct 1807.

21 Nov 1806   Josiah Reeves and Constandestion Brown. Min. Lewis Foster.

1 Apl 1805   Thomas Reeves and Betsy McCutchen, daughter of James McCutchen. Min. Robert Jones. M.R. 6 Apl 1805.

20 Dec 1809   William Rem and Susanah Jinkins. Sur. William Russay. Min. Thomas Whitlock.

19 May 1809   Abram Reynolds and Polly(Mary) Harbour. Sur. Benjamin Harbour. Min. Stephen Hubbard. M.R. 25 May 1809.

27 Nov 1848   Alexander P. Reynolds and Ruth Spencer. Sur. William Spencer. Min. Joshua Adams. M.R. 7 Dec 1848.

24 Sep 1849   Andrew J. Reynolds and Mary Conner. Sur. Peter Conner. Min. John Conner. M.R. 11 Oct 1849.

5 Feb 1799   Bartemus Reynolds and Mildred Taylor. Sur. David Taylor.

30 Sep 1831   C. H. Reynolds and Elizabeth C. Smith. Sur. W.F. Smith. Min. Joshua Adams. M.R. 6 Oct 1831.

5 Feb 1842   Fleming Reynolds and Tempy Joyce. Sur. James Joyce. Min. Joshua Adams. M.R. 8 Feb 1842.

14 Sep 1791 George Reynolds and Morning Wade, consent of her sister
Elizabeth Hilton and her husband Numan Hilton. Sur.
Joseph Reynolds. Wit. William McPeek and Sene Hilton.
Min. Robert Jones.

4 Feb 1808 Henry Reynolds and Susanah Clay. Sur. Daniel Edmonds.
Min. Thomas Whitlock.

31 Jan 1840 James Reynolds and Roxana Shelor, daughter of John
Shelor. Sur. Andrew Jackson Edens. Min. William Lawson.
M.R. 2 Feb 1840.

25 Sep 1827 John Reynolds and Ann Harbour. David Harbour states
that Ann has lived with his family for two years and
is of age. Sur. Joshua Harbour. Min. Joshua Adams.
M.R.30 Sep 1827.

25 Jan 1820 Meekins Reynolds and Polly Reynolds. Sur. Jesse
Reynolds. Min. Peter Frans. M.R. 26 Jan 1820.

7 Sep 1791 Middleton Reynolds and Elizabeth Murry. Sur. Moses
Reynolds and Joseph Reynolds. Min. William Dodson.
M.R. 8 Sep 1791.

4 Apl 1839 Thomas J. Reynolds and Charlotte Anglin. Sur. John H.
Washburn. Min. John Washburn. M.R. 7 Apl 1839.

16 Mar 1820 William Reynolds and Nancy Burnett. Sur. Isham Burnett.
Min. Stephen Hubbard. M.R. 23 Mar 1820.

9 Jan 1799 Capt. Holeman Rice and Edith Verdel, daughter of
Jackville Brewer. Sur. Samuel Morris,Jr.

18 Mar 1793 Robert Rich and Charlotte Salahorn, consent of her
guardian Robert Hooker. Sur. John Rea.

20 Dec 1834 Irvin Richardson and Permelia Lewis. Sur. Argelus
Lewis. Min. Thomas Whitlock.

29 Dec 1834 James W. Richardson, consent of John Gates,father, and
Sarah Boling, daughter of Gabriel Boling. Sur. John
Boling. Wit. George D. Richardson. Min. Jesse Jones.
M.R. 30 Dec 1834.

8 Jan 1808 Abner Rickman and Delilah Clark. Sur. Peter Rickman.
Min. Peter Frans. M.R. 14 Jan 1808.

8 Mar 1839 James Rickman and Elizabeth Viperman. Sur. John Ingram.
Min. John Conner.

14 Oct 1829 John Rickman and Polly Harris. Sur. James Harris.
Min. John Washburn. M.R. 15 Oct. 1829.

2 Mar 1805   John Rickman and Tabithia Harris. Sur. David S. Sims.
             Wit. David Sams.

25 Oct 1795 Thomas Rickman and Nancy Stephens, age 22.
             Sur. John Rickman.

23 Dec 1806 Thomas Rickman and Pattey Findley. Sur. Peter Findley.

25 Oct 1795 William Rickman and Abigal Gibson. Sur. John Rickman.

15 Jan 1843 William H. Rickman and Christina Holt. Sur. James G.
             Rickman. Min. Joshua Adams. M.R. 20 Jan 1844.

 2 Apl 1812 Asa Riddle and Mary East. Sur. Samuel Cannon.
             Min. Thomas Whitlock.

29 Jun 1805 Adam Rinehart and Sarah Young, daughter of John Young.
             Sur. Daniel Howell.

19 Jan 1812 Aaron Ritter and Susana Hardridge. Min. Thomas Whitlock.

 6 Sep 1815 Aaron Roberts and Anne Goard. Sur. Thomas Whitlock.
             Min. Thomas Whitlock.
             Robertson, Roberson
15 Dec 1820 Joshua Roberts and Elizabeth Smith. Sur. Thomas Whitlock.
             Min. Thomas Whitlock.

20 Aug 1796 David Roberson and Mary Henry, daughter of John Henry, Sr.
             Sur. John Henry, Jr.

25 Feb 1850 David J. Robertson and Nancy Robertson. Sur. William
             Roberson.

18 Sep 1849 Green M. Roberson and Mary Waller. Sur. George L. King.
             Min. Joshua Adams. M.R. 12 Sep 1849.

25 Oct 1847 James R. Roberson and Elvira P. Robertson. Sur. W. J.
             Robertson. Min. John Conner.

 8 Oct 1791 Nicholas Roberson and Molly Hilton, daughter of Samuel
             Hilton. Sur. Samuel Hilton. Wit. William McPeek.
             Min. Robert Jones.

16 Feb 1793 William Roberson and Sarah Lackey, daughter of John
             Lackey, Sr.. Sur. Henry Tuggle. Min. George Dodson.
             M.R. 21 Feb 1793.

24 Jan 1828 William Robertson and Isabel McAlexander, consent of
             mother, not named, and consent also signed by James
             McAlexander. Sur. William Burge, Jr.

22 June 1844 William H. Robertson and Mary J. Lackey. Sur. James
             Lackey.

Rogers, Roger, Rodgers

17 Aug 1828   Abram Roger(Koger?) and Dinah Litrell. Min.
Joshua Adams.

2 Jan 1849   Clement S. Rodgers and Ruth Blanchet. Sur. George S.
Rodgers. Wit. F.G. Smith. Min. Joshua Adams.
M.R. 4 Jan 1849.

30 Sep 1830   David Rogers and Patsy Allen. Sur. Anderson Allen.
Min. Bird Lowe.

2 Aug 1825   George Rogers and Lucy Newman. Sur. Winston Newman.
Min. Bird Lowe.

16 Sep 1794   George Rogers,Jr. and Nancy Lyon. Sur. William Rogers.

24 Nov 1852   George R. Rogers and Rebeca Jane, daughter of Isaac
Pike. Wit. Gabriel Pike.

24 Mar 1826   Hiram Rogers and Elizabeth Saunders. Sur. Robert
Saunders. Min. Bird Lowe.

3 Apl 1838   John T. Rogers and Hester J. Witt. Sur. Saunders Witt.
Min. Joshua Adams.

27 Nov 1823   Josiah Rogers and Sally Rogers. Sur. David Rogers.

3 Nov 1795   Robert Rogers and Milly Newman. Sur. Samuel Shelton.

20 Aug 1827   William Rogers and Elizabeth Newman. Sur. Winston
Newman.

20 Sep 1828   James Roe and Franky Hopkins. Sur. Thomas Reynolds.

29 Mar 1853   Crocket Roop and Baratha McAlexander. Min. John Conner.

26 Nov 1849   David C. Rorrer and S.A. Harbour. Sur. Mikel A. Rorrer.

20 Jan 1836   John Rorrer and Jane Handy, daughter of William Handy.
Sur. David Rorrer. Min. John Conner.

23 Oct 1841   Michael A. Rorrer and Elizabeth A. Ingram, daughter of
Rowland Ingram. Sur. John Slaughter. Wit. John Canaday.

30 Mar 1844   Thomas D. Rorrer and Arminda Davis. Sur. John W. Davis.
M.R. 4 Apl 1844.

15 Mar 1847   George W. Rosenbaim and Maria T. Foster. Sur. Isaac
Adams. Min. Owen Sumner. M.R. 9 Mar 1847.

13 Dec 1838   Charles Ross and Luvenia P. Foster. Sur. George C. Dodson.
Min. D. B. Nicholson. M.R. 20 Dec 1838.

24 Jul 1798   Daniel Ross and Nancy Ingram, daughter of James Ingram.
Sur. David Ross. Wit. Alexander Ingram.

23 Mar 1820   Daniel Ross and Joyce Harbour. Sur. David Harbour.
Min. Joshua Adams.

14 Feb 1833   David J. Ross and Elizabeth Turner. Sur. Shadrack
Turner. Min. John Turner.

 3 Nov 1853   Hardin D. Ross age 24, son of William and Mahaley
Ross, and Martha D. Conner age 17, daughter of
James and Hisiak Conner. Wit. E. J. Conner.

26 Jul 1804   Lewis Ross and Hannah James. Sur. John James.

20 Dec 1794   Nathaniel Ross and Milly Penn, daughter of Phillip
Penn. Sur. Samuel Staples.

12 Oct 1843   Peyton R. Ross and Mahala Turner,daughter of Thomas
Turner. Sur. Samuel G. Staples. Wit. Samuel A. Ross
and Joseph L. Turner. Min. Joshua Adams.

18 May 1837   Robert A. Ross and Amanda B. Turner, daughter of
Thomas W. Turner. Sur. David J. Ross. Wit. Peyton R.
Ross. Min. John Turner.

12 Oct 1843   Samuel A. Ross and Esther J. Harbour. Sur. John H.
Pedigo. Min. Joshua Adams.

13 Jun 1822   William Ross and Mahala Burnett. Sur. Isaac Adams.
Min. John Conner. M.R. 30 Jun 1822.

15 Sep 1798   Robert Rowan and Elizabeth Turner. Sur. Frances Turner.
Min. Jesse Jones.

26 Oct 1841   Michael Rowen and Elizabeth A. Ingram. Min. Joshua
Adams.

29 Aug 1811   James Russey,Jr. and Polly Cloud. Sur. Abraham Penn.

20 Oct 1805   William Russey and Marah Talbot. Sur. John Talbot.
Min. Thomas Whitlock.

27 Apl 1839   Jesse R. Salmons and Pamela Owens. Sur. David Owens.
Min. Jesse Jones. M.R. 19 Apl 1839.

27 Aug 1812   Jonathan Salmons and Patsy Martin, consent of Giles
Martin. Sur. Giles Martin.

 3 Jan 1814   Jonathan Salmon and Patsy Jones, consent of Jesse
Jones. Sur. Nathan Hall.

 2 Mar 1833   Russell Salmons and Sarah Rogers, daughter of John
Rogers. Sur. William Clark. Min. Julius Terrell.

 5 Jan 1802   William Salsberry and Nancy Elkins. Sur. William
Frazier.

5 Jan 1802   William Salsberry and Nancy Elkins.
Sur. William Frazier.

12 Apl 1836   Gabriel P. Sandefur and Martha Howell, daughter of
Samuel Howell. Sur. Capt. Mathew Sandefur.
Min. John Conner.

29 Sep 1827   William A. Sandefer and Nancy M. Sharp.
Sur. William Thompson.

1 Sep 1816   John Sands and Sally Wade. Sur. Samuel Philpott.
Min. Maning Hill. M.R. 7 Sep 1815.

16 Jan 1822   William Sands and Matilda Carter. Sur. Samuel Carter.
Min. John C. Traylor.

25 Mar 1850   William Satterfield and Charlotte A. Dalton, daughter
of James Dalton. Sur. William L. Murphy.
Min. G. W. Conner. M.R. 28 Mar 1850.

11 Apl 1844   Richard Sawyers and Lockey Puckett. Sur. Joseph McMillon.
Min. J. Boyd.

21 Jan 1813   John Scales and Sally Scales. Sur. James Scales.
Min. Maning Hill. M.R. 24 Jan 1813.

28 Dec 1843   Daniel Samuel Scott and Mary Ann Spangler.
Sur. John Spangler. Min. William Lawson.

18 Jul 1816   John Scott and Afferah Ayres. Sur. Elkanah Ayres.
Min. Thomas Whitlock.

15 Jun 1847   Joseph B. Scott and Mary Ann Shelton, daughter of
Herbert Shelton. Sur. Robert M. Clark.
Min. Joshua Adams.

21 Feb 1843   Richard H. Scales and Sophia R. Penn. Sur. S.G. Staples.

12 Aug 1793   Samuel Scurlock and Martha Terry, daughter of Elizabeth
Terry. Sur. James Scurlock. Wit. Richard Terry.

14 Oct 1792   John Senter and Nancy Lowell, daughter of William Lowell.
Sur. Henry Koger. Min. George Dodson. M.R. 19 Oct 1792.

20 Aug 1807   Charles Sharp and Matilda Anglin. Sur. Phillip Anglin.

23 Nov 1809   James Sharp and Polly Corn. Sur. Jesse Corn.
Min. Lewis Foster. M.R. 22 Nov 1809.

7 Dec 1796   John Sharp and Susanah Medley. Sur. John Medley,Jr.
Min. Isaac Adams.

29 Jul 1813   Joseph Sharp and Sally Shelton. Sur. Nathaniel Shelton.
Min. Peter Frans.

22 Feb 1798   Richard Sharp and Elizabeth Corn. Sur. Jesse Corn.
Min. Isaac Adams.

17 Aug 1796   Robert Sharp and Peney Shelton. Sur. Stephen Lyon.
Min. Isaac Adams.

19 Mar 1828   Samuel Sharp and Fanny(Frances T.) Lyon. Sur. Alex.
Murphy. Min. Bird Lowe.

20 Dec 1808   Thomas Sharp and Lucinda Reynolds. Sur. Abraham
Reynolds. Min.Peter Frans. M.R. 12 Jan 1809.

24 Feb 1811   William Sharp,Jr., and Peney Fitzgerald. Sur.
Harvey Fitzgerald. Min. Brett Stovall.

20 Dec 1834   Jesse N. Sheffield and Martha C. Knight, daughter of
Coleman Knight. Sur. Thomas Waller.

17 Nov 1839   Thomas C.T.J. Sheffield and Martha Martin, daughter
of Stephen and Sarah Martin. Sur. Robert Jarratt.
Wit. John Craig and James Massey.
Min. William M. Schoolfield. M.R. 21 Nov 1839.

11 Nov 1839   Floyd G. Shelor and Sarah F. Carter. Sur. Banes Carter.
The requests mentions Col. Carter.

2 Sep 1816   Jacob Shelor and Anna Tuggle, daughter of John Tuggle.
Sur. A. Staples. Min. Jesse Jones. M.R. 5 Sep 1816.

28 Nov 1837   Randolph Shelor, son of Jacob Shelor, and Polly Harris.
Sur. William Harris. Min. William Lawson.

29 Feb 1831   Thomas B. Shelor, of Floyd Co. Va., and Mary Barnard.
Sur. Isham Barnard. Min. Nathaniel Thompson.
M.R. 8 Mar 1831.

12 Feb 1825   Absolum Shelton and Polly Thompson. Sur. Rice Henderson.
Min. Joshua Adams. M.R. 3 Feb 1825

1 Aug 1842   Absolem Shelton and Susanah Blackard. Sur. Thomas
Blackard. Min.Joshua Adams. M.R. 28 Aug 1842.

12 Dec 1850   Alexander A. Shelton and Nancy Blackard.
Min. Joshua Adams.

8 Sep 1840   Anderson Shelton, William C. Shelton states that
Anderson is 22 yrs of age, and Mary Keaton. Sur.
William Keaton. Min. Joshua Adams.

28 Nov 1797   Archibald Shelton and Rodah Nolen, daughter of James Nolen. Sur. Robert Sharp.

17 Nov 1833   Eliphaz Shelton and Marriah H. Philpott. Sur. Milton R. Dodson. Min. Joshua Adams.

28 Aug 1839   Fredrick Shelton, son of Hudson Shelton, and Hetta Boling. Sur. John Boling. Min. John Conner.

6 Feb 1809   Frederick Shelton and Winny (Winnefred)Jones. Sur. Robert Sharp. Min. Peter Frans. M.R. 9 Feb 1809 and 12 Feb 1809.

10 Oct 1839   Gerald Shelton and Nancy Spencer. Sur. William Spencer. Min. Joshua Adams.

26 Sep 1819   Hamon Shelton and Sela (Priscilla) Fitzgerald, daughter of H. Fitzgerald. Min. Stephen Hubbard.

6 Jan 1825   Harbert Shelton and Sally Sharp. Sur. Peter Penn. Min. Bird Lowe.

9 Feb 1813   Hudson Shelton and Lucy Murphy. Sur. Claiborne Shelton. Min. Brett Stovall.

20 Feb 1841   Jacob Shelton and Sally(Sarah) Clifton, daughter of William Clifton. Sur. Hudson Shelton. Min. John Conner. M.R. 25 Feb 1841.

14 May 1841   James Shelton and Amanda Critz. Sur. William Critz. Min. Joshua Adams. M.R. 16 May 1841.

29 Mar 1832   James Shelton and Polly Frans, daughter of John Frans. Sur. David W. Smith. Min. John Washburn.

20 Dec 1828   John Shelton and Kitty Ayers, consent of Joseph Ayers. Sur. John Nowland. Wit. Harmon Magee and Francis Ayers. Min. Jesse Jones. M.R. 21 Dec 1828.

11 Sep 1817   Josiah Shelton and Winefred Shelton. Sur. John Frans. Min. Peter Frans. M.R. 27 Sep 1817.

15 Aug 1839   Levi Shelton and Phebe Allen. Sur. Anderson Allen. Min. John Washburn. M.R. 18 Aug 1839.

13 Jan 1831   Lewis Shelton and Sally Jones. Sur. Gabriel Jones. Min. Jesse Jones. M.R. 20 Jan 1831.

26 Aug 1812   Nathaniel Shelton and Betsey Roper. Sur. Peyton Harvile. Min. Peter Frans. M.R. 3 Sep 1812.

7 Nov 1852   Pines H. Shelton and Mary. O. Seales, daughter of John T. Seales. Min. D.G. Taylor.

23 Jun 1834   Samuel Shelton, son of Hudson Shelton, and Cynthia
Murphy. Sur. A. Murphy. Wit. William Shelton.
M.R. 24 Jun 1834.

15 Jan 1835   Thomas Shelton and Elizabeth Allen. Sur. Anderson
Allen. Min. Joshua Adams.

25 Nov 1834   Thomas N. Shelton and Martha A. Critz, daughter of
William Critz. Sur. Spencer F. Nowlin. Min.
Joshua Adams. M.R. 1 Jan 1835.

14 Dec 1838   Tyre Shelton and Rebecca Booker. Sur. William Booker.
Min. Bird Lowe.

17 May 1839   William Shelton and Frances Smith. Sur. D.W. Smyth.

28 Oct 1850   William Shelton and Sarah Freeman. Min. J. Adams.

19 Sep 1853   William H. Shelton and Mary E. Clark, daughter of
Eddy Clark. Wit. William H. Ayers and Rice O.Brim.

29 Sep 1816   James Sheppard and Rachel Bateman. Sur. Abraham Penn.

30 Oct 1841   Alexander Shockley and Mary Trent. Consent is given
by her guardian, John G. Lee. Sur. Daniel Harris.
Mr. Shockley is of Stokes Co. N.C..

17 Feb 1848   William A. Shouse and Sarah Collins. Sur. P.C. Joyce.
Min. Joshua Adams.

16 Jul 1833   Allman Short and Frances Smith. Sur. John D.Cheatham.
Min. Joshua Adams.

17 Jan 1836   Allman Short and Fanny Goard, daughter of John and
Ailey Goard. Sur. Allen Morrison

17 Jun 1844   Calton(Cotton) B. Short and Elizabeth Shelton.
Sur. Hudson Shelton. M.R. 20 Jun 1844.

13 Jan 1820   John Y. Short and Judith Thomas. Sur. Pleasant Thomas.
Min. Stephen Hubbard. M.R. 3 Feb 1820.

14 Feb 1828   Joseph Short and Polly Thomas, daughter of Charles
Thomas. Sur. James Bartlett. Wit. Nicoles Thomas.
Min. Stephen Hubbard. M.R. 21 Feb 1828.

29 Mar 1819   Obediah Short and Leoney Foley. Sur. Jeremiah Foley.
Min. John Conner. M.R. 1 Apl 1819.

21 Dec 1841   Hugh Sims and Elizabeth J. Soyers. Min. Martin Cloud.
M.R. 23 Dec 1841.

13 Jan 1794   Martin Sims and Nancy Adams. Sur. William Adams.

26 Aug 1823   Addam Simmons and Delilah Willis. Sur. Adam Ahart.
Min. Thomas Whitlock.

7 Apl 1830   Anderson Simmons, of Stokes Co. N.C., and Jane Burge.
Sur. William Burge. Min. Julius Terrell.

22 Nov 1797   Peter Simmons and Delilah Pruitt. Sur. Richard Pruitt.
Min. John Nunns. M.R. 9 Nov 1797.

18 Dec 1824   Richard Simson and Prudence Trine. Sur. Owen East.
Min. Thomas Whitlock.

10 Jul 1832   William Simpson and Mary Ann Worrel. Sur. D.C. Hill.
Min. Thomas Whitlock.

9 Apl 1815   Elijah Sisemore and Margaret George. Sur. Stephen
McMilion. Min. Thomas Whitlock.

12 Sep 1791   Robert Sisemore and Claran Freeman, daughter of
Agnes Freeman. Sur. William Hickinbottom.

17 May 1827   John Sites and Martha Murphy. Sur. Jesse Murphy.
Min. Bird Lowe.

3 Nov 1822   Isham Slate and Polly Chandler. Min. Maning Hill.
M.R. 3 Nov 1822.

27 Jul 1848   Isham James Slate and Rachel Mann. Sur. Frank
Collings. Min. Julius Terrell.

23 Dec 1828   Jeremiah Slate and Polly Bowman. Sur. Gilbert
Bowman. Min. Brett Stovall. M.R. 30 Dec 1828.

26 Apl 1835   William Slate and Malinda Bowman. Sur. Gilbert
Bowman. Min. Julius Terrell.

10 Oct 1813   Dandridge Slaughter and Susana Palmer. Sur. William
Hancock. Min. Jesse Jones.

21 Nov 1803   Ezekiel Slaughter and Letty Thompson. Sur. Dandridge
Slaughter. Min. Jesse Jones.

20 Sep 1821   John Slaughter and Elizabeth Jones, daughter of Jesse
Jones. Sur. Thomas Harbour. Min. Jesse Jones.
M.R. 16 Sep 1821.

25 Dec 1839   John Slaughter, son of Dandridge Slaughter, and
Rozinah Hall Ingram, daughter of Rowland Ingram.
Sur. James A. Ingram. Wit. Elizabeth Ingram.
Min. John Conner. M.R. 16 Jan 1840.

19 Apl 1826   Josiah Slaughter, son of John Slaughter, and Elizabeth
Koger. Sur. Joseph Koger. Min. Joshua Adams.

11 Aug 1825 Martin Slaughter and Mary (Polly) Conner. Sur. John
Conner. Min. John Conner. M.R. 21 Aug 1825.

26 Jan 1799 William Slaughter and Betsy(Elizabeth) Amos, dau of
Mary Amos. Sur. Jacob Saunders.

25 Aug 1796 John Sloan and Sarah Henry, dau of John Henry.
Sur. Alexander Lackey. Min. Robert Jones.

25 Aug 1796 William Sloan and Tilley Burnett, dau of Jeremiah
Burnett. Sur. James Lackey. Min. Jesse Jones.

10 Mar 1828 Allen Slusher and Mahala Harris. Sur. Reuben Harris.

19 Apl 1852 Oliver P. Slusher and Mary Jane Wood, dau of John R.
Wood. Wit. Richard Wood. Min. Jesse Jones.

21 Feb 1850 William C. Smart and Malinda Boyd. Sur. German Boyd.
Min. Joshua Adams. M.R. 28 Feb 1850.

6 Nov 1815 Augustine Smith and Mildred Stearman. Sur. Thomas
Whitlock. Min. Thomas Whitlock. M.R. 6 Nov 1815.

4 Jun 1803 Burril Smith and Pheby Bellar. Sur. Eli Bellar.

21 Jan 1853 Booker W. Smith and Salla A. Wilkes, dau of
Tempey J. Wilkes.

6 Sep 1841 Daniel Smith, son of Charles Smith, and Exoney
Hancock, dau of Martha Hancock. Sur. Thomas
Martin. Min. Joshua Adams. M.R. 13 Sep 1841.

8 Feb 1838 David W. Smythe and Adeline M. Smith.
Sur. W. T. Smith. Min. Joshua Adams.

26 Nov 1830 Ewell Smith and Drucilla Vaughters. Sur. Adam
Hall. Min. Thomas Whitlock.

29 Dec 1834 Ewell Smith and Marey (Masey) Mankins. Sur.
William Mankins. Min. Thomas Whitlock.

29 Aug 1836 Fowkles Smith and Mary Ann Hanby. Sur. A.A. Moir.
Min. Joshua Adams. M.R. 7 Aug 1836.

29 Mar 1829 George Smith and Sally Smith. Sur. and Min.
Thomas Whitlock.

6 Apl 1820 James Smith and Sarah Willis. Sur. Joshua Haynes.
Min. Thomas Whitlock.

22 Mar 1834 James Smith and Judy Bowman. Sur. John Thompson.
Min. Thomas Whitlock.

28 Oct 1802 John Smith and Rachel Packwood. Sur. Samuel Packwood.

30 Jul 1804 John Smith and Susanah Stanley, daughter of Zacheriah Stanley. Sur. Moses Hurt. Wit. Charles Mayberry. Min. Stephen Hubbard.

18 Aug 1848 John Williamson Smith and Susanah Boyd. Sur. John Boyd. Min. William Lawson. M.R. 7 Sep 1848.

18 Oct 1829 Levi Smith and Martha Sprouse. Sur. George D. Sprouse. Min. Maning Hill. M.R. 20 Oct 1829.

28 Sep 1848 Mainard Smith and Catherine Boyd. Min. William Lawson.

4 Apl 1812 Martin Smith and Polly Critz. Sur. William Critz. Min. Peter Frans. M.R. 9 Apl 1812.

10 Oct 1791 Nathaniel Smith and Polly Hanby. Sur. Thomas Mitchell.

5 Nov 1804 Peter Smith and Martha Hancock. Sur. Benjamin Hancock.

13 Jan 1805 Peyton Smith and Polly James. Sur. James Smith. Min. Peter Frans.

26 Dec 1822 Thornton Smith and Elizabeth Willis. Sur. Thomas Whitlock. Min. Thomas Whitlock. M.R. 26 Dec 1822.

15 Jan 1824 William Smith and Rosamond Wright. Sur. Thomas Boling. Min. Jesse Jones. M.R. 2 Feb 1824.

17 Oct 1843 William B. Smith, son of Charles Smith, and Lydia Ann Campbell, daughter of Ben J. Campbell. Sur. Thomas K. Campbell. Min. Arnold Walker.

Oct 1850 William D. Smith and Jane Mitchell. Min. Joshua Adams.

24 Nov 1840 Abraham Sneed and Rebecca (Polly) Turner, daughter of Francis Turner. Sur. Perrin Joyce. Wit. Samuel Sneed. Min. Jesse Jones. M.R. 17 Dec 1841.

5 Nov 1816 James Sneed and Sally Lackey, daughter of George Lackey. Sur. Isaac Adams. Min. Stephen Hubbard. M.R. 17 Nov 1816.

14 Sep 1807 John Sneed and Nancy Pedegoy(Pedigo). Sur. Edward Pedegoy. Min. Lewis Foster. M.R. 17 Sep 1807.

29 Jan 1838 John T. Sneed and Sally Foley. Sur. James Foley.

14 Sep 1815 Samuel Sneed and Easter Turner. Sur. Adam Turner. Min. Stephen Hubbard. M.R. 28 Sep 1815.

5 Sep 1849 Samuel Sneed and Elizabeth Moran, daughter of Nelson Moran. Sur. John Howell. Min. Jesse Jones.

4 Aug 1853   Samuel Sneed, son of Samuel Sneed,Sr. and Jane Sneed,
             and Nancy Wright, daughter of John N. and Elizabeth
             Wright. Min. Joshua Adams.

5 Feb 1798   Thomas Sneed and Sinthy Penn, daughter of Phillip Penn.
             Sur. Wilson Penn. Wit. Nathaniel Ross. Min.Isaac Adams.

8 Feb 1816   Thomas Snow and Leah Hall. Sur. James Smith.
             Min. Thomas Whitlock. M.R. 17 Feb 1816.

21 Feb 1848 Isaac Snuffer and Malinda Rakes, daughter of Samuel
             Rakes. Sur. Samuel Rakes. Min. Michael Hawry.
             M.R. 2 Mar 1848.

14 Feb 1799 William Soloman and Jane Phillips. Sur. Archibald Taylor

17 Apl 1816 James Sowder and Margret Gibbs. Sur. Thomas Whitlock.
             Min. Thomas Whitlock.

12 Jun 1815 Jesse Sowder and Jilsay Bullard. Sur. Thomas Whitlock.
             Min. Thomas Whitlock.

24 Oct 1843 Richard Spangler and Lucretia Scott. Sur. John Monday.

18 Feb 1818 John Spalding and Leony Foley. Sur. Patrick Foley.

7 Feb 1803   John Spawling and Rhoda Rakes. Min. S. Hall.
             M.R. 3 Mar 1803.

25 Aug 1806 Abraham Speckelmen and Charity Howell, daughter of
             Lenard and Susana Howell. Sur. David Howell.
             Wit. Jonathan Jones.

20 Feb 1830 James Spence and Nancy Watson. Sur. Martin Cloud,
             Jacob Grigg and Hugh Spence. Min. Thomas Whitlock.

29 Aug 1822 Abraham Spencer and Catherine Adams. Sur. John Spencer.

18 Dec 1826 Alexander Spencer and Polly Crum, daughter of John Crum.
             Sur. Samuel Brewer. Wit. William Crum & John Crum,Jr.

11 Jun 1818 Benjamin Spencer and Frankey Dotson. Sur. Carrington
             Dillon. Wit. William Spencer. Min. Peter Frans.
             M.R. 14 Jun 1818.

14 Aug 1835 Clark Spencer and Mary Purdy, daughter of Ezekiel Purdy.
             Sur. Marvel Spencer. Min. Joshua Adams. M.R. 23 Aug 1835.

28 Jul 1803 Daniel Spencer and Pheby Soloman, daughter of Drury
             Soloman. Sur. John Spencer.

16 Sep 1830 Elijah Spencer and Nancy Gourd, daughter of John Gourd.
             Sur. George Reynolds. Wit. Marvel Spencer.
             Min. Joshua Adams. M.R. 22 Sep 1830.

6 Aug 1850   German Spencer and Elizabeth Ann Grady. Min. Joshua Adams.

10 Dec 1846   Hardin Spencer and Nancy S. Reynolds. Sur. Peter Spencer.
Min. Joshua Adams.

21 Dec 1840   Jackson Spencer son of William Spencer, and Sarah Hopkins.
Sur. James Hopkins. Min. John Washburn. M.R. 24 Dec 1840.

23 Dec 1802   Jacob Spencer and Elizabeth Redman(alias Welch).
Sur. Joseph Going.

13 Oct 1842   Jarmon Spencer and Ruth J. Harbour. Sur. James Harbour.
Min. Joshua Adams.

12 Mar 1811   John Spencer and Lavinia Willis, daughter of William
Willis. Sur. Macajah Martin. Min. Peter Frans.
M.R. 14 Mar 1811.

 2 Mar 1824   John Spencer,Jr., and Delilah Ratliff, daughter of
Usly Ratliff. Sur. Abraham Spencer. Min. Joshua
Adams. M.R. 2 Mar 1824.

 3 Dec 1853   Levi Spencer, son of Marvel and Sarah Spencer, and
Naomi Marie Joyce, daughter of James and Susanah
Joyce. Min. Joshua Adams.

13 Oct 1842   Lewis Spencer and Priscilla Adams, daughter of Joshua
Adams. Sur. Anderson Purdy. Min. Joshua Adams.
M.R. 12 Oct 1828.

21 Nov 1839   Martin S. Spencer and Mary Tuggle. Sur. Henry Tuggle.
Min. Joshua Adams.

15 Feb 1816   Marvel Spencer and Sally Adams. Sur. John Adams.
Min. Peter Frans. M.R. 22 Feb 1816.

21 Sep 1842   Peter Spencer, son of Marvel Spencer, and Sabrinah
Pilson. Sur. Richard Pilson. Min. Joshua Adams.

 7 Jan 1851   Pinkney Spencer and Mary Jane Hagood, daughter of
Anderson Hagood. Min. William M. Schoolfield.
M.R. 21 Jan 1851.

13 Dec 1828   Thomas Spencer and Mary Adams. Sur. Joshua Adams.
Min. Joshua Adams. M.R. 11 Dec 1828.

28 Dec 1829   Thomas Spencer and Peggy Burnett. Sur. Jeremiah
Burnett,Jr. Min. John Conner.

 3 Oct 1817   William Spencer and Polly Adams. Sur. John Adams.
Min. Peter Frans. M.R. 5 Oct 1817.

 4 Feb 1839   William B. Spencer and Henrietta Parker, daughter of
John Parker. Sur. William Parker. Min. Joshua Adams.
M.R. 5 Feb 1839.

11 Dec 1851   William Lee Spencer and Tabitha Jane Wood.
              Min. Samuel J. Lackey.

14 Mar 1813   Peter Srader and Margret Wolfer. Sur. Thomas Whitlock.
              Min. Thomas Whitlock.

11 Feb 1852   Hiram Stanley and Lucy Come--. Min. Samuel J. Lackey.
              M.R. 29 Jan 1852.

 7 Apl 1827   John Stanley and Malinda Barnard. Sur. John Monday.
              Min. Brett Stovall. M.R. 13 Apl 1827.

12 Oct 1822   Moses Stanley and Eleanor Loe. Sur. Aaron Loe.
              Min. Stepehn Hubbard. M.R. 29 Oct 1822.

22 Feb 1834   Richard D. Stanley and Mary(Polly) Frans, consent of
              Daniel Frans. Sur. Samuel Clark. Wit. Cardwell Clark.
              Min. John Washburn. M.R. 27 Feb 1834.

 9 Jan 1849   William W. Stanley and Sarah Dodson, daughter of
              William Dodson. Sur. Frederick W. Dodson.
              Min. Joshua Adams. M.R. 11 Jan 1849.

17 Dec 1825   Joseph L. Stanley and Betsy Ann J. Poindexter.
              Sur. John B. Hudson. Min. John C. Traylor.
              Betsy Ann, the daughter of John Poindexter.

 7 Jan 1847   Dr. William C. Staples and Ann M. Penn. Sur. Samuel G.
              Staples. Min. John Rich. M.R. 20 Jul 1847.

 2 Dec 1823   Drinkard Stegall and Susanah Dehart. Sur. Joshua Dehart.
              Min. Stephen Hubbard. M.R. 9 Dec 1823.

28 Oct 1824   Masten Stegall and Polly Steagall. Sur. George Steagall.
              Min. Stephen Hubbard.

27 Nov 1848   Nathaniel Stegall and Martha Martin, daughter of Isaac
              Martin. Sur. Mathew Mabe. Wit. William Martin.
              Min. Joshua Adams. M.R. 1 Dec 1848.

11 May 1835   Elijah Stephens and Ann Jackson, daughter of George
              Jackson. Sur. Lewis Stephens. Wit. John Frasure and
              George Kington.

26 Jan 1826   Lewis Stephens and Orry Rogers. Sur. Hiram Rogers.
              Min. Bird Lowe.

30 Jul 1821   John Stewart and Jane Loggins. Sur. Tillman Loggins.
              Min. Peter Frans.

25 Mar 1822   John Stipe, son of Nancy Stipe, his father is deceased,
              and Susanah Turman. Sur. Thomas Howell.

27 Nov 1838   William A. J. Stockton and Exoney(Eoney) Hagood.
              Sur. Gregory Hagood. Min. John C. Traylor.
              M.R. 12 Dec 1838.

28 Oct 1839   James Stone and Maryan Stone. Sur. John Stone.

26 Mar 1816   John Stone and Susanah Stone. Sur. Thomas Stone.

11 Dec 1841   Joseph Stone and Malinda Jane Ferguson. Sur.
              Archibald Ferguson. Min. Joshua Adams.
              M.R. 15 Dec 1841.

 1 Apl 1848   Joseph Stone and Sarah Dillen. Sur. Jesse Dillen.
              Min. Joshua Adams. M.R. 13 Apl 1848.

 2 Jun 1823   Micajah Stone and Lucy Akers. Sur. William Lyon.

18 Oct 1853   Moses H. Stone, son of Littleberry & Nancy Stone,
              Ann Elizabeth Hollandsworth, daughter of German
              and Susan Hollandsworth. Min.Jeremiah Burnett.

       1824   Mr. Stone and Miss Aeris. Min. John C. Traylor.

 1 Nov 1841   Peyton Stone and Permelia Cox, daughter of
              Randolph Cox. Sur. James Cox.

17 Sep 1838   Samuel Stone and Martha Clark, daughter of John
              Clarke. Sur. Samuel Ingram. Wit. James Stone.
              Min. Joshua Adams. M.R. 20 Sep 1838.

       1804   Shadrick Stone, alias Shadrick Hall, and Caty
              Reynolds. Min. Jesse Jones.

17 Feb 1848   Stephen Stone,Jr and Cassia Ann Hollandsworth, daughter
              of Brice Hollandsworth. Sur. Barton Hollandsworth.
              Min. Joshua Adams. M.R. 28 Feb 1848.

 8 Aug 1839   Tandy Stone and Jane Hagood, daughter of Gregory
              Hagood. Sur. Charles Foster. Wit. Lewis Foster.

30 Jan 1821   Thomas Stone and Elizabeth Low. Sur. Aaron Low.

22 Apl 1823   Thomas Stone and Polley Slator. Sur. Thomas
              Hollandsworth.

 6 Apl 1841   Uciba(Eusibus) Stone and Jemima Cherry, daughter
              of John Cherry. Sur. Anderson Arnold.

17 Nov 1791   William Stone and Nancy Oneal. Sur. Edward Oneal.

20 Jan 1849   William Stone and Nancy Crum, consent of Nancy
              Crum. Sur. James Joyce. Min.Joshua Adams.
              M.R. 23 Jan 1849.

1822   William Stor and Miss Slater. Min.John C. Traylor.

11 May 1822   Archelous Stovall and Mary T. Sandefer, daughter of M. Sandefur. Sur. Nathan Reid. Min. Stephen Hubbard.

26 Jan 1793   Brett Stovall and Mary Hughes. Sur. Gabriel Penn.

16 Nov 1837   Joseph Stovall and Parmela Corn, daughter of Jesse Corn. Sur. Elam Williams. Min. Joshua Adams. M.R. 21 Nov 1837.

26 Mar 1841   Thomas J. Stovall and Sarah Tatum. Sur. H. Critz. Min. John W. Lewis. M.R. 7 Apl 1841.

29 Sep 1796   Jared Stow and Sally Hollandsworth. Sur. Thomas Hollandsworth. Min. Isaac Adams.

15 Nov 1802   Samuel Strong and Polly Adams, daughter of William Adams. Sur. Isaac Dodson. M.R. 16 Nov 1802.

8 Dec 1843   Ammon Stuart and Matilda Hurt. Sur. Rowland Hurt. M.R. 14 Dec 1843.

23 May 1811   William Stuts and Sarah Fitzgerald. Sur. Thomas Whitlock.

12 Apl 1816   Owen Sutfin and Sally Thompson. Sur. Henry Thompson. Min. John Conner. M.R. 13 Apl 1816.

21 Oct 1819   William Sutfin and Nancy Maberry(Mabry), daughter of Charles Mabry. Sur. William McPeek. Min. John Conner.

6 Oct 1816   William Sutfin and Lucy Blackhard. Sur. Clark Penn.

22 Nov 1810   John Switzler and Cary Lee. Sur. John Lee. Min. Brett Stovall.

5 Mar 1850   James B. Tate and Rachel E. Dalton, daughter of James Dalton. Sur. James H. Dalton. Min. Daniel G. Taylor. M.R. 14 Mar 1850.

13 Feb 1836   Edward Tatum and Ruth Foster, daughter of Charles Foster. Sur. George C. Dodson.

26 Oct 1839   Edward Tatum and Charlotte D. Critz, daughter of Gabriel Critz. Sur. J.C. Staples. Min. Joshua Adams. M.R. 17 Oct 1839.

11 Sep 1797   Jesse Tatum and Landal Parr. Sur. John Gates.

1 Mar 1797   John Tatum and Paissey Burge. Sur. Gabriel Penn.

11 Oct 1838   John G. (J) Tatum and Martha S. Foster, consent of Peter P. Penn. Sur. Clark Penn. Min. D. B. Nicholason, Methodist Episcopal. M.R. 23 Oct 1838.

29 Sep 1826   Thomas J. Tatum and Elizabeth M. Clark, consent of
G. Clark. Sur. Samuel Clark. Wit. Richard D. Stanley.
Min. Bird Lowe.

12 Apl 1850   William F. Tatum and Mary Ann D. Gray, daughter of
Daniel Gray. Sur. A. A. Moir. Min. Daniel G. Taylor.
M.R. 18 Apl 1850.

28 Mar 1828   Alfred Taylor and Rachel Wilson. Sur. Willis Luttrell.
Min. Joshua Adams. M.R. 2 Apl 1828.

12 Jan 1832   Anderson Taylor and Nancy Canaday. Sur. Jefferson
Taylor. Min. John Conner. M.R. 15 Jan 1832.

 8 Feb 1800   David Taylor and Nancy Penn. Sur. Jonathan Hanby.

22 Nov 1838   David P. Taylor and Malinda Dehart, daughter of
Elijah Dehart. Sur. E. J. Dehart.
Min. Jesse Jones. M.R. 27 Nov 1838.

14 Dec 1840   George W. Taylor and Hanah Maria Kasey. Sur. John N.
Kasey. Min. Joshua Adams. M.R. 24 Oct 1840.

25 Dec 1806   James Taylor and Tabitha Boaz. Sur. James Boaz.

23 Nov 1825   Jefferson Taylor and Mary Adams. Sur. William Ayres.
Min. Stephen Hubbard. M.R. 1 Nov 1825.

21 Oct 1828   John Taylor and Jane Via. Min. John Washburn.

26 Oct 1805   John Taylor and Elizabeth Pedigo, daughter of Joseph
Pedigo. Sur. Nathaniel Hilton. Min. Jesse Jones.

21 Oct 1828   John Taylor and Jane Ivie, daughter of Peter Ivie.
Sur. Jennings Moore. Wit. Francis Ivie.

 7 Mar 1815   Reuben Taylor and Nancy Gray. Sur. Powell Gray.
Min. Maning Hill.

12 Dec 1853   William A. Taylor, son of Jefferson & Mary Taylor,
and Adaline Adams, daughter of Notley P. & Sealy
Adams. Wit. John S. Adams. Min. G.W. Conner.

 5 Jan 1834   Benjamin Terry and Sarah Foley. Min. John Conner.

22 Jan 1852   Nathan B. Terry and Exoney Pendleton. Min. G.W. Conner.

 9 Feb 1825   Samuel Terry and Jane Hall. Sur. Nathan Hall.
Min. John Conner. M.R. 17 Feb 1825..but, lists the
bride as Jeney Helton.

12 Aug 1817   Reuben Thacker and Permelia Murphy, daughter of
Alex Murphy. Sur. A. Staples. Min. Peter Frans.
M.R. 13 Aug 1817.

11 Jan 1838 Adam Thomas and Sally Moran, daughter of Nelson Moran. Sur. David Owen. Wit. John Moran.

13 Oct 1853 Archibald J. Thomas and Elizabeth Ann Short. Min. Jesse Jones.

19 Jan 1813 Benjamin Thomas and Elizabeth Mills, daughter of Richard Mills. Min. Peter Frans. M.R. 21 Jan 1813.

17 Mar 1795 Charles Thomas,Jr. and Deborah Jordan, daughter of Thomas B. Jordan. Sur. Charles Thomas. Min. John Pedigo.

22 Dec 1841 Charles C. Thomas and Rebecca Dehart. Min. Jesse Jones.

18 Jan 1844 Edward Thomas and Elizabeth D. Brown. Sur. Martin Cloud. Min. Joshua Adams.

16 Dec 1819 Fleming Thomas and Delila Hall. Sur. John Hall. Min. Stephen Hubbard. M.R. 19 Dec 1819.

19 Nov 1845 George Thomas and Susan Thomas, daughter of Joseph Thomas. Sur. Joseph Thomas. Min. Jesse Jones.

16 Dec 1843 James Thomas and Cynthia Thomas. Sur. Fleming J. Canaday. Min. Jesse Jones.

17 Oct 1811 John Thomas and Polly Turner. Sur. Adam Turner.

12 Dec 1836 John W. Thomas, Jr. and Lucinda Moran, daughter of Nelson Moran. Sur. John J. Gough. Wit. John Moran and Elizabeth Moran. Min. Jesse Jones. M.R. 15 Dec 1836.

23 Jan 1851 Joseph Thomas and Oney Thomas. Min. John Conner.

14 Mar 1808 Nicholas Thomas and Polly Reeves. Sur. James Keaton. Min. Lewis Foster. M.R. 17 Mar 1808.

14 Dec 1826 Peter Thomas and Sarah Akers. Sur. Nathaniel Akers. Min. Stephen Hubbard. M.R. 31 Dec 1826.

17 Dec 1840 R. C. Thomas and Rebecca Dehart, daughter of Elijah Dehart,Sr. Sur. Crawford Turner.

9 Apl 1795 Richard Thomas and Elizabeth Ferrell. Sur. John Ferrell. Min. John Pedigo. M.R. 10 Apl 1795.

24 Nov 1825 Richard Thomas and Martha Turner. Sur. Adam Turner. Min. Stephen Hubbard.

15 Oct 1834 Richard Thomas,son of Pleasant Thomas, and Esther Harbour. Sur. Joseph Thomas.

3 Nov 1843 Robert A. Thomas and Eliza Jane Ivie, daughter of
           John W. Ivie. Sur. Jabez G. Dyer. Wit. John H. Ivie.
           Min. Joshua Adams. M.R. 7 Nov 1843.

4 Mar 1840 Samuel Thomas and Phebe Willis. Sur. Parker Hall.

7 Apl 1849 Samuel Thomas and MaryThomas, daughter of Joseph
           Thomas Sr. who acts as surety.

4 Jul 1846 Stephen Thomas and Sarah Janney, daughter of Isaac
           Janney. Sur. John Janney. Min. Joshua Adams.

26 Dec 1822 Washington Thomas and Elizabeth Taylor. Sur. Enoch
           Bridwell. Min. Maning Hill.

21 Mar 1806 Washington Thomas and Polly Frans. Sur. William Frans.
           Min. Maning Hill.

20 Apl 1844 Austin Thompson and Mary(Polly) Pike. Sur. Isaac Pike.
           Min. Julius Terrell. M.R. 22 Apl 1844.

15 Jul 1835 Claibourn Thompson, son of Elisha Thompson of Floyd
           Co,Va., and Mary Bolling, daughter of Gabriel Bolling.
           Sur. Gabriel Bolling. Wit. James Thompson.
           M.R. 28 Jul 1835.

27 Feb 1806 Francis Thompson and Eliza Hubbard. Sur. William
           Thompson. Min. Stephen Hubbard. M.R. 13 Mar 1806.

3 Oct 1797 Henry Thompson and Lucy Harris, daughter of Sara
           Harris. Sur. Nathan Morrison. Min. Jesse Jones.

13 Oct 1836 James Thompson and Sarah Barnard(Barnett).
           Sur. Nathaniel Thompson. Min. Nathaniel Thompson.
           M.R. 20 Oct 1836.

3 May 1819 Jesse Thompson and Frances Hill. Sur. Isaac W. Hill.
           Min. Jesse Jones. M.R. 13 May 1819.

6 Aug 1830 John Thompson and Patsey(Martha) Bowman. Sur. Tyre
           Bowman. Min. Thomas Whitlock.

16 Aug 1830 John Thompson and Nancy Vase. Sur. Greenville Willis.
           Min. Thomas Whitlock.

24 Dec 1844 Mathew S. Thompson and Mary F. Sandefur.
           Sur. S. G. Staples.

12 Jun 1836 Nelson Thompson and Elizabeth Bowman. Sur. Josiah
           Morefield. Min. Thomas Whitlock.

26 Nov 1849 Reuben Thompson and Elizabeth Laymen. Sur. George
           Layman. Min. G. W. Conner. M.R. 29 Nov 1849.

15 Oct 1832 Richard Thomson and Mahala Barnard. Sur. Isham Barnard.
             Min. Nathaniel Thompson. M.R. 30 Oct 1832.

19 Dec 1827 Thomas Thompson and Milly Lawson. Sur. William Lawson.

11 Mar 1824 William Thompson and Joanna E.M. Sandefer, daughter
             of M. Sandefer. Min. Stephen Hubbard.

26 Sep 1805 William Thompson and Hannah Hubbard. Sur. Dandridge
             Slaughter. Min. Stephen Hubbard. M.R. 3 Oct 1805.

24 Apl 1816 Jacob Tice and Jane Hall, daughter of Thomas R. Hall.
             Sur. Fleming Hall. Min. Jesse Jones.

18 Apl 1822 Nicholas Tice and Elizabeth Thomas. Sur. Pleasant
             Thomas.

 7 Jul 1823 William Tinch and Mary Purdy. Sur. William Hill.
             Wit. John Purdy.

28 Nov 1843 Aaron B. Tilley and Elizabeth Anglin. Sur. Andrew J.
             Allen. Phillip Anglin gives consent for Elizabeth.
             Min. Joshua Adams. M.R. 2 Dec 1843.

30 Oct 1794 Adam Tittle and Liddy Adams. Sur. Anthony Tittle,
             Jacob Adams,Jr., and Peter Adams.
             Min. George Dodson. M.R. 5 Nov 1794.

       1830 William Toler and Lucy Abington. Min. John C. Traylor.

25 Oct 1828 William Townley and Nancy Nichols, daughter of
             B. Nichols. Sur. Gregory Hagood.

20 Nov 1840 William Townley and Shermia(Shemina) Midkiff.
             Sur. William Watson. Min. John Conner. M.R. 22 Nov
             1840.

27 Jan 1827 G. W. Trammel and Nancy Brim. Sur. James Brim.

 8 Jan 1846 John S. Travis and Milly Shelton, daughter of Polly
             Shelton. Sur. George D. Marshall. Min. Joshua Adams.

 5 Jun 1819 Thomas J. Travis and Susan Abington, daughter of
             Bowls Abington. Sur. Robert Anglin.

13 Apl 1840 Abel Trent and Eliza Varner, daughter of Mary Varner.
             Sur. Caleb Harris. Min. John Washburn. M.R. 16 Apl 1840.

 5 Dec 1835 Field Trent and Sally Nowlin. Sur. James Nowlin.
             Min. Joshua Adams.

 6 Feb 1821 Zacheriah Trent and Nancy Purdy,daughter of Mary Purdy.
             Sur. Thomas Hollandsworth. Min. Peter Frans.
             M.R. 11 Feb 1821.

14 Dec 1840   James B. Tucker, of Surry Co.,N.C., and Jane Fowlkes, daughter of Anderson Fowlkes. Sur. Frances Lyon.

8 Mar 1843   John Tuder and Nancy Dillon, daughter of Carrington Dillon. Sur. Jesse Dillon. Min. Joshua Adams. M.R. 9 Mar 1843.

24 Jan 1840   William Tuder and Joicy Purdy, daughter of Ezekiel Purdy. Sur. Robert Tuder. Min. Joshua Adams. M.R. 28 Jan 1840.

31 Aug 1848   Anderson Tuggle and Frances Martin. Sur. Hardin Fulcher. Min. Joshua Adams.

15 Oct 1796   Charles Tuggle and Selah Simmons. Sur. Ruth Atkinson. Min. John Nunns.

20 Jan 1803   Henry Tuggle and Patsey Brammer, daughter of Burgis Brammer. Sur. John Tuggle. Wit. William Brammer.

29 Jul 1846   Henry Tuggle and Lucy A. E. Moir, daughter of A. A. Moir. Sur. A. A. Moir. Min. Joshua Adams.

27 Jan 1814   James Tuggle and Nancy Alexander. Sur. A. Turner.

5 Mar 1830   James Tuggle, son of James Tuggle, and Mecca(Micky) Frances. Sur. William A. Sandefer. Min. Bird Lowe.

6 Aug 1832   James Tuggle and Sarah Kendrick, daughter of Auslun?? Kendrick. Sur. Thomas Penn. Wit. Levi Smith. Min. John Washburn.

15 Jan 1852   Joel E. Tuggle and Leeanna McGhee. Min. Joshua Adams.

27 Dec 1816   John Tuggle and Nancy Sneed. Sur. David Perkins. Min. Jesse Jones. M.R. 5 Jan 1817.

27 Feb 1816   John Tuggle and Elizabeth Burnett. Sur. William Brammer.

16 Aug 1826   Adam Turner,Jr. and Lucey Nowlin. Sur. Richard Nowlin. Min. Stephen Hubbard. M.R. 24 Aug 1826.

10 Mar 1827   Admire Turner and Ruth Joyce. Sur. Alexander Joyce. Min. Maning Hill. M.R. 11 Mar 1827.

15 Mar 1838   Charles Turner and Violet Hall, daughter of Sarah Hall. Sur. Francis Turner. Min. Jesse Jones. M.R. 23 Mar 1838.

13 Jun 1791   Charles Crain Turner and Polly Frazer. Sur. George Corn.

14 Nov 1833 Crawford Turner and Susanna Ross. Sur. Daniel Ross.
            Min. Stephen Hubbard. M.R. 26 Nov 1833.

   Dec 1853 Creed O. Turner, son of O. Turner. Wit. Tazwell A.
            Turner and George Turner (Consent note).

25 Nov 1852 Fleming Turner and Nancy Rakes, daughter of Lucinda
            Rakes. Wit. Samuel J. Rakes. Min. John Conner.

16 Jan 1817 Francis Turner and Nancy Thomas, daughter of Charles
            Thomas,Jr. Sur. Adam Turner. Min. Stephen Hubbard.
            M.R. 21 Jan 1817.

15 Dec 1825 George Washington Turner, son of John Turner, and
            Lucy Thomas. Sur. Richard Thomas. Wit. Shad. Turner.
            Min. Stephen Hubbard. M.R. 22 Dec 1825.

24 Dec 1847 Greenwood Turner and Rebecca Ayers, daughter of
            Thomas J. Ayers. Sur. William H. Ayers.
            Min. Joshua Adams.

12 Dec 1809 Jackson Turner and Susanah Short. Min. Jesse Jones.

27 Jan 1796 James Turner and Elizabeth Harris.
            Sur. Alexander Lackey.

26 Dec 1796 James Turner and Ann Reeves, daughter of George
            Reeves. Sur. Samuel Staples. Wit. Thomas Reeves
            and John Turner.

 2 Nov 1801 James Turner of Henry Co. Va., and Elizabeth Koger,
            consent of John Koger. Sur. David Tittle.

18 Dec 1848 Jefferson Turner and Susan C. Short, daughter of
            John Short. Sur. Francis Turner and John Short.

 5 Jan 1793 John Turner and Judah(Judith) Roberson, daughter
            of David Roberson. Sur. William Roberson. Wit.
            James Lackey. Min. Robert Jones.

15 Oct 1804 John Turner and Nancy Burnett, consent of John
            Burnett. Sur. James Hall. Min. Stephen Hubbard.

27 Jul 1820 John Turner and Scyntha Poore. Sur. Lewis Turner.
            Min.Maning Hill.

17 Oct 1805 John Turner and Lucy Nolen. Min. William H. Robertson.

31 Mar 1814 John Turner and Sally Burnett. Sur. William Burnett.

13 Sep 1838 John B. Turner and Exoney Via, daughter of William
            Via. Sur. John Turner. Min. Joshua Adams.
            M.R. 19 Sep 1838.

20 Feb 1850   John G. Turner and Nancy Thomas, daughter of
Delilah Thomas. Sur. Francis Turner. Wit. William
F. Hall and America Thomas.

12 Oct 1805   Joseph Turner and -----. Sur. Francis Nowlin.

16 Dec 1830   Richard Turner and Celia George. Sur. Micah Jonsen.
Min. Joshua Adams. M.R. 21 Dec 1830.

8 Feb 1840   Robert Turner and Elizabeth McGuffin. Sur. Joseph C.
McGuffin.

28 Jan 1813   Shadrack Turner and Judith Burnett, daughter of
John Burnett. Sur. John Cox. Min. Lewis Foster.
M.R. 18 Feb 1814.

30 Dec 1851   Stephen H. Turner and Malissa R. Turner.
Min. Daniel G. Taylor.

22 Feb 1847   Tazwell A. Turner and Mary Jane Carter, daughter of
Banes Carter. Sur. John P. Carter.

5 Dec 1825   Thompson Turner and Nancy Fitzgerald. Sur. John
Gilbert. Min. Bird Lowe.

2 Jan 1817   William Turner and Elizabeth Philpott(on Bond is
listed as Turner). Sur. James Via. Min. Stephen
Hubbard. M.R. 2 Feb 1817.

26 Dec 1850   William Turner and Mary J. Vaughan. Min. G. W. Conner.

5 Feb 1846   William Turner and Mary Frances Ayers. Thomas Ayers
certifies that Mary Frances is of age. Sur. William
Ayers. Min. Joshua Adams.

20 Feb 1817   Ratf---umphy ???? and Bridget Grimes.
Min. John Conner.

24 Oct 1842   Phillip Vass and Nancy Richardson.
Sur. James Richardson.

23 Oct 1805   Edmond Vancel and Rachel Landreth. Sur. Elihu Ayers.
Min. Thomas Whitlock.

7 Apl 1849   David Vaughan and Sally Parr. Sur. Herbert Shelton.
Min. G. W. Conner. M.R. 8 Apl 1849.

30 May 1831   David Vaughan and Fanny Martin. Min. John Conner.

21 Mar 1845   John Vaughn and Catherine Baize. Sur. John Beiys.

26 Sep 1848   Joshua A. Vaughn and Caroline Matilda Hollandsworth,
dau of German Hollandsworth. Sur. Samuel Harris.
Wit. Chesley Hollandsworth. Min. Joshua Adams.

23 Feb 1829   Thomas Vaughan and Tabithia Martin, daughter of Moses Martin. Sur. Jefferson Taylor. Wit. George R. Davis and John Martin. Min. Joshua Adams.

5 Feb 1795   William Thomas Vaughan, son of Agnes Vaughan, and Martha(Patsey) Reynolds. Sur. Bartlett Reynolds. Min. Isaac Adams. M.R. 11 Feb 1795.

15 Oct 1835   Wilson T. Vaughan and Susanah Dehart. Sur. Elijah Dehart. Min. Joshua Adams. M.R. 12 Nov 1835.

17 Oct 1792   Jonathan Vess and Elizabeth Heron, daughter of Andrew Heron. Sur. James Heron. Wit. Benjamin Fletcher and James Pigg. Min. George Dodson. M. R. 18 Oct 1792.

19 May 1838   Anderson Vest and Rodah Cockram. Sur. Edward Cockram.

25 Mar 1833   Henry T. Vest and Elizabeth Palmer. Sur. John D. Vest.

4 Aug 1839   John Vest and Delphia Martin. Sur. William Martin. Min. Joshua Adams. M.R. 5 Aug 1839.

8 Oct 1824   Littleberry Vess(Vest) and Nancy McGee, consent of Mary Mac gehee. Sur. John Gustler. Wit. David Underwood. Min. John Washburn.

13 Mar 1828   Alexander Via and Fanny Wright. Sur. Elijah Dehart. Min. Stephen Hubbard. M.R. 23 Mar 1828.

26 Oct 1835   Fleming Via and Mary Corn, daughter of Jesse Corn. Sur. Jesse Corn. Wit. Permelia Corn. Min. Joshua Adams. M.R. 1 Nov 1835.

5 Mar 1818   James Via and Nancy Godard. Sur. William Via. Wit. William Martin. Min. Stephen Hubbard.

14 Dec 1827   James Via, Jr. and Polly Dehart. Sur. Thomas Dehart. Min. Stephen Hubbard. M.R. 16 Dec 1827.

5 Apl 1829   Isaac Via, son of Josiah Via, and Patsey Cockram, daughter of Edward Cockram. Sur. Edward Cockram. Wit. Joel Barber.

16 Aug 1816   Richard Via and Franky Via, daughter of William Via. Sur. John Thomas.

7 Sep 1836   Robert Via and Elizabeth Spencer, daughter of Benjamin Spencer. Sur. Benjamin Spencer. Min. Joshua Adams.

27 Apl 1850   Sparrel Via and Mary Cockram, daughter of Edward Cockram. Sur. Edward Cockram.

30 May 1800   William Via and Elizabeth Ingram. Sur. Alexander
Ingram. Min. Nathan Hall. M.R. 6 Jun 1800.

30 Aug 1850   William Via, Jr. and Mary Hooker. Sur. John Martin.
Min. Joshua Adams.

 8 Sep 1827   William Via, Jr. and Charity Chambers.
Sur. John Chambers.

23 Dec 1851   Elijah D. Via or Viars and Nancy Akers.

22 Mar 1831   Daniel Vipperman and Nancy Clifton. Sur. Thomas
Grogan and John Cassell.

 5 Oct 1848   Daniel Vipperman and Martha Hall. Sur. Joseph Hall.
Min. G. W. Conner.

27 Dec 1836   Nicholas Vipperman and Martha Rickman. Sur. John R.
Rickman. Wit. Caleb Griffith and William Griffith.
Min. John Conner. M.R. 28 Dec 1836.

13 Mar 1823   Jacob Wade and Susanah McBride. Sur. G. Washington.
Min. Jesse Jones. M.R. 3 Apl 1823.

18 Dec 1808   James Wade and Nancy Thomas. Sur. Benjamin Thomas.
Min. Maning Hill. M.R. 21 Dec 1808.

19 Dec 1841   Marshall Wade of Franklin Co. Va., and America H.
Jones Via, daughter of James Via. (Her mother was
a Jones). Sur. James Via. Wit. E. S. Corn.

22 Aug 1816   William Wade and Betsy Shelor. Sur. Elkanah Ayers.
Min. Thomas Whitlock.

 5 Jan 1793   Benjamin Walden and Betsy(Elizabeth) Frazer, daughter
of Robert and Elizabeth Frasher. Sur. Giles Martin.
Min. George Dodson. M.R. 17 Jan 1793.

28 Apl 1802   Moses Walden and Mary Smallman. Sur. Moses Godard.

17 Jul 1791   Nathan Walden and Nancy Frazer. Sur. Robert Frazer.

30 Sep 1807   Richard Walden and Sarah Cruise. Min. Lewis Foster.

13 Aug 1792   William Walden and Margaret King. Sur. Samuel King
and Moses Walden.

14 Mar 1818   William Walden and Mary Cooper. Sur. Hutson Akers.

28 Mar 1848   James A. Waller and Jane Hanby. Sur. Hardin H. Hanby.
Min. Joshua Adams.

 8 Mar 1830   Arnold Walker of Henry Co.Va.,and Jane Cahill. Sur.
Capt. Edward Philpott. Min. John Turner.
M.R. 9 Mar 1830.

6 Jan 1829   James T. Walker and Onah(Oney) Morrison.
             Sur. Thomas Morrison. Min. Jesse Jones. M.R.
             28 Jan 1829.

28 Dec 1844   John Walker and Ruth Hanby. Min. Joshua Adams.

18 Sep 1851   Linville Walker and Permelia Martin.
             Min. Joshua Adams.

9 Nov 1828   Samuel Walker and Sarah Smith. Sur. Tandy Walker,
             and William East. Min. John Turner. M.R. 8 Nov 1828.

16 Mar 1792   John Ward, son of Thomas Ward, and Frances(Franky)
             Sublett, daughter of James Sublett. Sur. William
             Sublett.

1 Dec 1794   Thomas Ward,Jr. and Elizabeth Sisem. Sur. Thomas
             Ward,Sr. Min. Isaac Adams.

31 May 1804   William Ward and Nancy Coomer, daughter of Richard
             Coomer. Sur. Richard Davidson. Wit. Dandridge
             Slaughter.

26 Aug 1804   William Ward and Mildred Landreth. Sur. Samuel
             Cannon. Min. Thomas Whitlock.

16 Jul 1811   James T. Ware and Mary Hardredy. Sur. Levy Johnson.

1 Oct 1797   Phillip Ware, son of Samuel Ware, and Patsey Mayo.
             Sur. John Philips. Min. Isaac Adams.

8 Nov 1807   William Ware and Elizabeth Corn, daughter of George
             Corn,Sr.. Wit. George Corn.

2 Dec 1834   John H. Washburn and Rozanah J. Reynolds, daughter
             of Thomas Reynolds. Sur. Thomas J. Reynolds.
             Min. John Washburn,Sr. M.R. 4 Dec 1834.

22 Dec 1846   David Washington, son of Soloman Washington, and
             Ann(Anna) Pendleton, daughter of Prier Pendleton.
             Sur. James Dillon. Min. G. W. Conner.

7 Feb 1848   Hiram Watkins of Henry Co. Va., and Leminia Harbour,
             daughter of James Harbour. Sur. James W. Ross.
             Min. Joshua Adams.

10 Jan 1828   James Watkins and Sarah Collings. Sur. Joshua Watkins.
             Min. Joshua Adams.

16 Nov 1819   James Watts and Elizabeth Sharp. Sur. Peter Cassady.
             Min. Brett Stovall.

3 Dec 1837   Jonathan Watson and Harriett Clark, daughter of
             Michael Clark. Sur. William Gustler.

19 Dec 1850   John S. Watson and Leoney Morrison.
              Min. Daniel G. Taylor.

10 Mar 1816   Thomas H. Watson and Fanney McKinzey. Sur. John
              Sharp. Min. H. Fitzgerald.

11 Mar 1830   Floyd Webb and Polly Critz. Sur. Hamon Critz.
              Min. John Jones.

10 May 1807   Giles Webb and Rachel Horton. Sur. Abraham Penn.
              Min. Thomas Whitlock. M.R. 15 May1807.

13 Jan 1812   Henry Webb and Catharine Harrel. Sur. Jesse
              Harrel. Min. Thomas Whitlock.

25 Nov 1844   Henry Webb, son of Jacob Webb, and Susan M.
              Shelor. Sur. John Shelor. Wit. Lucy Webb
              and Jacob Horton.

20 Dec 1804   John Webb and Susanna Parr. Sur. William Parr.

17 Oct 1815   John Webb and Hannah Cox. Sur. Abraham Penn.
              Min. Thomas Whitlock.

10 Feb 1812   John Webb and Lockey R. Smith, daughter of
              Nathaniel Smith. Sur. Samuel Lackey.
              Min. Brett Stovall. M.R. 13 Feb 1812.

20 Apl 1823   Silvester Webb and Rachel Thomas. Sur. John
              Jones. Min. Maning Hill. M.R. 10 Jun 1823.

16 Sep 1812   Valentine Webb and Betsy Abshear. Sur. Jacob
              Griggs. Min. Thomas Whitlock. M.R. 11 Sep 1812.

28 Jul 1825   William Webb,Jr. and Betsy(Elizabeth) Gray.
              Sur. Daniel Gray. Min. Bird Lowe.

 9 May 1840   Mifflin Weeks and Eury Hutson. Sur. Fleming
              Canaday. Wit. William Underwood.

26 Dec 1833   Benjamin Well and Elizabeth Griffin.
              Min. Silas Minter.

10 Oct 1827   George Wells and Elizabeth Knighton, daughter of
              John Knighton. Sur. John C. Knighton.

23 Dec 1849   George Wells and Elizabeth Mitchell, daughter of
              James H. Mitchell. Sur. Gressom Hagood.
              Min. W. M. Schoolfield.

 7 Apl 1827   Reuben Wells and Nancy Thomas, daughter of
              Washington Thomas. Sur. William Frans.
              Min. John Washburn. M.R. 11 Apl 1827.

25 Apl 1792   William M. Wells and Elizabeth Clark,daughter of
              John Clark. Sur. William Deal. Wit. Isaac Going
              and Elisha Wells. Min. George Dodson.
              M.R. 6 Apl 1792.

29 Sep 1828   Joshua West son of Hester West, and Mary(Polly) Hurt. Sur. John Hurt and John Terry. Min. John Conner. M.R. 2 Oct 1828.

21 Dec 1849   Edward Jefferson Whalen, son of Pleasant Whalen, and Emily Balisle, daughter of Barnabas Balisle,Sr. Sur. Pleasant Whalen. Min. Joshua Adams.

3 Sep 1841   Moses Whorley and Milly Lewis, daughter of Alvin Lewis. Sur. Hamon Critz.

7 Jan 1829   Alexander White and Patsy Willis. Sur. Greensville Willis. Min. Thomas Whitlock. M.R. 7 Jan 1828.

29 Dec 1847   Thomas White and Louisa Brian, daughter of William Brian. Sur. William Brian .Wit. Martha Brian and Sally Brian. Min. Jeremiah Burnett.

8 May 1833   Jorial Whitlock and Anna Cockram, daughter of Edward Cockram. Sur. Brice Cockram. Wit. Mary Cockram and David Cockram. Min. Stephen Hubbard.

10 Apl 1844   Martin Whitlock and Ruth Willis. Sur. Martin Cloud. Min. J. Boyd.

8 Mar 1804   Richard Whitlock and Sarah Hancock. Sur. Paul Chiles Ingram. Min. Reuben Short.

10 Jan 1827   Thesterton Whitlock, consent of Sarah Whitlock, and Nancy Martin daughter of Mary Chivers. Sur. Henry Whitlock. Wit. Elizabeth Price.

1 Sep 1823   Pleasant Whitlow and Peggy Carter. Sur. John Koger. Min. John C. Traylor.

13 Oct 1849   John B. Whitten and Mary Ann Jackson, daughter of James A. Jackson. Sur. Thompson C. Washburn. Min. Joshua Adams. M.R. 16 Oct 1849.

11 Oct 1849   Andrew Jackson Wigginton, son of George Wiggington, and Martha R. Hudnall, daughter of Richard Hudnall. Wit. Charles W. Hudnall. Min. D. G. Taylor. M. R. 21 Feb 1849.

28 Dec 1805   Israel Wilks and Mary Coombs. Sur. Amos Coombs. Min. Robert Jones. M.R. 29 Jan 1805.

29 Jun 1826   Allen Willard and Fanny Collins, daughter of Elizabeth Collins. Sur. Jefferson Pennington. Min. Bird Lowe.

22 Jan 1827   John Willard and Elizabeth Nelson. Sur. Allen Willard. Min. Bird Lowe.

25 Sep 1794   Aaron Williams and Elizabeth Lee, consent of John Lee.
Sur. James Bartlett. Wit. John Brammer.

7 Sep 1845   Benjamin M. Williams and Caroline Vanhook. Sur.
Anthony M. Dupuy. Min. William M. Schoolfield.
M.R. 8 Sep 1845.

19 May 1838   Caleb F. Williams and Elizabeth Gilbert. Sur. Phillip
Askew. Min. John Washburn. M.R. 31 May 1838.

12 Dec 1813   James Williams and Jane Reeves, daughter of George
Reeves. Wit. Elisha Packwood. Min. Stephen Hubbard.

26 Aug 1823   John Williams and Sally Hilton. Min. John Conner.

23 Dec 1822   John B. Williams and Sally Helms. Sur. Jacob Helms.

16 Jul 1845   John B. Williams and Easter Foley, daughter of
Christopher Foley. Sur. John Cassell. Wit. Elizabeth
Foley. Min. Joshua Adams. M.R. 17 Jul 1845.

31 Dec 1850   Marshall G. Williams and Amanda Whaling.
Min. John Conner.

5 Feb 1840   Sparril D. Williams, consent of J.B. Williams, and
Oney Branch. Sur. James Branch. Min. Joshua Adams.
M.R. 6 Feb 1840.

21 Dec 1833   Berryman Willis and Elizabeth Griffin, daughter of
Richard Griffin. Sur. Bluford Griffin.

27 Dec 1821   James Willis and Mahalia Wright. Sur. Marvel Bowling.
Min. Stephen Hubbard. M.R. 27 Dec 1821.

12 Apl 1802   Joel Willis and Anna Askew, daughter of Daniel Askew.
Sur. Isaac Dodson.

12 Jan 1802   John Willis and Jane Redman. Sur. Ignatious Redman.

14 May 1792   Joseph Willis and Peggy Walker, whose parents are
deceased. Sur. David Rogers. Wit. Humb. Lyon and
Henry Smith.

4 Jun 1794   Joseph Willis and Sally Nowling, daughter of James
Nowling. Wit. Joel Willis.

17 Oct 1792   Thomas Willis and Leta Fain, daughter of William
Fain. Sur. James Pigg. Wit. David Willis.
Min. George Dodson. M.R. 5 Nov 1792.

13 Dec 1795   William Willis and Levinia Davidson, daughter of
David Davidson. Sur. Joel Willis. Wit. David Willis.

18 Jul 1792   John Wilmouth and Elizabeth Mullins, daughter of Ambrose Mullins. Sur. Abraham Penn. Min. George Dodson. M.R. 19 Jul 1792.

4 Feb 1826   Charles Wilson and Jane Anglin, daughter of Elizabeth Anglin. Sur. Elisha Anglin. Wit. William McMillion. Min. Joshua Adams.

23 Jan 1817   Sollamon Wilson and Rachel Martin. Sollamon Wilson went off 2 years and 4 months later with one of Rachel's sisters. She has not heard of him for seven years, and according to Rachel's sister he is now dead. 1 Apl 1828.

12 Oct 1807   William K. Wilson and Fanny Johns. Her father lives in Montgomery Co. Va., and Fanny is residing with her Uncle Elijah Lyon. Sur. Robert Johns.

28 Oct 1818   Elijah Wimbush and Mary Stovall, daughter of Brett Stovall. Sur. Archelaus H. Stovall. Min. Maning Hill. M. R. 29 Oct 1818.

6 Dec 1846   William H. Wimbush and Rebecca E. Reynolds, daughter of Thomas Reynolds. Sur. Peter M. Reynolds. Min. Joshua Adams. M.R. 10 Dec 1846.

21 Apl 1853   John Wimmer and Mary B. Cloud. Wit. Martin Cloud. Min. William Lawson.

28 May 1841   Burwell Winfree, consent of Dorcas Winfrey, and Orinai Hutson. Sur. Mifflin Weeks. Wit. William Underwood and Elizabeth Underwood.

23 Nov 1828   James Witcher of Pittsylvania Co.,and Nancy Corn. Sur. Jesse Corn. Wit. Ephram Witcher. Vincent Witcher, guardian for James Witcher, gives his consent. Min. Stephen Hubbard.

4 May 1843   Adam H. Witt and Permelia Foley, daughter of James Foley,Sr. Sur. Saunders Witt. Wit. Richard B. Foley. Min. Joshua Adams.

14 Jul 1820   Saunders Witt and Viley Helms. Sur. S. G. Staples. Min. John Conner. M.R. 20 Jul 1820.

12 Oct 1809   Silas Witt and Matilda Willis. Sur. William Adams.

12 Jul 1819   William Witt and Fanny Carter. Sur. Abram Staples. Min. Peter Frans.

23 Feb 1799   William Witt and Lucy Reeves, daughter of George Reeves. Sur. Richard Thomas. Wit. Samuel Packwood. Min. Joseph Pedigo. M.R. 24 Feb 1799.

6 Jan 1846   William Witt and Virgina Potter, daughter of
William Potter. Sur. Samuel Staples.
Min. Joshua Adams.

28 Dec 1829 Asa Wood and Polly Allen. Sur. Andrew Allen.
Min. John Washburn. M.R. 3 Jan 1830.

10 Mar 1826 Alexander Wood and Bethenia Brammer, daughter of
John Brammer. Sur. William Brammer.

23 Sep 1830 Edward Wood and Mary Moran. Min. Jesse Jones.

8 Jul 1853   Gabriel Wood age 19, son of Jeremiah and Mary
Wood, and Louella Akers age 18, daughter of
Fleming and Nancy Akers. Wit. Fleming Akers.
Min. G. W. Conner. M.R. 14 Jul 1853.

13 May 1853 Isaac Wood and Lavinia E. Akers. Wit. Fleming
Akers and Sarah Ann Akers. Min. G. W. Conner.

4 Dec 1853   James Wood and Elizabeth Meredith. Min. Jesse Jones.

15 Jun 1824 Jeremiah Wood age 21 and Polly Dehart, daughter of
Gabriel Dehart. Sur. Stephen Hubbard.
Min. Stephen Hubbard. M.R. 15 Jun 1824.

4 Oct 1821   John Wood and Lucinda Dehart. Sur. James Dehart.
Min. Stephen Hubbard. M.R. 4 Oct 1821.

27 Nov 1848 John Wood and Martha J. Hall, daughter of Rowland
Hall. Sur. William W. Hall.

19 Dec 1850 John Wood and Martha Davenport. Min. Joshua Adams.

10 Dec 1809 John Wood and Jenny Glaspy. Sur. John Glaspy.
Min. Lewis Foster. M.R. 7 Dec 1809.

22 Apl 1828 Peter Wood, son of Richard Wood, and Nancy Moran.
Sur. Isaac Adams. Wit. Jesse Viars.

8 Sep 1823   Richard Wood and Nancy (Fanny) Brammer. Sur. John
Brammer. Min. Stephen Hubbard. M.R. 9 Sep 1823.

Oct 1850   Richard A. Wood, son of Alexander Wood.(Consent).

17 Oct 1850 Richard Wood Jr, and Lucinda Wood. Min. G.W. Conner.

5 Feb 1852   Richard Wood and Judith Ann Short. Min. Jesse Jones.

17 Nov 1844 Stephen Wood and Rachel Thomas. Sur. Joseph Thomas.
Min. Jesse Jones.

20 Apl 1851   William G. Wood and Jincey Collins. Min. Joshua Adams.

28 Sep 1846   George Woody of Henry Co. Va., and Elizabeth J. Turner.
              Sur. John Turner. Min. Arnold Walker.

 4 Jan 1840⁻ Thomas B. Woolwine, son of John Woolwine of Montgomery
              Co.,Va., and Sally (Sarah) Adams. Sur. Notley P. Adams.
              Wit. Phillip Woolwine. Min. John Conner. M.R. 6 Jan
              1840.

12 Sep 1822   Shadrack Woosley and Peggy Duvize. Sur. John Hancock.
              Min. Stephen Hubbard. M.R. 5 Sep 1822.

31 Jul 1848   Abner Wray age 30, and Nancy Kelly, an orphan.
              Sur. Samuel C. Ingram. Wit. John Cherry.
              Min. Jeremiah Burnett.

 2 Sep 1796   Joseph Wren and Rebecca McGuffey; consent of Joseph
              McGuffey. Sur. Henry McGuffey.

28 Sep 1846   Daniel E. Wright and Elizabeth Dillard, daughter of
              James Dillard. Sur. John E. Wright.
              Min. Joshua Adams.

17 Jan 1835   Hiram Wright and Mary Hughes. Sur. Laban Wright.
              Min. John Conner.

18 Jan 1846   John B. Wright and Mary Collings. Sur. John Collins.
              Min. Joshua Adams.

 9 Jan 1816   John Wright and Nancy Slaughter. Sur. John Slaughter.
              Min. Stephen Hubbard.

16 Apl 1823   Josiah Wright and Susanah Hixon. Sur. Thomas R. Hall.
              Min. Stephen Hubbard. M.R. 15 May 1823.

30 Sep 1847   Josiah Wright and Sarah Lynch Spencer. Sur. Abraham
              Spencer. M.R. 4 Oct 1847.

14 Oct 1840   Jubal Wright and Emily W. Martin. Sur. James Martin.
              Min. Joshua Adams. M.R. 20 Oct 1840.

14 Jan 1835   Reuben Wright and Delilah Hall. Sur. Russell Hall.

 9 Apl 1845   Robert Wright and Mary Conner. Sur. Chesley Rakes.
              Min. G. W. Conner. M.R. 13 Apl 1845.

13 Jan 1847   Turner Wright and Sarah Dixon, daughter of Martha
              Dixon. Sur. John Janney. Wit. Isaac Janey.

14 Sep 1809   Christopher Young and Margaret Strange, daughter of
              John Strange. Sur. John Strange,Sr.
              Wit. Thomas Joyce.

15 Jan 1833   George Young and Bethane Hall. Sur. Martin Cloud.

4 Feb 1840   George(John) Young and Adelpha Turner. Sur. John
             Turner. Min. Michael Howry.

26 Nov 1828   William Young, son of Peyton Young,Sr., and Elizabeth
             Foster. Sur. Lewis T. Foster. Wit. Peyton Young,Jr.
             Min. John Turner.

13 Nov 1815   Christopher Ziglar and Sarah Mills, daughter of
             Richard Mills. Min. Maning Hill. M.R. 16 Nov 1815.

9 Nov 1828   Leonard C. Zeglar and Zilpha Jones. Sur. Jesse Jones.
             Min. John Jones.

29 Jan 1831   Reuben Ziglar and Lucy Frans, daughter of John Frans.
             Sur. Gabriel Jones. Wit. John G. Lee.
             Min. John Washburn. M.R. 10 Feb 1831.

3 Jan 1851   Richard Ziglar and Catherine Abington, daughter of
             Elizabeth Abington. Min. Daniel G. Taylor.
             M.R. 9 Jan 1851.

15 Sep 1847   John N. Zentmeyer and Martha Penn. Sur. S. G. Staples.
             John Zentmeyer of Floyd Co. Va..Min. John Rich.

12 Oct 1836 John Cassell, son of William Cassell, and Lucinda
Duvall, daughter of John Duvall. Sur. Mark Plaster.
Wit. Jonas Plaster and James Murphy. Min. Joshua
Adams.

 8 Dec 1841 Michael Cassell and Mary Turner, daughter of Lewis
Turner. Sur. John Cassell. Wit. Caleb T. Williams.
Min. Joshua Adams.

21 Oct 1843 William S. Cassell, son of William Cassell,Sr., and
Catherine Edwards, daughter of Brice Edwards. Sur.
Samuel G. Staples. Wit. Jonas Plaster, Austen J.
Cassell and Levina Cassell. Min. Joshua Adams.
M.R. 31 Oct 1843.

        1819 John Castle and Polly Carter. Min. Brett Stovall.

    Jan 1808 James Ceath and Anney Morrison. Min. Wm. Robertson.

14 May 1807 William Ceeton and Susanah Hollandsworth.
Min. Lewis Foster.

 8 Aug 1832 John Chambers and Mary Burch. Sur. Samuel Howell.
Min. John Conner.

15 Oct 1791 Isaac Chandler and Elizabeth Stultz, daughter of
George Stultz. Min. Henry Merritt, elder of the
Methodist Church.

10 Dec 1794 John Chandler and Elizabeth Bennett. Sur. Eliphaz
Shelton.

28 Dec 1830 Seaton Chandler and Hannah Beasley, daughter of
Thomas Beasley. Wit. Hardin Beasley. Min.
Brett Stovall. M.R. 11 Jan 1831.

 9 Sep 1809 William Chandler and Polly Harris. Sur. John Hughes.
Min. Brett Stovall. M.R. 18 Sep 1809.

29 Jun 1852 Alexander C. Chaney and Hester Ann Wilkerson, daughter
of T. P. Wilkerson. Min. William M. Scholfield.

15 Apl 1851 Mathew H. Chaney and Charlotte Woods. Min. William M.
Schoolfield.

22 Oct 1793 John Chapman and Milley Keaton. Sur. William Keaton.
Min. George Dodson. M.R. 27 Oct 1793.

14 Oct 1840 William Chappell and Lydia Deen, daughter of Henry H.
Deen. Sur. Eli Hiatt.

 3 Jan 1828 Joseph Cheatham and Martha Morris, daughter of William
Morris. Wit. Rebecca Bradley and Mary Cheatham.
Min. Joshua Adams. M.R. 5 Jan 1828.

NOTE: This was originally Page 20 A and due to pagination had to be transferred
to the end of the book.

BLACKARD, BLACKHARD
Lucy 116
Nancy 106
Susanah 106

BLACKBURN
Nancy 25
Priscilla 33
Sally 32

BLANCET, BLANCHET, BLANSETT
J. 63
Margaret 1
Martha 88
Polly 31
Rachel 4
Ruth 103

BLANKS
Elizabeth 54

BLEVINES
Elizabeth 87

BOAZ
Agnes 93
Anna 89
Polly 43
Tabitha 117

BOLEN, BOLLING, BOWLIN,
BOWLEN, BOWLING
Frances 51
Hetta 107
Leony F. 59
Lucinda 10
Mary 22
Mary 119
Matilda 41
Mincey 78
Mincey 83
Nancy 25
Sally 96
Sarah 101

BOLT
Elizabeth 54
Winifred 44

BONDURANT
Salley 19

BONS
Patience 95
Rachel 12

BOOKER
Elizabeth F. 49
Nancy 20
Phebe 47
Rebecca 108

BOOTH
Anna 86
Angeline 56
Dinah (Dianna) 58
Rachel 58
Susanah 32
Tamer 86

BOSTICK
Betsy 70

BOWMAN, BOMAN
Elizabeth 51
Elizabeth 119
Gelah 16
Gillah 15
Jane 35
Jency 16
Judy 110
Leatha 38
Lockey 55

BOWMAN, BOMAN, cont'd.
Malinda 109
Mary 60
Mima 12
Nancy 67
Nancy 35
Patsey (Martha) 119
Polly 109
Sarah 78

BOYD
Catherine 111
Malinda 110
Mary 36
Nancy 24
Ony (Laony) 4
Susanah 111

BRAMMER
Bethaniah 43
Bethenia 131
Elizabeth 86
Elizabeth Ann 8
Frances 18
Kiziah 75
Kiziah 76
Letha 79
Lucy 33
Margaret 86
Mary 13
Mary 65
Mary 65
Nancy 8
Nancy 83
Nancy (Fanny) 131
Patsey 121
Rachel 13
Ruth 24
Sarah 2

BRANCH
Barbara 65
Nancy 87
Oney 129

BRANSON
Mary 57

BREAM
C. 78

BREWER
Maria 84

BRIAN
Louisa 128

BRIDGES
Nancy 83
Sally 15

BRIMM, BRIM
Kesiah 12
Lucy 11
Nancy 120

BROWN
Caty 100
Constandestion 100
Elizabeth D. 118
Jane 92
Mary 67
Peggy 38
Tabithia 67

BRYANT, BRIANT
Jane 27
Nancy 81
Sarah 28

BULLARD
Jilsay 112

BURGE
Jane 109
Paissey 116

BURCH
Mary 20

BURNETT
Betsy 62
Elizabeth Eleanor 10
Elizabeth 26
Elizabeth 68
Elizabeth 81
Elizabeth 121
Eliza 74
Frances 7
Jane 11
Jane (Jinny) 50
Judah 69
Judith 123
Lucy 64
Mahala 104
Mary 53
Milley 66
Nancey 30
Nancy 101
Nancy 122
Peggy 113
Permelia 26
Polly 13
Polly 92
Polley 90
Rhoda 56
Ruth Mayo 58
Ruth 93
Sally 122
Sarah 75
Sarah Ann 50
Tilley 110

BURRESS
Frances 36
Nancy Jane 60

CAHILL
Jane 125

CAMPBELL
Lydia Ann 111
Martha 24

CANADAY, CANNADAY
Delila 85
Elizabeth 99
Elizabeth 18
Martha 83
Nancy 117
Polly 50
Susannah 17

CANNON
Nancy 7

CARDWELL
Elizabeth 22

CARTER
Eleanor 34
Elizabeth 40
Fanny 130
Frances 90
Hannah 79
Hannah C. 71
Jencey 26
Louisa E. 82
Lucinda 61
Lucy 61
Malinda 95
+ Mary 21
Matilda 105
Nancy 38
Nancy N. 91

CARTER, cont'd.
Patsy	23
Peggy	128
Polly	4
+ Mary Jane	123
Polly	20
Sally	51
Sarah	42
Sarah F.	106
Sarah Jane	19
Susanah	14

CASSELL
Elizabeth	76
Martha Jane	44
Sally	96

CHAMBERS
Charity	125
Elizabeth	84

CHANDLER
Mary	57
Polly	109
Sally	88

CHANEY
Seley	12

CHEATHAM
Martha	84

CHERRY
Ann	4
Jemima	115

CHITWOOD
Delilah	95
Elizabeth	93
Necey	86
Polly	94
Sally	94

CHRISTIAN
Elizabeth	64
Polley	41

CLARK
Ann	70
Delilah	101
Elizabeth	7
Elizabeth	23
Elizabeth	127
Elizabeth C.	37
Elizabeth M.	117
Elmira R.	66
Elvia	54
Frances	7
Harriett	126
Jane P.	59
Jinsey	94
Lucy	48
Martha	16
Martha	115
Mary	51
Mary C.	18
Mary E.	108
Nancy	65
Roxy	80
Ruth	42
Sally	22
Sally	23
Sally F.	24
Sally N.	67
Sarah C.	72
Sarah J.	68
Susan	93

CLAY
Elizabeth	85
Lucy	10
Nancy	56
Susanah	101

CLEMMONS
Agnes	99
Mary	31

CLEVOR
Rebecca	98

CLIFTON
Lucinda	41
Martha	31
Nancy	11
Nancy	125
Sally (Sarah)	107

CLOUD
Elizabeth Jane	7
Jeston	36
Mary B.	130
Polly	104

COALSON
Jemly	47

COCKRAM
Anna	128
Arta	98
Bashabay	36
Delila	98
Frances	77
Mary	124
Nancy	13
Patsey	124
Rodah	124
Ruth	24
Sarah	13

COCKRAN
Kiziah	74

COLE
Polly	55

COLLINS, COLLINGS
Dida	91
Eleanor	90
Elizabeth	40
Fanny	128
Jane	85
Jincey	132
Joanna	11
July	47
Lydia	97
Mary	132
Nancy	95
Ossie	8
Sarah	108
Sarah	126

COME--
Lucy	114

CONNER
Emilia (Milly)	64
Exoney	1
Exoney	1
Exony L.	34
Judah	98
Judith	65
Lock	47
Martha D.	104
Mary	100
Mary	132
Mary (Polly)	110
Milly	32
Nancy	31
Sally	58

CONSOLVENT
Polly	30

COOK
Elizabeth	37

COOMBS
Mary	128

COMMER
Nancy	126

COOPER
Elizabeth	11
Mary	125

CORN
Drucilla	73
Elizabeth	1
Elizabth	77
Elizabeth	106
Elizabeth	126
Elizabeth T.	26
Malinda	49
Mary	124
Mary (Polly)	3
Mary (Polly)	84
Milly	62
Nancy	21
Nancy	67
Nancy	130
Parmela	116
Phoebe	77
Polly	105
Sarah	69
Susanah	70
Susannah	21
Susannah (Saran)	29

COTHER
Nancy	20

COVINGTON
Martha	7

COX
Elizabeth	48
Elizabeth	50
Elizabeth	17
Febe	38
Hannah	127
Leah	17
Mary	93
Mary	95
Nancy	37
Peggy	48
Permelia	115
Polly	16
Sally	9
Sarah	85

CRADDOCK
Dicy	48
Lucinda	29
Nancy	55
Nancy M.	27
Patsy	62
Susannah	28

CRITZ
Amanda	107
Charlotte D.	116
Elizabeth (Betsy)	6
Martha A.	108
Mary	4
Mary	81
Mary Jane	41
Nancy	30
Nancy	38
Polly	111
Polly	127
Sarah	30
Susan	28

CROSS
Susannah	75

CRUISE, CREWS
Elizabeth	59

CRUISE, CREWS, cont'd.

Frances	65
Lucinda	98
Lucy	28
Mahala	24
Polly	76
Sally	40
Sarah	125
Sarah Jane	3

CRUM

Polly	112
Nancy	115

CRUSENBURY

Milly	61

CRUTCHEN

Sophia	42

CRUTCHER

Charlotte	94
Franky	56

CUSTER

Martha	98

DALTON, DAULTON

Charlotte A.	105
Eliza	86
Jane	20
Rachel E.	116

DANGER

Barbary	80

DANIEL

Clarey	57
Luvenia	29
Mary	43
Nancy	3
Nancy	20
Polly (Nelly)	33
Rebecca	53
Sally	88
Tempy	3

DAVENPORT

Martha	131

DAVIDSON

Avice	35
Elizabeth	40
Levinia	129

DAVIS

Arminda	103
Frances	5
Nancy	14
Rhoda	55

DEAL

Liddy (Elizabeth)	19
Nancy	71
Polly	92
Rachel	77
Susannah	34

DEEN

Elvira	3
Lydai	20

DEHART

America	9
Elizabeth	64
Elizann	9
Hannah	68
Lucinda	15,32
Lucinda	131
Malinda	117
Mary	21
Nancy	25

DEHART, cont'd.

Nancy	64
Polly	53
Polly	124
Polly	131
Rebecca	44
Rebecca	46
Rebecca	118 (2)
Sally	98
Susanah	66
Susanah	114
Susanah	123
Susanah Malinda	9

DENNIS

Nancey	5

DENNY

Frances	96

DETHERAGE

Sara	90

DICKERSON

Elizabeth	44
Polly	23

DICKINSON

Nancy	48

DILLARD

Elizabeth	132
Rebecca	11
Sarah	15

DILLEN, DILLON, DILLION

Elizabeth	13
Jane	97
Martha	95
Nancy	48
Nancy	121
Sarah	115

DINKINS

Rebekah	1

DIXON

Sarah	132

DOCKERY

Mary	19

DODSON, DOTSON

Agnes	48
Frankey	112
Lucinda B.	87
Mary	92
Sarah	114
Sarah Jane	22

DONATHAN

Mary	34

DOVITY

Mary	71

DUNCAN

Julia	35
Polly	45

DUNN

Nancy	8

DURHAM

Nancey	91

DUVIZE

Peggy	132

DUVALL

Lucinda	20

EAST

Elizabeth	26
Frances	15
Frances	54
Marey	54
Mary	102
Sarah	36
Susanah	15
Ursley	90

EDENS, EADINS, EDENS

Abigail	28
Leveny	19
Lydia	55
Lydia	84
Mary	93
Nancy	40
Sarah	43

EDDS

Elizabeth	2

EDMONDS

Jane	54

EDWARDS

America	4
Catherine	20
Elizabeth	52
Jane	52
Leviny	20
Lucy	20
Mary Ann	37
Nancy	22
Nancy	82
Polly L.	89
Susan	78
Susanah (Lucinda)	24
Tabitha	28

ELGIN

Nancy	65
Susanna	32

ELKINS

Arty	43
Nancy	104
Nancy	105

ELLIOTT

Betsy(Elizabeth)	100
Luvena	45
Malinda	34
Tempy	74

ELLYSON

Lucinda	54

EMERSON

Lucinda	54

EMERSON

Susan	76

EPPERSON

Catherine	72
Susanah	71

FAIN

Leta	129
Martha	58

FALKNER

Winney	57

FARRELL

Sally	21

FARRIS

Polly	93

FENDER
          Hander   18

FENDLEY, FINDLEY
          Judith   54
          Patty   102
          Prudence   77

FERGUSON
          Amanda P.   96
          Malinda Jane   115
          Maryan H.   48

FERRELL
          Elizabeth   118

FINNEY
          Ellenor   38
          Mary   88
          Nancy   4

FITZGERALD
          Frances Elizabeth 81
          Jane   45
          Peney   106
          Polly   42
          Nancy   123
          Sarah   116
          Sela (Priscilla) 107
          Stacy   9
          Stacy   18

FITZPATRICK
          Elizabeth   95
          Rebecca   6

FLEMING
          Nancy   71

FLETCHER
          Elizabeth   77

FLIPPEN
          Annis   25
          Mary   5
          Sally   89

FLOOD
          Lidia   70

FOLEY
          Bregit   46
          Easter   129
          Emeline Adeline   41
          Leony   112
          Leoney   108
          Letitia   41
          Lity   11
          Lucinda B.   10
          Nancy   41 (2)
          Nancy (Nanny)   83
          Permelia   130
          Rachel   31
          Ruth   10
          Sally   111
          Sarah   117

FOSTER
          Elizabeth   87
          Elizabeth   133
          Exoney   1
          Jane   6
          Lucinda   34
          Luvenia P.   103
          Martha S.   116
          Maria T.   103
          Mary   67
          Ruth   116

FOWLKES
          Jane   121

FRANCES
          Mecca (Micky)   121

FRANKLIN
          Sally   68

FRANS
          Charlotte F.   62
          Elizabeth   69
          Harriett   85
          Lucy   133
          Mary (Polly)   114
          Nancy   28
          Nancy   75
          Polly   107
          Polly   119
          Polly   74
          Sally   5
          Susan   75
          Susan   94

FRAZER, FRASURE
          Ann Mariah   76
          Betsy (Elizabeth) 125
          Malinda   46
          Martha   96
          Miss   77
          Nancy   125
          Polly   121
          Sarah E.   28

FREEMAN
          Any   24
          Caran   109
          Sarah   60
          Sarah   108

FRY
          Sarah F.   95
          Zady   25

FULCHER
          Elizabeth A.   79
          Jane   44
          Polly   37

FULKERSON
          Mildred   100
          Mildred   41
          Nancy   35
          Rachel   46
          Sally   19
          Susanah C.   40
          Virginia   43

FUSON
          Elizabeth   1
          Sally   9
          Sally   50
          Sally   86

GAINES
          Nancy   51
          Sarah   21
          Susannah   67

GARRISON
          Mary   55

GATES
          Martha   31

GEORGE
          Celia   122
          Eliza   97
          Letha   36
          Margaret   109
          Martha   36
          Martha   73

GIBBS
          Margret   112

GIBSON
          Abigal   102

GILBERT
          Barbara Ann   91
          Elizabeth   129
          Jane   62
          Lucinda   5
          Polly   20
          Sarah   29

GILLENWATERS
          Polly   8

GLASGOW
          Matilda   2

GOARD
          Anne   102
          Fanny   108
          Nancy   12
          Rachel P.   15

GLASPY
          Jenny   131

GODARD
          Elender   61
          Elizabeth   61
          Miss   99
          Nancy   124

GOING
          Elizabeth   100
          Margaret   38
          Mary (Martha)   18
          Nancy   46
          Pegge   1
          Penai   92
          Rebecca   39

GOSSETT, GUSSETT
          Elizabeth   91
          J.   72
          Phebe   33

GOURD
          Nancy   112

GRADY
          Elizabeth Ann   113
          Frances   46
          Lucy   9

GRAHAM
          Malvina   14
          Martha   51

GRAY
          Betsy (Elizabeth) 127
          Elilzabeth   80
          Jane   67
          Mary   76
          Mary Ann D.   117
          Martha J.   79
          Matilda   79
          Nancy   117

GREEN
          Morning   57
          Nancy   51
          Polly   51

GREER
          Mary Jane   80

GREGORY
          Margaret   46

GREGSBAY
          Abigail   2

GRIFFIN
Elizabeth 127
Elizabeth 129
Nancy 4

GRIFFITH
Elusha 96
Jane 96

GRIMES
Bridget 123

GRUIN
Polly 51

GUILLIAM
Sarah 80

GUNTER
Elizabeth 75

GUSLER
Catherine 62

HAGOOD
Ann 82
Elisabeth 42
Exoney (Eoney) 115
Jane 115
Mary Jane 113
Nancy 84
Sophia 19
Susannah 21

HAILE, HALE
Anna 71
Hannah 26
Keziah 93

HAIRSTON
Elizabeth P. 49
Sarah A. 16

HALL
Anna 14,17
Arteminca (A.E.) 84
Bethane 133
C. 83
Catherine 78
Charlotte 86
Deborah 19
Delilah 132
Delila 118
Elizabeth 66
Exoney E. 23
Frances 47
Frances 76
Jane 117
Jane 120
Jemimah 16
Jinny 53
Judah 50
Judith 50
Julina 49
Leah 112
Lucinda 46
Lucinda 76
Martha 16
Martha 125
Martha J. 131
Mary 53
Matilda 62
Nancy 50
Polly 17
Rozinah 66
Sabrinah 49
Sally 93
Sarah 4
Serna 11
Vina (Levinah) 50
Violet 121

HAMM
Sintha 11

HAMMONS
Mary 69
Polly 9
Selah 47

HAMPTON
Nancey 92

HANBY
Emily 75
Jane 84
Jane 125
Mary Ann 110
Nancy 23
Nancy D. 70
Nancy 82
Polly 111
Ruth 126
Sally 86

HANCOCK
Celia 51
Elisabeth 50
Elizabeth 60
Elizabeth 85
Exoney 110
Judith 81
Lucy 93
Martha 37
Martha 111
Mary 85
Olive 28
Polly 23
Sarah 128

HANDY
Caty 28
Hannah 52
Jane 103
Martha 10
Martha 92
Nancy 59
Sally 38
Sarah 10
Selah (Celia) 81

HANDRIDG
Susana 8

HANEY
Miley 47

HANNAH
Polly 3

HARBOUR
Ann 101
Elizabeth 96
Esther 63
Esther 118
Esther J. 104
Jane 73
Joyce 64
Joyce 104
Leminia 126
Levina 11
Mary 85
Mary Elvira 16
Matilda J. 29
Permela C. 97
Polly 90
Polly (Mary) 100
Rachel 96
Ruth J. 113
S.A. 103
Sarah 50
Sarah 93
S.J. 93

HARDREDY-HARDRIDGE
Mary 126
Susana 102

HARREL
Betsey 12
Catharine 127
Hannah 28

HARRIS
Agnes 45
Celia 51
Charlotte 7
Charlotte 92
Elizabeth 5
Elizabeth 27
Elizabeth 36
Elizabeth 52
Elizabeth 59
Elizabeth 62
Elizabeth 84
Elizabeth 122
Elizabeth L. 81
Eliza 12
Jane 38
Judith 16
Leony 5
Lottey 21
Lucy 13
Lucy 51
Lucy 119
Luvinia 37
Mahala 110
Martha 12
Martha 83
Mary 9
Mary 70
Mary 89
Miss 71
Nancy 11
Nancy 77
Nancy 86
Patsy 93
Polly 20
Polly 101
Polly 106
Prudence 20
Rebecca 5
Rhoda 30
Sally 32
Sally 52
Sally 68
Sarah 8
Sarah 80
Tabithia 92
Tabithia 102

HARRISON
Harriet 42
Polly 28

HASLIP
Nancy 72

HART
Catherine 88
Mary 25
Sally 59

HATCHER
Agnes 64
Sally (Sara) 51

HAYNES, HANES
Adaline 87
Charlotte 76
Clare 84
Nancy 42
Polly 35
Sarah 19
Susanah 60

HAZELWOOD
    Ruth   89

HELMS
    Anna   4
    Sally   129
    Viley   130

HENRY
    Mary   102
    Sarah   110

HENSLEY
    Eliza J.   2
    Polly   38

HENSON
    Anney   45
    Anney   68

HERD
    Sally   14

HERON
    Elizabeth   123

HICKMAN
    Nancy   62

HICKS, HIX
    Elizabeth   88
    Martha   97
    Nancy   13

HIETT, HIATT
    Easter   31
    Martha   44
    Martha   45
    Maza   13
    Nancy   88

HIGH
    Jayne   66

HIGHTOWER
    Jane   26

HILL
    Elizabeth   72
    Elizabeth   88
    Frances   119
    Jane   14
    Jane   72
    Nancy   21
    Nancy   78
    Zanly   93

HINES
    Lucy F.   82
    Mary   9
    Susan J.   42

HIXON
    Susanah   132

HODGES
    Ann (Anna)   56
    Anny   45

HOLLIDAY
    Sally   95

HOLLANDSWORTH
    Ann Elizabeth   115
    Betsey   56
    Caroline Matilda   123
    Cassie Ann   115
    Elizabeth   80
    Febey   35
    Julia   98
    Mahaley   80
    Martha Ann   74
    Martha Ann Susan   98

HOLLANDSWORTH, Cont'd.
    Mary   61
    Mary   98
    Milly   4
    Nancy Mariah   34
    Polly   48
    Priscilla   81
    Rebecca   3
    Sally   116
    Sarah   27
    Sarah   62
    Susanah   20
    Susanah   61
    Susannah   27
    Susannah   71

HOLT, HOELT
    Christina   102
    Hannah   97

HOPKINS
    Franky   103
    Cinsey (Jane)   47
    Jane   44
    Malinda   71
    Malinda   37
    Martha   92
    Mary Ann   98
    Sally   86
    Sarah   113

HOOKER
    Eliza   79
    Martha   92
    Mary   125
    Nancy   92
    Polly   95

HORNE
    Rosanah   45

HORNSBAY
    Nancy   78

HORTON
    Rachel   127

HOUCHINS
    Agnes   3
    America   37
    Margaret (Peggy)   21
    Nancy   38
    Polly   61

HOWELL
    Charity   112
    Darkes (Dorcas)   69
    Lucy   44
    Martha   105

HUBBARD
    Anna   14,93
    Catherine   31
    Eliza   119
    Elizabeth   10
    Elizabeth   93
    Hannah   120
    Judith C.   23
    Judy   27
    Kiziah   57
    Lucy   13
    Lucy   57
    Lucy   86
    Mary   3
    Nancy   98
    Susanna   13

HUDSON
    Lucy R.   69
    Mary   62
    Mary   40
    Nancy   70

HUDNALL
    Angeline   43
    Elizabeth (Betsy)   26
    Elmira   22
    Martha R.   128

HUET
    Sally   96

HUFF
    Polly   78

HUGHES
    Agnes   18
    Charlotte   74
    Mary   116
    Mary   132
    Matilda   33
    Nancy   52
    Patsy   17
    Sally   79
    Sarah   63

HUNT
    Elizabeth   81

HURST
    Delilah   90

HURT
    Mary (Polly)   128
    Matilda   116
    Mildred (Milly)   17
    Nancy   74

HUTCHINGS
    Martha   96

HUTSON
    Eury   127
    Orinai   130

HUTTS
    Sarah Ann   71

HYLTON, HILTON, HELTON
    Elisabeth   8
    Elizabeth   38
    Elizabeth   56
    Lucy   65
    Martha   55
    Mary Ann   21
    Molly   102
    Nancy   38
    Sally   72
    Senney   2
    Sally   129
    Sophia   91
    Susannah   33
    Temperance   38
    Ursly   75

INGRAM
    Elizabeth   124
    Elizabeth A.   103
    Elizabeth A.   104
    Franky   82
    Nancy   44
    Nancy   79
    Nancy   103
    Ony   1
    Rozinah Hall   109
    Ruth   82
    Sally   67
    Sarah   1

IVIE
    Ann B.   72
    Eliza Jane   119
    Jane   117
    Martha E.   35
    Sarah Ann   72

McGUFFEY
- Rebecca 132

McKINZEY
- Fanney 127

McMILION, McMILLION
- Rebecca 12
- Ruth 50
- Sally 57

McPEEK
- Elizabeth 61

NANCE
- Nancy 6
- Virginia E. 48

NELSON
- Elizabeth 128
- Mary 41

NEVELLS
- Rebecca 84

NEW
- Martha 16
- Sally M. 56

NEWMAN
- Elizabeth 103
- Ersley 41
- Lucy 103
- Milly 103
- Nancy 40
- Ona 76
- Ruth 36

NICHOLS
- Elizabeth 78
- Lucy 39
- Nancy 120

NOE
- Elizabeth 78
- Mary 65

NOLEN, NOWLIN, NOWLING, NOWLAND
- Biddy 1
- Conah 89
- Elizabeth 90
- Elizabeth 90
- Hannah 53
- Kizia 54
- Lucy 121
- Lucy 122
- Mary 17
- Nancy 43
- Rodah 107
- Ruth 90
- Sally 10
- Sally 70
- Sally 120
- Sally 129

NORMAN
- Mary 70

ONEAL
- Nancy 115

OVERBY
- Martha 7

OVERMAN
- Polly 46

OWEN, OWENS
- Maryan 83
- Pamela 104
- Sarah 89

PACK
- Elizabeth 46
- Locky 84
- Martha 12
- Milly 89
- Nancy 63

PACKWOOD
- Eady 87
- Elizabeth 54
- Elizabeth 97
- Exony 44
- Nancy 30
- Rachel 110

PALMER, PARMER
- Belinda 55
- Elizabeth 30
- Elizabeth 123
- Sarah 32
- Susana 109

PARR
- Jane 24
- Landal 116
- Nancy 94
- S. (Arency) 10
- Sally 123
- Sarah 70
- Susanna 127

PARKER
- Henrietta 113
- Mary 83

PEDIGO, PEDIGOY, PEDDIGOE
- Bathsheba 24
- Elizabeth 117
- Hannah 100
- Keziah 37
- Lucy 22
- Nancy 111
- Polly 59

PENDLETON
- Ann (Anna) 126
- Elizabeth 65
- Exoney 117
- Mary 10
- Mary J. 60
- Sarah 77

PENN
- Ann M. 114
- Barbara Ann 93
- Bettie F. 66
- Eliza 49
- Elizabeth (Betsy) 6
- Frances 33, 7
- Frances J. 94
- Lucinda Catherine 94
- Luvinna 28
- Martha 133
- Martha A.C. 42
- Mary A. 94
- Milly 104
- Nancy 117
- Patsy 95
- Polly 39
- Polly 42
- Sinthy 112
- Sophia R. 105
- Ruth 1
- Ruth 80

PENNINGTON
- Mary 48
- Nancy 17
- Rhody 34

PERKINS
- Anney 91

PHILLIPS
- Elizabeth 30
- Jane 112
- Sarah 9

PHILPOTT
- Cerina 42
- Elizabeth 123
- Elizabeth Gravitt 81
- Elvira G. 75
- Jane 18
- Jane 34
- Julia B. 19
- Marriah H. 107
- Mary Ann 35
- Polly 28
- Ruth 80
- Sarah F. 77
- Sinai 73

PIGG
- Sally 34

PIKE
- Mary (Polly) 119
- Rebecca Jane 103

PILSON
- Elizabeth 68
- Esther 1
- Margaret 59
- Margaret 63
- Nancy 68
- Sabrinah 113

PLASTER
- Elizabeth 53
- Polly 43
- Violet 47

PLYMALE
- Anna 37

POINDEXTER
- Ann E. 54
- Betsy Ann J. 114
- Emily 88

POOR, POORE
- Mariannah 70
- Milly 49
- Polly 47
- Polly 70
- Polly 85
- Rhodah 92
- Sally 69
- Scyntha 122

POTTER
- Ann T. 9
- Martha J. 44
- Virginia 131

POWELL
- Mary 46

PRICE
- America 78
- Delany 15
- Lucy 89
- Nancy S. 93
- Ruth 38
- Sarah 9
- Sarah 76

PROFFIT
- Elizabeth 79

PRUITT
- Delilah 91

PRUNTY
- Julia A.F. 7

PUCKETT
   Elizabeth   80
   Lockey   105
   Mary W.   8
   Nancy   75
   Sarah   81

PURDY
   Catherine   61
   Joicy   121
   Lavicy   27
   Mary   112
   Mary   120
   Matilda   99
   Nancy   120
   Polly   27
   Polly   40
   Ruth   61

QUALLS
   Jane   91

RAKES
   Anna   50
   Elizabeth   6
   Elizabeth   14
   Jane   49
   Judy   48
   Malinda   112
   Mary   23
   Mary   18
   Polly Malinda 44
   Rhoda   112
   Rocksana   98
   Zina   29

RANDALS
   Mary   34

RATLIFF
   Delilah   113
   Jemima   10
   Jemima   16
   nancy   99

REA
   Elizabeth   75
   Sally   8

REED
   Lucinda S.   96

REDFORD
   Eady   94

REDMAN
   Elizabeth   113
   Jane   129
   Nancy   49

REEVES
   Ann   122
   Jane   129
   Lucy   130
   Polly   118

REID
   Mary Ann   94

REYNOLDS
   Caty   115
   Caty   50
   Celey   80
   Elizabeth   53
   Frances   74
   Jenny (Jean) 85
   Leony   1
   Leviny   90
   Lucinda   106
   Matilda   35
   Martha (Patsey) 123
   Milly   6

REYNOLDS, Cont'd.
   Milley   83
   Milly (Amelia) 91
   Nancy   19
   Nancy   45
   Nancy S.   113
   Penca   29
   Polly   4
   Polly   21
   Polly   101
   Rebecca E.   130
   Rozanah J.   126
   Ruth   53
   Sarah   46
   Susan J.   73
   Susanah   19
   Susanah   48

RICHARDSON
   Charity   61
   Nancy   123

RICKMAN
   Catherine   39
   Lucinda   76
   Martha   125
   Sally   39
   Susannah   39

RIDDLE
   Elizabeth   7

ROBERSON, ROBERTSON
   Catherine R. 94
   Elizabeth   43
   Elizabeth   35
   Elvira P.   102
   Jane   25
   Judah (Judith) 122
   Lucinda   35
   Lucy   25
   Mary   79
   Nancy   87
   Nancy   102
   Rachel   43
   Rebecca   60
   Sally   60
   Sally R.   68

ROGERS, RODGERS
   Elizabeth   9
   Elizabeth (Betsy) 58
   Lucy   58
   Milly   44
   Orry   114
   Ruth   35
   Ruth   58
   Sally   103
   Sarah   104
   Sarah R.   89
   Susanna   79
   Susanna Jane 28
   Susanna Jane 29
   Verlinka E. 44

ROPER
   Betsey   107

RORRER
   Mary E.   85

ROSS
   Aney   26
   Dicey   97
   Elizabeth P. 22
   Jane   77
   Keziah   25
   Malinda   68
   Martha   19
   Martha   72
   Susanna   122

ROWAN
   Martha Eliabeth 28

ROWARK
   Sally   26

RUDER
   Jane   40

RUSK
   Sarah   77

RUSSELL
   Elizabeth 64
   Selyan   40

RYALL
   Nancy   84

SALAHORN
   Charlotte 101

SALMONS
   Charlotte 99
   Sally G. 21
   Susanah 54

SANDEFER, SANDEFUR
   America H. 46
   Eliza B. 22
   Elizabeth C. 66
   Joanna E.M. 120
   Mary F. 119
   Mary T. 116

SANDERS
   Mary   69

SANDS
   Nancy   87

SAUNDERS
   Elizabeth 103
   Mary W. 3
   Nancy   9

SAYERS
   Elizabeth 25
   Matilda 36
   Susanah 97

SCALES
   Elizabeth 57
   Sally   105

SCOTT
   Lucretia 112
   Lyda   88
   Margaret 82
   Mary W. 6

SCRUGGS
   Amanda 91
   Sarah   47

SEALES
   Mary O. 107

SHARP, SHARPE
   Elizabeth 126
   Fanny   57
   Frances 89
   Jane   44
   Louvenia 96
   Lucy   44
   Lucy   73
   Nancy   26
   Nancy M. 105
   Peggy   39
   Ruth   29
   Sally   107

SHARP, Cont'd.
   Sahar   47
   Veny   17

SHELOR
   Betsy   125
   Roxana   101
   Susan M.   127

SHELTON
   Charlotte   89
   Elizabeth   58
   Elizabeth   89
   Elizabeth   90
   Elizabeth   108
   Frances   39
   Luvena   28
   Mary Ann   37
   Mary Ann   105
   Milly   120
   Nancy   90
   Nancy   99
   Olive   90
   Peney   106
   Polly   51
   Polly C.   6
   Sally   89
   Sally   106
   Winefred   107

SHEPPARD, SHEPHARD
   Emily E.   5
   Louisa   61

SHORT
   Elizabeth Ann   118
   Frances   47
   Judith Ann   131
   Susan C.   122
   Susanah   122

SIMKINS
   Kitty   38

SIMMS, SIMS
   Anna   88
   Elizabeth   48
   Ellenor   88
   Ginsey   42
   Oney D.   88
   Polly Lessonby   48

SIMMONS
   Selah   121

SIMSON
   Jane   12
   Mary   36
   Winney   56

SISEM
   Elizabeth   126

SISEMORE
   Betsey   36

SITTON
   Perscilla   92

SLATE
   Mary   35
   Nancy   25

SLATER, SLATOR
   Miss   116
   Polley   115

SLAUGHTER
   Helen   45
   Judith   16
   Lucy   33
   Martha   53
   Mary E.   56

SLAUGHTER, Cont'd.
   Nancy   132
   Naomi   25
   Ruth   73
   Susanah   26
   Thena   2

SMALL
   Darkas   18

SMALLMAN
   Mary   125
   Nancy   61

SMART
   Jemima   99
   Martha J.   67

SMITH
   Adeline M.   110
   Becky   68
   Delila P.   68
   Eava (Eve)   58
   Elizabeth   102
   Elizabeth C.   100
   Embersetta   5
   Frances   108
   Frances   108
   Harriet   78
   Jency   68
   Letha   79
   Lockey R.   127
   Mary Ann   40
   Nancy   40
   Nancy   44
   Nancy   46
   Nancy   58
   Polly   11
   Polly   33
   Ruth A.   21
   Sally   110
   Sarah   126
   Sarah   16
   Sarah F.   69
   Susanah N.   16

SNEED
   Jane   112
   Judith   73
   Judith   90
   Martha   43
   Martha   63
   Mary   90
   Nancy   121
   Polly   43

SNIDER
   Sally   63

SNOW
   Amendey   88

SOLOMAN
   Phebey   112

SOYERS
   Elizabeth J.   108

SPANGLER
   Mary Ann   105

SPALDIN, SPALDING
   Mary   5
   Nancy   92

SPENCE
   Morning   97

SPENCER
   Delilia   46
   Elizabeth   30
   Elizabeth   62
   Elizabeth   124

SPENCER, Cont'd.
   Frances   62
   Lucinda   34
   Lucinda   2
   Lucy   31
   Malinda   21
   Martha   33
   Martha Jane   70
   Martha W.   90
   Mary   70
   Maryan M.   97
   Matilda   26
   Matilda J.   42
   Nancy   98
   Nancy   107
   Peggy Susanna   98
   Polly   33
   Polly   74
   Priscilla Ruth   74
   Ruth   39
   Ruth   100
   Sally   27
   Sarah Lynch   132

SPROUSE
   Amelia   19
   Martha   111
   Nancy   81

SPROWIL
   Jane   92

STALEY
   Susanah   60

STANLEY
   Catherine   8
   Catherine   83
   Maryann Elizabeth   21
   Susanah   111

STAPLES
   Eliza L.   16
   Martha   60
   Mary M.   86
   Keziah C.   100
   Ruth P.   100

STEARMAN
   Mildred   110

STEGALL, STEAGALL
   Anis   27
   Elizabeth   51
   Milly C.   99
   Nancy   67
   Phebey   . 75
   Polly   114
   Sally   20
   Sally James   32

STEPHENS, STEVENS
   Elizabeth   45
   Nancy   95
   Nancy   102
   Polly   72

STEWART
   Esa   72
   Matilda   39

STICKLEMAN
   Elizabeth   99

STONE
   Martha   21
   Maryan   115
   Milly   17
   Nancy   42
   Susanah   115
   Susannah   99

STOVALL	
Jane	22
Mary	130
Matilda	30
Serenor	53

STRANGE, STRANG	
Elizabeth	8
Margaret	132
Nancy	12
Sarah	74

STUART	
Bethenia F.	21
Columbia S.	49
Nancy D.	97

STULTZ	
Elizabeth	20

SUBLETT	
Frances (Franky)	126
Patty	67

SUMNER	
Charity	99

SUTFIN	
Ann	17

SURRAT	
Sally	15

SWIGGETT	
Charlotte	61

TALBOT	
Marah	104

TATE	
Frances A.	45

TATUM	
Elizabeth	23
Elizabeth	51
Martha R.	5
Nancy W.	66
Sarah	116

TAYLOR	
Carolinae	64
Denty M.	47
Eliza Ann	31
Elizabeth	32
Elisabeth	35
Elizabeth	119
Exony Timinda	32
Mary	32
Mildred	100
Penelope	52
Permela	82
Sarah Ann	43

TERRY	
Elizabeth	87
Elizabeth Belinda	55
Levinah	54
Martha	105
Polly	17
Polly	63
Sally	37

THACKER	
Darkis	62
Philida	63

THOMAS	
Catherine	64
Cynthia	118
Deborah	32
Deley	18
Dorothy R.	98

THOMAS, Cont'd.	
Elizabeth	1
Elizabeth	53
Elizabeth	120
Jane	85
Judith	108
Judy	2
Lucinda (Susan)	73
Lucy	122
Mary	72
Mary	119
Matilda A.	30
Nancy	122
Nancy	125
Nancy	127
Oney	118
Polly	53
Polly	90
Polly	108
Rachel	131
Rebecca	82
Sarah	68
Susan	118
Susanah	18
Susanah	48
Susanah	69 (2)

THOMSON, THOMPSON	
Anna	47
Anny	75
Betsy	91
Elizabeth	37
Fanny	65
Frances	8
Garten	18
Letty	109
Mary	4
Mary (Polly)	68
Malinda	74
Mildred	98
Mildred	99
Polly	75
Polly	106
Sally	12
Sally	49
Sally	116
Susannah	67

TITTLE	
Ann	1

TRENT	
Mary	108
Mildred	54
Nancy	54
Phoeby	30
Sarah	91
Susannah	86

TRINE	
Prudence	109

TUCKER	
Eliza	24
Sarah N.	25

TUDER	
Martha	33

TUGGLE	
Anna	106
Elizabeth	10
Elizabeth	41
Elizabeth	72
Frances	14
Mary	93
Mary	113
Miss	15
Nancy	72,17
Polly	76
Rachel	59
Sally	69
Sarah	56
Seley	87

TUNE	
Elisabeth	2
Elisabeth	31

TURMAN	
Frances	51
Susanah	114

TURNER	
Adelpha	133
Amanda B.	104
Betsy	49
Easter	111
Elizabeth	104
Elizabeth J.	132
Evaline	92
Exoney	50
Frances	58
jane	17
Jane	66
Jemimah	66
Judith	57
Mahala	104
Mahala	5
Malissa R.	123
Malinda	70
Martha	118
Mary	20
Mary Ann	89
Nancy	95
Peggy	17
Permelia	20
Polly	118
Rebecca (Polly)	111
Ruth	73
Sally	50
Sinai	58
Sinai P.	88
Susanah	114

VAH---	
jane F.	23

VANCEL	
Catherine	74

VANHOOK	
Caroline	129

VARNER	
Ann E.	54
Eliza	120

VASE	
Nancy	119

VAUGHTER, VAUGHTERS	
Drucilla	110
Margaret	12
Martha	49
Sally	50

VAUGHAN, VAUGHN	
Charlotte	65
Elizabeth	55
Elizabeth Jane	92
Mary J.	123

VERDEL	
Edith	101

VEST	
Nancy S.	99

VIA	
America H.	125
+ Exoney	122
Franky	124
Jane	117
Martha	32
Nancy	3
Sally	99
+ Elizabeth	81

VIPPERMAN
    Elizabeth   101
    Ruth   24
    Sally D.   17

WADE
    Ann   2
    Louisa   100
    Milly   59
    Morning   101
    Nancy   77
    Sally   105
    Sarah   59

WALDEN
    Perninah   27
    Sally   27
    Sarah   75

WALKER
    Keziah   37
    Lucinda   23
    Peggy   129

WALLER
    Mary   102

WARD
    Frances   75

WARE
    Polly   26

WASHBURN
    Elizabeth   78
    Sally   52

WASHINGTON
    Ann   91

WATSON
    Nancy   112
    Roxey   91
    Rosesey   3
    Sophia   31

WEAVER
    Martha   97

WEBB
    Mary   95
    Nancy   73

WEDDLE
    Sarah   55
    Sarah   56

WELCH
    Elizabeth   113

WELLS
    Dolly A.   84
    Louisa   69
    Lucy G.   57

WHALEN, WHALING
    Amanda   129
    Mary   41
    Sarah   49

WHITE
    Alesley   60
    Mary   15

WHITLOCK
    Peggy   96

WILKERSON
    Hester Ann   20

WILKES
    Salla A.   110
    Sally Ann   41

WILLARD
    Nancy   74

WILLIAMS
    Becky   58
    Jane   43
    Levina Ann   52
    Miss   59
    Nancy   53
    Sally   53

WILLIS
    Delilah   109
    Elizabeth   111
    Jane   88
    Lavinia   113
    Matilda   130
    Patsy   128
    Phebe   119
    Ruth   128
    Sarah   110

WILSON
    Mary   65
    Permelia   82
    Rachel   117

WINFREE, WINFREY
    Dorcas   14
    Nancy   13

WITT
    Elizabeth   47
    Elizabeth   52
    Hester   64
    Hester J.   103
    Lucinda   41
    Lucy   64
    Mary Ann   53
    Patsey   36
    Ruth   47

WOLFER
    Margret   114

WOOD, WOODS
    Agga   87
    Anna   23
    Anna   65
    Charity   59
    Charlotte   20
    Delila   57
    Judith   24
    Lucinda   2
    Lucinda   131
    Mary Ann   58
    Mary Jane   110
    Tabitha Jane   114

WOODALL
    Jane   28

WRIGHT
    Elizabeth   22
    Fanny   124
    Mahalia   129
    Mary P.   65
    Polly   29
    Rosamond   111
    Ruth   79
    Temperance   30

WRAY
    Martha   84

YATS
    Catherine   6

YEATES
    Lavina   63

YOUNG
    Frances   59
    Harriet E.   66
    Sarah   102

* * END * *

www.ingramcontent.com/pod-product-compliance
Lightning Source LLC
Chambersburg PA
CBHW021831020426
42334CB00014B/577